Philip Jaisohn

The First Korean American – A Forgotten Hero

서재필 기념 재단

The Philip Jaisohn Memorial Foundation

Philadelphia, PA

Cover: Stillness at Sunset
Oil on Canvas (24" x 11")
Sim Joo Yoon (윤심주)
Ehwa Women's University, College of Art.
Exhibited at the Aegis Gallery in Saratoga, CA 2012.

To People
Who Sacrificed Their Lives
For Korea's Independence

CONTENTS

Editorial Note

In 1983, Professor Channing Liem (임창영) authored a biography of Dr. Philip Jaisohn (서재필 徐載弼) for the Philip Jaisohn Memorial Foundation in Philadelphia, Pennsylvania. As the original biography is now out of print and no longer available, there is a need to make it accessible to today's readers.

This book is a revised edition, created to bring Professor Liem's valuable work to a modern audience. To enhance its appeal and readability, relevant photographs and editorial notes—sourced from online archives—have been incorporated into the text.

To date, approximately 20 biographies of Dr. Philip Jaisohn have been published in Korea, all written in Korean. However, most of these authors never had the opportunity to meet Dr. Jaisohn personally. This book, authored by Professor Liem—who spent nearly 20 years in direct conversation with Dr. Jaisohn and, after his passing, became the custodian of his personal letters and documents—is, to my knowledge, the only biography that truly captures Dr. Jaisohn's own voice. It conveys not only his hopes and triumphs but also his sorrows and struggles, offering readers an intimate and authentic portrait of his life.

I hope that visitors to the Philip Jaisohn Memorial Hall in Media, a southern suburb of Philadelphia, will find this volume helpful in deepening their understanding of Dr. Jaisohn's legacy. It is with great joy that I celebrate the 50th anniversary of the Philip Jaisohn Memorial Foundation through the publication of this biography. As the editor, the four months I spent preparing this revised edition in early 2025 were deeply fulfilling, and I wish to extend my heartfelt gratitude to the Foundation for allowing me the privilege of immersing myself in the extraordinary life of Dr. Jaisohn.

Editor, Young-il Cho
Professor, Drexel University
Board member, Philip Jaisohn Memorial Foundation, Philadelphia

About the Author: Channing Liem (임창영)

Born in Korea on October 30, 1909, Channing Liem received both traditional and modern education before coming to the United States for further studies. He attended Lafayette College and Princeton University, earning a Ph.D. in Politics from Princeton. He also pursued graduate studies at New York Theological Seminary and conducted post-doctoral research at Yale University.

Dr. Liem taught at Princeton University, Chatham College, and the State University of New York at New Paltz. In addition, he served as Minister and Director of the Korean Church and Institute in New York City.

As early as 1937, at the outbreak of the Second Sino-Japanese War, he joined fellow Korean exiles in the United States in actively campaigning for Korea's independence. During World War II, while contributing to the U.S. war effort as a consultant to the Office of War Information and the Office of Censorship, he was appointed by Syngman Rhee as Director of Education—and later as Chairman—of the Korean Commission in Washington, D.C. He resigned from the post shortly thereafter.

Following Korea's liberation from Japanese rule, Dr. Liem chose not to return to Korea. Instead, with the encouragement of figures such as Professor Albert Einstein and New York City Mayor Fiorello LaGuardia, he established the American Foundation for Korean Education. Its mission was to support the training of Korean scientists and technical experts to assist in Korea's postwar reconstruction.

In late 1947, Channing Liem returned to Korea, where he served as secretary to Dr. Philip Jaisohn, Chief Adviser to the Commanding General of the U.S. Army Forces in Korea.

Following Syngman Rhee's election as the first President of South Korea, Liem returned to the United States and accepted a faculty position at Chatham College. As the Rhee administration grew increasingly autocratic and corrupt, Liem felt compelled to speak out against it. Opposition leaders in Seoul, operating in secrecy, kept him informed of the true political conditions in South Korea. This enabled him to provide accurate and timely information to the American public.

In 1960, after nationwide student-led demonstrations brought down the Rhee regime, and the Democratic government of Prime Minister Chang Myon was established, Liem was appointed South Korea's Ambassador to the United Nations. During his service at the UN, he was also dispatched as a special envoy to newly independent nations in Southwest Africa.

However, the Democratic government was overthrown less than a year later, in May 1961, by a secret military coup led by General Park Chung-hee. Upon learning of the coup, Liem resigned from his UN post and returned to academic life in the United States. He declined subsequent offers of government positions from the Park administration and instead dedicated himself to advocating for the restoration of democratic governance in South Korea and the peaceful reunification of the Korean peninsula.

To further this cause, he collaborated with Korean nationalist leaders in the United States, Europe, and Japan to establish the Overseas Korean Union for Democracy and Unification, where he served as Chairman of the Central Committee.

He also served as Honorary Co-Chairperson of the Board of Directors of the Philip Jaisohn Memorial Foundation.

Among the honors he received were a gold medal for excellence in oratory from Lafayette College; the Sanxay and Mills Fellowships from Princeton University; a Ford Faculty Fellowship at Chatham College; honorary membership in the Mark Twain Society; and a Certificate of Meritorious Service from the Government of the Republic of Korea.

Introduction

This is the story of a man whose impact on the modernization of Korea and of Korean-American relations was unrivaled by any of his contemporaries. However, because he chose to work behind-the-scenes, he remained little known until recently. His Korean name was Soh Jai-pil (서재필), but after arrival in America, he changed it to Philip Jaisohn.

One day in 1926, the *Dong A Ilbo* (East Asia Daily) published a report under the headlines: 'At age 60. Soh Jai-pil (徐載弼) *paksa* (Dr. Philip Jaisohn) Reenters Medical School.' It stated that the veteran independence leader having lost his personal fortune in a four-year campaign for...(deleted by Japanese censors), was back in medical school, the University of Pennsylvania, for refresher courses in order to resume his practice. I was stunned as I had thought that nothing could force him out of the fight for Korean independence. Now that the man on whom millions had pinned their hope for a free Korea quit the struggle, who would take his place? Continuing with this article, however, I also learned of his impaired health. He had not only lost his fortune, but his health also. Disappointed though I was in the seeming hopelessness of the cause of Korea's independence, my admiration for him grew all the greater. By showing his determination to rebuild his professional career at his advanced age, coupled with poor health, he was proving himself a man of indomitable will and of extraordinary wisdom. As an ancient Chinese sage taught, one who would conquer the world must first master himself and provide his family's needs. Jaisohn was a warrior and statesman in the truest sense, I said to myself. 'God willing, I hope to meet him someday.'

The dream came true in 1931. I had come to America the year before and entered Lafayette College in Easton, PA. The first semester ended early in February 1931, and the second semester was not due to begin for a week. One day during the recess, I was browsing in the periodicals room of the college library. On the front page of the latest Lafayette Alumni Bulletin was a picture of a group of men. It attracted my attention because one of them was an Oriental gentleman - a rare occurrence in those days.

Reading the article next to the picture, I noticed that the gentleman was described as Dr. Philip Jaisohn, a member of the Lafayette Class of 1892 and speaker at their Reading Alumni Luncheon. Although I had never heard of the name before, the description about him was very intriguing. The article went on to introduce him as a native of Korea who had served as an adviser to the King of Korea and concluded with his statement that he was a resident pathologist at Saint Joseph's Hospital of that city. The more I pondered, the more it appeared that he might be Soh Jai-pil *paksa*. Impatient to verify this, I hurried back to my room and wrote him a letter. After introducing myself, I asked him whether I was correct in assuming that he was the Soh Jai-pil *paksa* of Korea, and if true, I might have the pleasure of calling on him at a time of mutual convenience.

His reply came by return mail. Yes, he was Soh Jai-pil, he wrote. He said he had heard of my being at Lafayette from Dr. William Lewis, President of the College, and added that he would be glad to see me any time I could make it to Reading. I answered him right away, thanking him for the prompt and gracious answer, and promised to visit him as soon as possible. The long-awaited opportunity came in May when I had an invitation to attend a meeting in a town not far from Reading. I wrote to him asking if it would be convenient for him to see me on the first Saturday in May, as I would be passing through the city that day. Again, he replied promptly, saying although he planned to go home that day (it was customary for him to spend weekends with his family in Media, PA), he would be glad to see me as he could easily postpone his departure till after my visit.

That day was balmy. Saint Joseph's Hospital, a stately brick building, was surrounded by a well-tended lawn and looked homey. As I approached the main entrance, there were two large lilac trees standing on both sides. They were in full bloom and looked as if they were inviting me in. Inside, I was greeted by a polite man who led me into Dr. Jaisohn's office on the main floor and told me that he would be down from upstairs shortly. I sat there surveying the room. It was not large but clean, typical of a physician's office: a microscope, a paper pad and a pen on the desk, bookcase against a wall filled books and journals, and the smell of antiseptics. Having long visualized the man as an internationally known crusader for Korea's independence, it was something of a rude awakening to find that he was engaged in a fight with microorganisms in that tiny office. With all due respect for the medical profession, I could not help feeling that he was too valuable a person to waste his time there. He should be fighting against Japanese imperialism, liberate Korea, and help bring justice to mankind, I thought.

Suddenly I got up, lest Dr. Jaisohn walk in and find me absent minded. Stepping out into the corridor and taking a few steps toward the lobby, I caught sight of him. He was slowly descending the stairs at the far end. Though gray-haired and somewhat lean, he looked younger and more vigorous than I had anticipated. Tall, erect, broad shouldered and with a high forehead, he was handsome. He had an impressive bearing which made him look very distinguished. On noticing me, he walked briskly toward me, shook my hand and said: "Is this Mr. Liem? Glad to see you." And he led me into his office. We sat facing each other. He sat on his swivel chair by his desk and I on a straight chair against the wall. He puffed at his cigar without saying a word, but stared at me, expressionlessly through his tortoise-shell glasses. He did look forbidding. Some people meeting him for the first time received the impression that he was cold and stern, but that was only apparent and not real.

I had only two hours. Anxious to make the most of it, I began our conversation. "Dr. Jaisohn, you have no idea how great an honor and pleasure you are bestowing on me by allowing me to come to meet you." His seemingly stern look mellowed as he replied to my remark with the gentlest sounding four words: "The pleasure is mutual." Then, in his quiet, avuncular solicitude, he proceeded to ask how I was getting along in college, whether it was not too difficult to adjust to the American way of life, etc. Then, without lecturing me in a way Oriental elders were wont to do, he gave me the most valuable lesson on how to become a successful person by means of a brief personal reminiscence. When a youth, he said "he had good intentions, but he was in too much of a hurry to achieve his good purpose and failed miserably". It was in reference to the abortive *Kapsin coup* (갑신정변 1884) in which he played a major role. In consequence, he made-up his mind to hold on to a noble aim, but endeavor to reach it as best he could, taking one day at a time. As I listened to him, I concluded that he was of a happy blend of the best of the Orient and the Occident.

His ability to make his visitor feel at home was remarkable. Knowledgeable on all subjects under discussion, yet deferent to the opinions of others, he was a good listener as well as a gifted conversationalist. Having a whole lot of questions to ask, yet finding the time flying by, I was afraid I might be brusque to the point of rudeness. He said: "You are my guest and I'll be happy to answer any question you ask, if I can."

It was not necessary for me to ask him many questions, for what he had to tell me was of great importance, and he told it so interestingly. At the same time, he was always ready to be interrupted and showed himself a good listener. Touching on a person's career or occupation, he said that 'people choose it because they either like it or must'. He cited his own case by saying that he had become a physician pathologist because he was fascinated by what caused disease and how it could be cured. Once, he had also dabbled in politics and joined in a reform movement in Korea because he felt compelled to do so. "If one is interested in an occupation and it is one that is beneficial for one's fellow men, one should choose it; if a small voice within beckons one to a career because it is of value to one's community or country, one should respond to the call", he said. As for himself, he found it entirely satisfying to be a physician. On two occasions, too, he felt called upon to help cure

Korea's ills, and in so doing he sustained a loss of non-inconsiderable fortune and health. But he hastened to add that he had no regrets, as it was for worthy cause.

I asked him if he thought the cause of Korea's independence was doomed. He answered that such was by no means the case. Korea's freedom, he asserted, was more than a political issue. It was a moral imperative, The rape of a nation which, he said, was what Japan had committed in Korea was a declaration of war on God. No power on earth could defeat God, he said. If the Korean people refused to desert God by uniting on God's side, he was sure that Korea would be liberated. He said, "once I thought that a group of my friends and I, with the King of Korea as hostage, could transform a decadent Korea overnight into a modern, strong nation. I was wrong. A unified endeavor by an awakened people is indispensable to a free Korea."

And he went on to reminisce about the abortive coup of 1884, his flight abroad, of a 12-year struggle to obtain an education in America, and of a second try at reform of Korea.

Our two hours visit quickly ended while I sat listening to Dr. Jaisohn in absorbing interest. When I reluctantly got up to take my leave, he walked out to the hospital entrance, bade me a warm farewell and urged me to keep in touch with him. I know he meant what he said, and I gave him my promise. My contact with him through correspondence and personal association in the ensuing 20 years was the most valuable lesson in my life. If the pages which follow enable the readers to catch a glimpse of it, I will feel my labor amply rewarded.

New Paltz, N.Y.
June 24, 1983   Channing Liem
                 林 昌榮

CHAPTER ONE:
EARLY ENVIRONMENT

Philip Jaisohn, with his liberalism, was an anomaly in the feudal Korea of his time. Born in what was known as the Hermit Kingdom, he found its fierce isolationism intolerable and pioneered the movement for international intercourse. He called for a responsible rule in the face of an absolute monarchy to which Korea had been subjected for thousands of years. He championed the equality of all persons at a time when his people considered the hereditary aristocratic system as divinely ordained. He introduced such words as *toknip* (independence) and *minju* (democracy) into the Korean vocabulary, raising the eyebrows of powers and electrifying the rank and file.

The origin of Korea's isolationism is shrouded in antiquity. However, it was neither absolute nor always strictly enforced. Korea had never applied it to China, as she regarded the latter as her 'older brother.' Until the late mid-19th century too, it was enforced with considerable laxity, now allowing some foreigners to enter the country and reside in a designated area, such as the Japanese were in *Pusan*, now ignoring occasional smuggling in of literature on the *sohak* (Western learning or Christianity) by Koreans, and now looking the other way while some Occidental missionaries slipped into the country in violation of the law. In 1783, a young Korean named Yi Seung-hoon, who had been converted to Roman Catholicism by some Jesuits he met while he was a student in Peking, brought back with him a number of books about Christianity. Though this was illegal, he was not punished. On the contrary, he was able to propagate this new and intriguing faith among some of his fellow young *yangbans* (양반, aristocrats). Additionally, during the early 19th century, a dozen foreign missionaries stole themselves into Korea and quietly conducted evangelistic activities without harassment by Korean officials. Even when Korea tightened her isolationist policy, China was made an exception, and the Japanese settlement in *Pusan* was merely quarantined.

What was Korea like when Jaisohn was born?

Firstly, about the time of Jaisohn's birth, however, the Korean government began to stiffen the enforcement of the exclusion laws. By the latter part of the 1860s, the government not only spurned contact with foreign nationals, but it also sternly forbade contact between Koreans and foreigners. Even with China, people-to-people association was put to an end, and when Pecking's envoys made official visits to Korea, Korean hosts escorted them along so carefully segregated routes that they were scarcely able to meet the people or observe the country. Travel abroad by the people, let alone the possession of literature on any other country except China, was liable to capital punishment. Foreigners entered Korea at their own peril.

Hence, there existed only mutual ignorance and misunderstanding between Koreans and foreigners. Following the opening of China and Japan in 1842 and 1854, respectively, the victorious Western powers sought to do likewise in Korea, but in view of her fiery opposition, that was considered not worth the cost involved and they gave it up.

But their decision to leave her alone lasted only for a while, for their frustration merely deepened their curiosity about the Hermit Kingdom. Was she so fabulously rich that her people were determined to keep foreigners out? Or was she so miserably poor and weak that the people feared an easy conquest of her by the foreigners. They turned to Chinese officials for an answer, but the latter were little better informed. So, the Western 'barbarians' were left to believe what they preferred. Whatever their views about 'the last untouched land in East Asia' might be, they were unanimous in wishing to open her up for exploitation in one way or another.

If the Occidentals were so ignorant of Korea and her people, Koreans were equally uninformed about the 'Western Barbarians' and their countries. For example, one day in 1855, a group of quaint, hairy seamen staggered ashore near a coastal village called *Tongchon, Kangwon* province. Exhausted after many days of ordeal on the stormy seas and finally thrown overboard from their ship-wrecked craft, they begged the villagers for food by means of sign language. The villagers, though fearful of punishment by their government for violating anti-foreign laws, were moved by human compassion and gave them not only food but dry clothing and shelter as well. It was relatively easy for the strangers to explain that they were hungry by sign language, but it was an entirely different matter to explain their nationality. Not knowing who they were, the Koreans nevertheless gave them food and shelter for days until messengers from Seoul came to escort them to Peking. Only when the escort took them to the Chinese capital did they learn that the strangers were Americans. What else did they know about America? Nothing beyond the fact that the Chinese characters described her as *'Mei Quo'* (美國, Beautiful Country).

The next episode illustrates how mutual ignorance leads to tragic consequences. In mid-summer, 1866, a Mr. Preston, an American, fitted out a ship named S.S. General Sherman with light arms and an assortment of merchandise, and along with a crew of several nationalities, he sailed for Korea with the avowed purpose of opening her up for trade.

- But he arrived in the wrong place at the wrong time and employed a wrong method to accomplish his purpose.
- He docked in *Pyongyang* instead of *Inchon* which was the proper place. He arrived in the northern city at the end of the rainy season when the floodwater on the *Taedong River* had begun to recede, making it dangerous for his ship.
- And the people of *Pyongyang* had no power to accede to his request for trade without the permission of the Government in Seoul.

The governor of *Pyongyang* scolded Preston for intruding on his city, but agreed to convey the Americans request to Seoul, warning that the answer, which was almost certain to be in the negative, would not arrive for weeks, if at all. Indeed, the message from Seoul was for the governor to drive the 'barbarian pirates' away. However, before the arrival of the message, tragedy had already befallen the American ship. No sooner had the monsoon ended than the flood of the *Taedong River* receded, grounding the General Sherman in the river. To compound the Americans problem, their provisions had been exhausted. They tried to buy foodstuffs, but Korean merchants would not sell any in the absence of their government's permission. Faced with the choice of either starving to death or robbing, they opted for the latter. The irate Koreans retaliated by burning down the American ship with her entire crew trapped in her. Preston and his crew suffered the consequence of their ignorance of and their cavalier attitude toward the Koreans.

Unfortunately, in action as well as attitude, Preston was typical of all Americans who followed him. And for this, the United States was to pay a heavy price. As the Sherman turned into *Taedong River*, Korean coast guards and onlookers on the shore frantically waved it away, but the captain ignored them, perhaps seeing that the Koreans were hostile to them, and sailed on. Actually, the Koreans were trying to tell the Americans that 'it was too dangerous to go up the river.'

When the news of the fate of the American ship reached Seoul, the reaction of the Government was equally cavalier. It acted as if Korea had defeated the United States. After a jubilant celebration over the 'victory' against the 'Ocean barbarians,' it went smugly on pursuing its head-in-sands policy. Its refusal to ponder the implication of the Western expansionism which was sweeping through India, China and Japan, and its failure to prepare the nation for the expected assault of the Western tide led to the ultimate fall of Korea to foreign domination.

Photo: General Sherman, a U.S. naval ship. (General Sherman Incident, 1866)

The Regency of Taewon-gun

<u>Secondly</u>, the Korea of the time of Jaisohn's birth may be characterized as the '*Taewon-gun time*.' Although the Prince himself was the originator of her militant isolationism, the Taewon-gun time was more inclusive. It represented his relentless drive toward three goals:

- Korea for Koreans,
- the Koreans for the might of the House of *Yi*, and
- the might of the House of *Yi* for his own glory.

Lacking wealth or the know-how, he tried to achieve his goals through mainly isolationist policies. In the beginning, through luck and daring, his isolationism proved successful and brought him popularity. However, his simplistic means of bringing glory to the House of *Yi* and him, which will be described later, ended in disaster.

Prince Heungson, who received the title Taewon-gun when his son became the 26th King of Korea in 1864, was a dominant figure during the stormy decade of 1864 - 1873. He was born in an impoverished family of the royal clan in 1820 and experienced bitter privations while growing up. Barred from government position under an edict of the founder of the *Yi* Dynasty, and since it was thought demeaning for Prince to engage in manual labor, he led the life of a mendicant. To those from whom he begged for drink for himself and rice and fuel for his family, he always promised to remember them when he gained control of the government. He asserted that when he became powerful, he would wipe out corruption from the government and rule with justice for all people. Though most of his listeners or benefactors dismissed him, with good reason, as an idle dreamer, some who discerned unusual qualities in him were intrigued.

Deep inside of him, he was serious. Nursing consuming hatred against the *seido*, (a clan blessed oligarchy) of the Kims of *Andong*, which was in absolute control of power at the time, he vowed to himself to bring it down some day. On the surface, however, he maintained an air of indifference and employed all his princely charm to be on good terms with the mighty Kims, and borrowed money and clothing from them, never intending to repay or return them, and they knew that he never intended to.

In the early 1860s. King Choljong, who had been put on the throne by the Kims when he was 18, was seriously ill and was without a son. Dowager Queen Cho, who as the senior member of the royal household, had the power to designate Choljong's successor should he die without leaving a son, also held a secret grudge against the Kims for having replaced the Cho *seido* (her own clan) with their own. In utmost secrecy, Prince Heungson met the Dowager Queen and made to her a proposal. If, in the event of the King's demise without leaving a son, she would designate his second son as the next King, he would not only make her regent but also see to it that her clan replaced the Kim *seido*. The Dowager Queen accepted his proposal.

Having secured the agreement, the beggar prince now went around feigning insanity. He played this new role so convincingly that before long everyone who knew him believed that he had gone completely mad. One day he would walk in the homes of high officials and help himself with clothing, shoes and money. The next day he would be found 'punch drunk' following brawls with riff-raffs (i.e., disreputable or worthless people) of Seoul. He often spent nights on the streets or in shacks in company with derelicts.

Early in January 1864, King Choljung died unexpectedly. He had no living son. The Kims of *Andong*, whose *seido* had begun nearly a century before, were caught off guard. But Dowager Queen Cho was not. She had a trusted aide to attend to the king, day and night. No sooner had he collapsed while strolling in the palace garden than she learned it and rushed to him to take possession of the royal seal. The king had died. With the seal in her hand, she convened an emergency meeting of senior ministers, announced her intention to designate Myong-bok, the 'crazy' prince's 12-year-old second son, as King Choljung's successor.

Photo: Royal seals used by the *Joseon* dynasty

At first, Kim Moon-keun, head of the Kim *seido*, demurred, but realizing that she had the authority and sensing that her mind had been made-up, he concurred. His primary objection was that the king-designate had a living father. However, he and his fellow clansmen thought it best to make the most of the bad situation by reassuring themselves that his father was so insane that he was 'as good as dead.' Thus, the shy little son of the 'crazy prince' became the 26th monarch of the *Yi* Dynasty with the royal title of Kojong, and the 'crazy prince' was given the august title, Taewon-gun. Nobody expected him to realize what it meant.

To everybody's surprise, however, Taewon-gun calmly let it be known that he was not only in full command of his mental faculties, but also that he was taking charge of the ship of state. He named Dowager Queen Cho regent. He also announced that he would be the 'adviser to the regent.' He said nothing about replacing the Kim *seido* with Cho's, but by action he made it clear that there would be no more *seido* by any clan.

That the Taewon-gun was able to get away with the power grab in violation of the laws and traditions of the realm was proof not only of his charisma and daring, but also of how anxiously the nation had been waiting for a change. After centuries of life under the corrupt, rapacious and repressive *seido* system, especially the last one, any kind of regime was a welcome change. The Taewon-gun promised much more.

He vowed to break the monopoly of power by the *norons* (party of the Elder Theoreticians) of which the Kim *seido* had been the center. He promised to liberalize the right to a government career whereby qualified non-*yangbans*, especially the people of northern Korea, could be hired.

Pointing to his own background of poverty, he promised social justice and called on the people to shun wasteful and luxurious ways of life. He even warned *kisaeng* (기생) girls not to indulge in fancy, expensive dresses. Above all, he vowed to restore the might and glory of the royalty, the House of *Yi*. He was not only a man of words; he was a man of action. No sooner had he assumed the office of 'adviser' to the Regent, then he drove out the entire body of corrupt, inefficient officials and replaced them with new ones. He ignored his promise made to Dowager Queen Cho concerning replacement of the Kim *seido* with that of the Chos.

However, his implementation of the promises proved erratic, superficial, and ill conceived. He did open the door to government service to all political groups and even to commoners, but this was hardly more than tokenism, and those recruited were obliged to serve only at his pleasure. It is true too, that he abolished the feared *sowons* (scholars' academies) which numbered over 600 and had in fact become little autonomous governments with virtual powers of taxation. This was loudly applauded by the peasants, but it was becoming more and more evident that the motive behind the Taewon-gun's 'daring action' was to concentrate all powers of the realm in his hand. It also came to light that he did not practice what he preached about avoiding luxury and frivolities. Almost nightly there was feasting in *Wunhyon* Palace, the Taewon-gun's residence, with expensively dressed *kisaengs* in attendance.

What dismayed the people was the way he went about restoring the 'might and glory' of the royalty. One was domestic in nature and the other was foreign. Let us first examine the former.

Taewon-gun's Domestic Policies

In 1865, he commenced the rebuilding of the *Kyongbok* Palace which was gutted during the Japanese invasion of the 1590s. Granted that this would help lift the physical image of the House of *Yi*, the facts were, however, that the National Treasury was empty, and that after decades of blunder and plunder by greedy officials, the people were thoroughly impoverished. The estimated cost of the project, $7,400,000, represented an astronomical sum in those days, which was expected to be borne by taxpayers. Worse yet, the sum did not include the cost of labor and included only the cost of some of the materials. Labor and such materials as timber and stone were to be 'donated' by the people. Indeed, the people were forced to pay through the nose in taxes, labor materials, toll charge for entrance into Seoul by peddlers and in losses owing to the government's flooding the nation with debased coins. By the time the palace was rebuilt, the edifice stood not as a proud symbol of royal grandeur, but as a reminder of the Taewon-gun's tyranny

As if the economic squeeze were not enough, the Taewon-gun proceeded to literally draw the blood and tears out of the people with his diabolical anti-Christian crusade referred to above. Being staunchly conservative, he had no use for the 'Western teaching.' Neither had he shown any violent antipathy toward it. In fact, he had at one point thought of enlisting the assistance of a leading French missionary in dissuading Russia's attempt to open trade relations with Korea. In other words, in pursuing his primary aim of keeping Korea to himself, he was willing to take advantage of anything, including Christianity, after making it clear that its existence was at his pleasure.

He thought of the religion as a mixed blessing to him. As a fast-growing faith, it attracted some of Korea's leading *yangbans* and the more they immersed themselves in religious affairs, leaving politics alone, the better for him. On the other hand, some converts became zealots and went about preaching against idolatry and burning ancestral shrines as objects of idolatry. This caused loud outcries by the people against the Christians, and Taewon-gun could not remain oblivious to it.

When the leading French missionary to whom the Taewon-gun had indirectly requested for mediation declined, saying he could not intervene in political affairs, the strong man of Korea took it as a personal effrontery. The French missionary did not care or was unaware of the fact that he was in the country on the Taewon-gun's sufferance. The latter had to act now to set the facts straight or he would soon be at the mercy of the Christians, he concluded. In February 1866, he stunned Korean Christians, whose number was estimated at more than 20,000 and about a dozen foreign missionaries with these orders:

- that all Korean Christians should forthwith renounce their faith;
- that all foreign missionaries should immediately depart from Korea; and
- that all who disobeyed the order would be executed.

A swift mass arrest followed, in which Nam Jong-sam, a friend of Taewon-gun himself, and his 84-year-old father were included. Also apprehended were nine French missionaries. Father Berneux, leader of them, was kept for three days in a filthy, unheated cell where he was subjected to severe physical torture to force him to admit to crime. On the fourth day, he was brought to the Taewon-gun, who reminded him that he had committed a capital crime by entering Korea and proselytizing the Koreans. He ordered the missionary to admit it and leave Korea. If he refused, he would be executed. The missionary refused, insisting that since he had come to the country in obedience to God's command, he was innocent, adding, "Your Highness is acting in defiance of God." The Taewon-gun, angered by what he considered was Berneux's impudence, ordered him beheaded. Also martyred between February and July of that year were all eight missionaries and tens of thousands of Korean Christians, including Nam Jong-sam.

Photo: Statue commemorating Bishop Berneux, who was martyred during the *Byeongin* Persecution (병인박해) of 1866, at the *Galmaemot* (갈매못) Martyrs' Shrine. (*Daejeon* Diocese) (2023)

Retaliatory Actions by France and the United States

One of the three missionaries whose lives were spared by Koreans who risked their own in order to hide them in their homes, made his escape to China and reported the news to the French Minister in Peking. M. Bellonet, proud Minister of Napoleon III, thundered and anger: "The King of Korea, by harming my people, has sentenced himself to death. I'll see that the sentence is carried out," and ordered Admiral Roze to Korea to punish the 'Korean King.'

Roze left for Korea with a fleet of three warships. The approach of the French fleet near *Inchon* threw Seoul into a frenzied turmoil, but the Taewon-gun was not moved. Roze returned to China for reinforcement. Returning with a fleet of five warships, he blockaded the coast of *Inchon*, but when Seoul showed no signs of readiness for negotiation, he ordered the seizure of a town on *Kanghwa* Island. Storming into it, Roze's troops looted everything of value, books, art pieces, etc. in the local government building. Still, Seoul remained defiant. After two weeks of fruitless waiting, Roze sent a scout party of 120 towards Seoul. But at *Yanghwajin* they were ambushed by Korean troops, and the surprised French soldiers hastily retreated, leaving behind a score of their fallen comrades. The Korean casualty consisted of five dead and wounded. The Taewon-gun, now confident of victory, sent an aide to Roze with an explanation of his reasons for the punishment of the French missionaries and told him to leave. In reply, Roze presented two conditions for leaving,

- namely the payment of reparations for the killing of the missionaries, and
- punishment of those guilty of the crime.

The Korean ruler did not even bother to answer. Roze, vowing to teach the Koreans a lesson, ordered the island of *Kanghwa* occupied and sent a scout team of 60 to its capital for a probing action. However, as the team neared the capital, 500 Korean defenders jumped on them from behind and inflicted heavy casualties. The surprised invaders turned tail and fled. It was obvious that Roze could not vanquish the Koreans without a much larger force than he had under his command, but since

France's involvement in the Indo-China War at the time obviated it, he had no choice but to admit failure and turn back. Thus, the Taewon-gun won the first round of his campaign to keep Korea for Koreans, to enhance the might of the House of *Yi*, and to build himself up as the proud symbol of the unconquerable Kingdom of Korea and her royalty.

He was not allowed to bask in his victory for long. Another 'barbarian nation,' whose identity was unknown, loomed on the horizon to challenge him. Since the Sino-Russian Treaty of 1860, which extended Russia's eastern frontier to the Korean border, Russian traders made frequent incursions into Korea. They proved troublesome to local Koreans. And it was in order to put an end to these intrusions that the Taewon-gun had sought the assistance of the French missionaries, but meeting with refusal, retaliated against them. However, the 'barbarian nation' that was a serious challenge to him was not Russia.

It was America of which the strongman of Korea had scarcely any knowledge. America's challenge was probably 'in a fit of absent-mindednesses' for it is doubtful that Washington was aware of the Sherman affair described earlier. The United States expedition into Korea in 1871 to seek redress of losses in the Sherman affair and to conclude a treaty of commerce was ill-conceived and ill-executed. Washington sent Commodore Rogers with a fleet of five ships, which was the size of the French fleet that was too inadequate to bring Korea to her knees. It sent Frederick Low, American Minister in Peking, who did not believe that the mission would succeed, to negotiate a diplomatic treaty with Korea.

On arrival at *Inchon*, however, Low dispatched a note to Seoul, requesting a diplomatic dialogue, while simultaneously Rogers sent military vessels up the *Han River* estuary towards Seoul. The Taewon-gun, viewing this as a provocation, ordered the fort commander on *Kanghwa Island* to repulse the invaders. The U.S. ships were fired at and the Americans, taking it as an insult to their flag, stormed the fort with forces many times larger than the Koreans. The Korean defenders fought back with tenacity until they were killed to the last man. The American honor was vindicated, but they had to return without accomplishing their objective - conclusion of a commercial and diplomatic treaty with Korea.

Photo: The U.S. warship Monocacy during the *Shinmiyangyo* (1871)

As the exultant Taewon-gun led the nation in celebrating the 'victory,' his detractors called him a maniacal anti-foreignist or megalomaniac or the combination of both, while his admirers hailed him as the savior of Korea and of Korea's honor. A more sober assessment of the man would have been that he was neither of these. Though he was egregiously in error in trying to stamp out Christianity in Korea by force, it was not his anti-foreignism which led him to it. It was due to his conviction that Korea already had all the religions she needed without

Christianity, and more importantly, that the religion posed a direct challenge to him as the ruler of the country.

 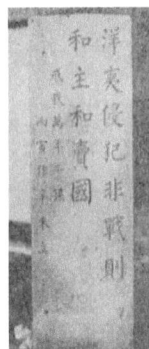

Photo (Left): U.S. sailors standing guard on the banks of the *Han* River during the *Shinmiyangyo* (1871). (Right): The *Cheokhwabi* (Anti-Foreign Stele) erected by Taewon-gun to declare the rejection of foreign influence.

(**Editor's Note**: Inscription on the *Cheokhwabi*:
洋夷侵犯 非戰則和 主和賣國
'When the Western barbarians invade, not fighting them means advocating peace; to advocate peace is to sell out the nation.')

It should be remembered that he observed Korea's tradition of bestowing hospitality to foreigners when their presence in their country was accidental. Thus, in July 1866, when he was in the midst of the campaign to drive out all foreign missionaries and to stamp out Christianity, he ordered safe conduct for the crew of the S.S. Surprise, an American ship which had been shipwrecked off the coast of *Sonsapo*, *Whanghae* province. No doubt, too, there were not a few Koreans heartened by his daring defiance against the foreigners in order to keep Korea free of foreign meddling and of the 'outlandish' Western teaching. However, for most of the people, he was an object of, and a cause for, fear. There was pervasive fear among the people. Even as they hailed him for the victories over the French and American forces, they were unable to dispel the fear that the Western challenge was by no means over and that the next time around, Korea might not be so fortunate.

Feeling particularly uneasy were classical scholars who were as conservative as the Taewon-gun yet were aware of the British victory over China in the Opium War and of the successful U.S. pressure on Japan to enter treaty relations. Both China and Japan were mightier than Korea by far. If the Western powers could humble them, was it reasonable to suppose that the Taewon-gun really administered defeat on France and the United States? Many of them were overwhelmed with fear on another ground. They witnessed some of their Catholic neighbors being taken away in chains, never to return home alive, and others fleeing to the mountains in ghastly terror. If the Taewon-gun could ruin the lives of so many because they had accepted a religion of which he did not approve, would he not also do likewise with them if and when they displeased him?

There was still another cause of fear among the people. It was common knowledge that there existed a deepening tension between the Taewon-gun and his followers on the one hand, and the King and his partisans on the other. The latter were bitter because, among other reasons, the father of the King was clinging to power despite the fact that the King had reached the age entitling him to take over the reins of the Government. The Taewon-gun feared that the moment the King 'took charge' of the Government, the queen would be the real ruler. This would inevitably lead to the *seido* by her clan - the Mins - with all the evils inherent in the system. Nevertheless, that sooner or later the smouldering feud between the two factions would erupt into a bloody, enervating conflict appeared inevitable and the people shuddered at the thought.

Yangban System

The third characteristic of Jaisohn's early years was a rigid social stratification in Korea, commonly referred to as the *yangban* (양반) system. The term *yangban* came into use during the *Koryo* dynasty (918-1392 AD). King Kwangjong (950- 975 AD) instituted a system which came to be known as *kwago* (과거, government service examination) whereby he recruited his aides on the basis of merit. This had been advocated by Confucius. His aides thus chosen fell into two categories, civilian *(munban)* and military *(muban)*. Possibly due to the common interest and mutual affinity, the officials of the *munban* class settled on the eastern *(동, tong)* side of the Royal Court, while those of the *muban* class settled on the western *(서, so)* side.

Accordingly, in time civilian officials and their families were called *tongban,* while the military officials and their families of civilian class were called *soban.* Subsequently, as both groups multiplied in number and were forced to reside in whatever areas that were convenient, they merged into one and were known as *yangban* (both groups). Initially, there were only two classes in the country, the royalty and the commoners. The *yangban* was not a class; it was a group consisting of high officials, and an official leaving government service ceased to be a *yangban*.

However, during the *Yi* dynasty (1392-1910), the class system gradually underwent a change.

- First, *yangban* became a social class. It consisted of not only office holders but also their families.

- Secondly, it was subdivided into three – *yangban*, *jung-in* (중인, middlers), and *so-in* (소인, petty ones).

- Thirdly, a qualified hereditary class system developed whereby the 4th generation offspring of the royalty moved down to *yangban*, the 4th generation offspring of a *yangban* assumed the status of *jung-in* and so on. Below the royalty and the three grades of nobility were two additional classes, namely *sang-in* (상인, commoners) and *chon-in* (천인, slaves). The son of a *yangban* by a concubine became a *so-in*.

Photo: The class system of the *Joseon Yi* Dynasty. Commoners bow to a *yangban* (nobleman) riding a horse accompanied by his attendants.

Although in theory the royalty stood at the top under the hereditary, hierarchical class system, in reality, the distinction between it and *yangban* was blurred. At the lower levels (excluding the *chon-in),* upward social mobility was possible. Thus, even an impoverished commoner could take the *kwago* (government service examination) and if successful, received appointment to government position. Stories abound depicting brilliant but poor commoners grinding through sleepless nights for years and years under an improvised lamp of fireflies in squash flower in order to prepare for the *kwago*, passing it with flying colors and becoming *yangbans*.

By the time of Jaisohn's birth, however, the class system had frozen into such rigidity as to nearly approximate the caste system of India. Interclass contact between *yangban* and the lower classes was virtually nonexistent. While members of all classes except *chon-in* were eligible for the *kwago* examinations, members of each could take only the *kwago* intended for their class. Thus, *jung-ins* took the *kwago* designed for them and if successful, they were eligible for middle level government positions. *So-ins*, upon passing the *kwago* of their class, were eligible for minor government positions. Although the commoners were qualified for a low level *kwago*, in practice they never aspired for it as even the preparations for it were too costly for them.

The examination was on the mastery of Chinese classics written in cumbersome Chinese characters, and one must devote many years of intensive study before trying it. Under such a system, the commoners who constituted over four-fifths of the population were de-franchised. Moreover, although male slavery was outlawed by the Government following the Korea-Japan War of the 1590s, which significantly reduced the male population, an ancient tradition persisted under which there existed in those days a class known as *chon-in*. Its precise size remained unknown, but judging by the fact that they were engaged in such lowly occupations as domestic help, butchering, tanning, entertaining, etc., one must estimate that it was larger than the *yangban* class.

Hence, nearly 90 percent of the people enjoyed no rights at all as citizens of the country. As an indigent nobleman, Taewon-gun knew how the masses felt about injustice and promised to rectify it if he ever were in a position to do so. However, upon assuming power, he failed to take any action on it. As a lad of preschool age, Jaisohn was baffled when someone admiring his musical talent sighed that Jaisohn, being a *yangban*, could not become a singer. Shortly thereafter, he was sent to Seoul to live with a rich uncle and to prepare for *kwago*. There, he was startled to find scores of people surrounding him. He thought they were his relatives, but they were servants waiting to serve him. He was scared. And so, he found the name Taewon-gun on everyone's lips, some praising him and others cursing him, and wondered why. Then he saw them both agreeing that the Regent was the most feared man in the country. "Everybody is afraid of him," they said.

CHAPTER TWO:
BOYHOOD

Sang Kyong (Double Luck)

The year *Kehae* in the Lunar Calendar was a lucky one for Soh Kwang-Un and his wife *Hampyong Yi Si*. Earlier that year, Kwang-Un had passed his *kwago* (government service examination) and was appointed to the magistracy of *Tong-bok* district in *South Cholla* province. On November 28th of the year *Kehae*, too, a healthy boy, their second son, was born. It was thus a doubly lucky year, and that jubilant parents named him Sang Kyong, meaning Double Luck. This, however, was his pet name. His legal name, decided upon following consultations in a family council, was Jai-pil (載弼, meaning assumption of service).

Though Sang Kyong was born in *Kanaeri* in *Tong-bok* district, *South Cholla* province, his paternal ancestral home was in *Non-san*, *South Chungchong* province, where the Soh clan had lived for generations. *Kanaeri* was the hometown of his maternal grandparents. As was customary those days, Mrs. Soh Kwang-un gave birth to all their children at her parents' house in *Kanaeri*. Sang Kyong was descended from two of Korea's most illustrious families and was born to wealth. On his father's side, Jaisohn's 8th generation grandfather was Prince Dalsung, father-in-law of King Young-jo. In addition, the Soh clan had produced numerous high officials and renowned scholars.

On his mother's side, his grandfather Yi Ki-dae was a descendant of the founder of the *Yi* dynasty, and Ki-dae himself was reputedly one of the wealthiest men in *Cholla* province. His house, destroyed during the Korean War, was said to be a showplace in southern Korea. Situated on a plateau halfway up *Mang-il bong*, (sunrise peak), the house was in reality a compound of seven large buildings in whose center was a lotus pond filled with fish of many varieties. In the middle of the pond was an islet on which stood a small villa. It was in this villa that Sang Kyong was born. From this villa on a clear day, one had a fine view of the towering *Mudung san* (peerless mountains) in distant *Kwangju*. According to an ancient saying, Sang Kyong's birth here was a happy omen, for a child born in a place which offers a good view of a famous mountain far away was said to be destined to grow up to become a great man. To this day, the inhabitants of *Kanaeri* are said to believe that Jaisohn was the proof of this.

Happy Childhood

Till the age of seven, Sang Kyong spent a great deal of time there. He was a favorite of his grandparents. Gregarious and energetic, he enjoyed running races, wrestling and rolling downhill with his playmates in his grandparent's homestead. It was fun too, listening to the farmers singing folk songs as they worked in the field and learning to sing with them. They encouraged him to sing with them, remarking that he had a 'beautiful, melodious' voice. During breaks he joined the farmers in dancing in a circle, and they told him he would make a great *kwangdae* (entertainer) and remarked: "What a pity you were born a yangban." Since entertaining (singing, dancing, and acrobatics) was a profession of the lowest social class in those days, they knew well that he would not be permitted to indulge in such fun for long.

Photo: The birthplace of Soh Jai-pil in *Kanaeri, Mundeok-myeon, Boseong-gun, Cholla-nam-do*.

On a hot summer day, it is said, when Sang Kyong was about six, it chanced that a magistrate of a neighboring district was passing by *Kanaeri* with his entourage. On reaching a huge elm tree on the edge of the village, the magistrate stopped for a rest in its shade. Emerging from his sedan chair, he sat under the tree, fanning himself with a large fan. No sooner had he seated himself on a mat than the village tots gathered around him and gazed at him and his sedan chair with unsophisticated curiosity. Among the throngs of children were Sang Kyong who watched as the fat pot-bellied magistrate wearing a large horse-hair hat was guarded solicitously by his fawning servants. The other children did likewise. Soon the servants, anxious for peace and quiet for their master, barked at them to go away and be quiet. All except Sang Kyong scampered away in fright, for they remembered their parents telling how vicious government officials were. The look of the magistrate and the yell of his attendants proved, they thought, how true their folks were.

But Sang Kyong did not move. He was not scared. In fact, he thought the whole scene amusing and stepping closer to the magistrate, he looked straight into his eyes. For a few moments, His Honor surveyed the little challenger sternly but soon mellowed and invited the lad to sing in the song. "I'd be glad to, sir," Sang Kyong answered. But first, may I borrow your fan? I can sing better if I can use it for accompaniment." The magistrate was momentarily taken aback by Sang Kyong's audacity. But realizing that the request was for his own entertainment, he complied. Sang Kyong, took the fan, flipped it open with a surprising dexterity, and sang one of his favorite songs, accompanying it with a rhythmic swing to and from. He sang with gusto in a clear strong voice. The magistrate and his retainers were impressed and requested an encore, and Sang Kyong cheerfully obliged. When the magistrate asked the child his name, the latter answered: "My name is Soh Jai-pil but my parents and grandparents call me Sang Kyong because in the year I was born, two lucky things happened to my family. My father passed his kwago and I was born." "That is very interesting," said the official, "Mark my words, Sang Kyong, someday you will become a great man."

Adopted into the *Andong* Kim Family

When Sang Kyong was 7, the patriarchs of the Soh Clan decided that one of their clansmen Soh Kwang-ha, who was without a male heir, needed to adopt a boy in order to continue his family line unbroken.

Since tradition required that this adoptee must be of the same generation as that of Kwang-ha's son, had he had one, Sang Kyong was selected. Accordingly, he went to live with his adoptive parents, Soh Kwang-ha and Kim Si of the famous Kims of *Andong*. From then on, he was allowed to visit his natural parents, but it was all but impossible to visit his maternal grandparents at *Kanaeri*.

His adoptive parents told him that playing with the children of poor peasants was a frivolity a son of a *yangban* should shun. Thus, sooner than most youngsters, Sang Kyong was made to realize that he was born not to enjoy life, but to fill a role assigned to him for the maintenance of a social system. He had never been asked whether he wished to be adopted by another family. The decision was made by his clan oligarchs for the continuation of the family name of one of his relatives. Understandably, it seems that his relationship with his adoptive parents was not one of mutual affection. In later years, reminiscing about his early boyhood, he remarked that his memory of them was vague.

It soon became apparent that Kwang-ha's motive in adopting Sang Kyong was not only to perpetuate his family name, but also to bring fame and fortune to his family through his adopted son. The lad was bright, comely and healthy. All he needed to become great was to pass the *kwago,* the license to a government career. For this, he used to study under the best possible teacher of Confucian classics available and to be acquainted with the right kind of people who would help advance his career. This was possible only in the capital city and Kwang-ha and his wife decided to send him off to Seoul. "Son," they told Sang Kyong one day, "We are sending you to Seoul. As a fisherman who wishes to catch big fish must go to a big sea, one who wishes to acquire great fame must go to the big city."

There, Sang Kyong's adoptive parents told him he would be living with his uncle's family, and his rich and powerful uncle would see to it that he studied under the finest teacher. Sang Kyong dutifully obeyed, and shortly thereafter he bade farewell to his adoptive parents and went to Seoul. There he lived with Kim Sung-keun and his family in a palatial house. Mr. Kim, who was the brother of his adoptive mother, was a cabinet minister and leading member of the Kims of *Andong*, a clan that had virtually ruled Korea until the Taewon-gun's rise to power. One of the wealthiest men in Korea, he owned several sumptuous houses in the nation's capital as well as elsewhere. The one where Sang Kyong went to live was located near *Wun-Hyon* Palace, the residence of Regent Prince Taewon, father of the King, and was almost as pretentious as the Prince's. Of this house, Jaisohn later said:

> In Seoul, I lived with my uncle and their son Pyong-uk in their palatial house. The first thing I remember was sitting in a fine Korean style house. In the men's quarters, there were many servants in addition to eight private secretaries. The women's quarters were in a separate building connected by a passageway, and only women were allowed in there. Male relatives could visit them, but their arrival had to be announced. In the men's quarters there were, in addition to my uncle's suite, rooms for his assistants and their aides, an audience chamber, a room for our ancestral tablets and the school for my cousin, myself and a half dozen other boys.

At *Kanaeri*, Sang Kyong had displayed gregarious and daring traits. In Seoul his other qualities were revealed, chief among which were 'concern for other people and self-reliance.' The concern for others so characteristic of his later career could be gleaned from his dealings with the staff of Minister Kim's household, which he later recounted. He wrote of his first day's experience at his uncle's house:

> The room was full of people I did not know. They were looking at me and laughing. I was much offended seeing them enjoy themselves at my expense, but later I learned the reason. When I was very small, I was not able to eat meat as I was allergic to it, so I was largely raised on grain, vegetables and fruits. Upon being transported to this rich relative's house, I was offered all kinds of meat. I refused the offer. When they asked why, I said that meat made my skin itch. They laughed, saying they had never heard of such a thing.

The room full of people referred to by Jaisohn were mostly Minister Kim's house servants. Having never eaten enough meat to satisfy their appetite, they had no opportunity to find out if one could be allergic to it. Hence, they thought that Sang Kyong was being funny when he said meat made his skin itch. However, he soon sensed that they laughed not only out of amusement but also to persuade him to take some. They feared that otherwise he would become weak, and that Minister Kim and his wife would blame them for it. Not wishing to cause them trouble, Sang Kyong forced himself to take meat, taking a small quantity at first and gradually increasing the amount. Thus, he built up an immunity in his system.

'Self-reliance' was another characteristic of Sang Kyong's, which became manifest shortly after his arrival in Seoul. As early as he could remember he had always washed, dressed and undressed himself, although there were servants in his natural parents' and adoptive parents' houses. His cousin, on the other hand, seemed quite content to let the servants attend to all his ablutions, and they proposed to do likewise for him. Both he and his cousin were of the same age. At first, he spurned their offer. Then, not wishing to disconcert the routine, he allowed himself to be treated 'like a toy.' Try as he did to tolerate this, he found it more and more revolting, and finally he told him politely that he would take care of his own washing and dressing.

Education System

Education among the aristocrats of Korea in those days was an esoteric affair. A tutor was hired by a family to teach Chinese characters and Confucian classics to their sons and sometimes their friends' sons in one of their rooms. Girls were not allowed to attend classes with boys but were taught by either their parents or a hired teacher. In the latter case, the teacher taught his female pupils sitting in a room separated from them by a curtain. The tutor could be heard, but he and the girls did not see each other.

Mr. Kim set aside a chamber in the male quarters of his house to serve as the school for his son, Sang Kyong, and a half dozen sons of his friends. Then he hired a well-recommended tutor and told him to make good scholars out of them. Jaisohn remembered how surprised he was by the contrast between his schoolmates here and the boys he used to play with in *Kanaeri*. The former looked and acted like fairies, while the latter were real humans. One of his schoolmates was carried to the school in a sedan chair wearing a wool-lined white silk robe. He was Yi

Wan-yong who, later as Prime Minister, signed away Korea's independence in 1910.

Sang Kyong and Pyong Uk, his cousin, arose at 7:00 a.m. After washing and dressing, they had breakfast consisting of soup, rice and meat or fish and by 8:30 a.m. they were in their school. The school schedule was:

8:30 to 10:30,   learning and reading Chinese characters and
                     beginners' lessons;
10:30 to 11:00, recreation;
11:00 to 12:00, Chinese calligraphy;
12:00 to 13:00, lunch.

The afternoon schedule was similar to the mornings. Following supper, Sang Kyong and Pyong Uk returned to the school and spent several hours reading their daily lessons over and over again till they learned them by heart. The aim of education was twofold:

- cultivation of the boy's moral character and
- preparation for the *kwago*.

In practice, the later aim was far more important. Under the umbrella title of *kwago*, there were various types and levels of it, such as

- Royal kwago,
- Provincial kwago,
- Civilian kwago and
- Military kwago.

However, all of them stressed the mastery of Confucian classics. In due course, the examinations degenerated into contests for rote memorization of the classics. Those capable of reciting passages selected for them by examiners were declared as having passed the *kwago* to which they were entitled, and those reciting the passages flawlessly passed them with the highest honor. The textbooks which Sang Kyong and his fellow students used in the beginning were:

- One Thousand Characters 千字文, a concise story of the universe in 1,000 characters.
- Lessons for Juniors 童蒙先習, elementary ethics and five human relationships.
- Primary Learning 初學, a serial history of China.
- Little Classics 小學 and The Four Books and the Three Classics 四書三經, for intermediate pupils.

Since each student was tutored individually, bright ones naturally moved ahead faster, and Sang Kyong, who was perhaps the brightest in his school, learned all the beginner's texts and many of the Confucian classics reserved for upper-level scholars during the six years he spent at his uncle's school. This was something most of his schoolmates could not do in twelve years.

Sang Kyong's amazing progress in his study was not because the subjects he took were stimulating and interesting. As a matter of fact, education in Korea at the time was utterly uninspiring. The curriculum consisted of subjects that were anything but relevant to the students. There were no sports, arts, sciences or current affairs in it. There were brief periods of recreation, but there was neither an athletic field where they could run races nor equipment with which they could engage in sports. Their tutor, an unathletic man, considered physical exercise as a waste of time and regarded it as his duty to keep the pupils chained to the floor virtually all day, day after day, and to see to it that they learned and recited their lessons. Worse yet, the students went to school each morning dreading physical punishment. Under the old tradition, the teacher's authority to punish his pupils whenever he saw fit, and in any manner, whatever was never questioned, and this tutor exercised it freely.

Picture: A *seodang* (private school) teacher and students.

Sang Kyong was not free from the dread either, because his uncle had told the teacher to employ any means deemed necessary to make scholars out of his son, his nephew, and all the rest. Daily routine at Minister Kim's school began with a 'bow down' to the teacher. The teacher would sometimes whack a pupil just for clumsiness in bow-downing. A long bamboo stick never left his hand. He used it to point out significant passages in the text as well as to administer punishment to inattentive or dozing pupils.

To Sang Kyong, the teacher's draconian behavior was more distracting than helpful to his pupils and soon found a way to 'tranquilize' him. He was a portly man suffering from a mild case of asthma and was prone to doze off when sitting still, especially in the midst of a continuous din. After teaching the boys their daily lessons, he would announce: "Reading period!" This was the most boring period of all, but the sound of their reading aloud on and on made him drowsy, and he would soon doze off. As long as there was a noise of reading in the room, he remained asleep. Noting this, Sang Kyong and the rest divided themselves into two groups and took turns reading as loudly as if the whole student body was; while one group read this, the other relaxed.

Fortunately for Sang Kyong, not only did he have a photographic mind, which made memorizing easy, but he also had a penetrating perception which enabled him to appreciate the spirit of the teaching contained in the Classics. He realized that the essence of Confucian teaching was the pursuit of wisdom and virtue, not the memorization of it by rote. Hence, in spite of the uninspiring teaching, he derived much benefit out of his education. The other lads obviously did not. Born and bred in wealth and spoiled by their doting servants, perhaps they found their school life too uninteresting. They were accustomed to doing as they pleased. They knew they would pass the *kwago* anyway because their fathers were rich and influential, so they merely pretended to study.

Joyful Times of Childhood

Sang Kyong did not have much fun out of playing with his schoolmates. Dressed in expensive clean robes and transported to and from school in sedan chairs, they seem to regard any form of exercise as physical labor. So, he played with the children of his uncle's house employees. The games he was fond of playing were quoits and coin hitting. Coin hitting consisted of making a hole in the ground and pitching coins into the hole from a distance of 15 feet or so. The aim was to hit the hole or land nearest to it. The one landing nearer the hole than his opponents got all the coins.

There was one exception to his monotonous life in Seoul during this earlier period. That was paying occasional visits to *Suwon* where his paternal grandfather was the Governor. The Governor's residence was located in an exclusive place surrounded by hundreds of acres of land. Here he could release his excess energy to his heart's content by running races with his grandfather's hunting dogs or riding a donkey which his grandfather had bought for him. This spacious estate with hundreds of varieties of trees, thousands of rocks, plants, flowers and all kinds of animals, provided an ideal laboratory for its inquisitive mind. He went there as often as he could.

Though his study of Confucian classics emphasizing social ethics and past civilization was not without some attraction, he was much more curious about things present and tangible: Botany, zoology, mineralogy, physics, chemistry, as well as geography, anthropology, and sociology. Walking in the woods, he was in the company of the plants and animals, lying on the grassy fields and gazing at the stars, sun and moon. He thirsted for the secret of their ability to stay afloat and of their power to give off light and heat.

The Government Service Examination

At about the age of thirteen, Sang Kyong had covered all seven books of the Confucian Classics, 四書三經. That is, he was able to recite most of them. Everyone suggested that it would be well for him to take the *kwago,* because the sooner he tried, the more opportunity to pass it he would have. Not many pass it the first time. At this time there was an announcement that a Royal *Kwago* - reserved for the sons of high *yangbans* - would be held. Sang Kyong was persuaded to try it. He was the youngest among the candidates, of whom there were nineteen.

On the day of examination, he followed the other candidates into the royal palace. The King was on hand. They were ordered to kneel before His Majesty, one at a time. After that, the examining officials placed before them question sheets, each of which contained a different title, volume of the classics and selections from which the candidates were told to recite. One at a time, the candidates were called before the judges, who ordered each to announce the passages from the classics he was to recite. Some performed passably, some sat tongue tied. When Sang Kyong's turn came, he stepped forward, knelt, and no sooner had he announced his passages than he recited them as if he were reading from the texts. The examiners, marveling at his brilliance, declared him the winner of the highest award.

A bright government career lay ahead of him. With the meritorious *kupje* (passing of the *kwago)*, Sang Kyong was no longer addressed by that name, though only in his early teens, he was *Toryong Nim* (Your Honor) to his house servants and Jai-pil to his friends and peers.

CHAPTER THREE:
YOUTH

In 1864, the Taewon-gun, as described earlier, engineered the ascension to the throne of his second son as the 26th ruler of the *Yi* dynasty and made himself 'Adviser' to the regent dowager Queen Cho of Korea. From then on, he became so dominant that he was called Regent Taewon-gun. He was also the most controversial figure in their realm, with a few of the people hailing him as a reformer but most intensely fearing and hating him. It is said that mothers hushed their crying children by warning: "The Taewon-gun is coming." Hence, when he was forced into retirement a decade later, almost everyone, including young Jaisohn, heaved a sigh of relief. When King Kojong reached adulthood in 1867, the Dowager Queen, who was the regent in name only, declared the regency ended, but the Taewon-gun continued to exercise power, causing the people to assume erroneously that he was the regent. In fact, he was often referred to as the 'regent prince.'

The Mins' Faction

Nevertheless, it soon became clear to the people that the Taewon-gun's ouster meant to them merely jumping from the frying pan into the fire. His capricious and oppressive rule was replaced by an equally corrupt and detestable rule - the *seido* of the Min clan. The chief difference between the Taewon-gun regency and the Min *seido*, though, was that the latter was headed by a woman, Queen Min. From 1874 to 1895, when she met her violent death at the hands of Japanese killers, this domineering woman exercised her royal husband's powers as thoroughly as her father-in-law had. Though she was the most talked of person for over two decades, only a handful of people knew her in person. Presumably for fear of assassination, she never made public appearances. Nor did she allow photographs of herself to be taken. Even when holding meetings with ministers, she hid herself behind a bamboo screen.

Superstitious though she was, she was a remarkably intelligent woman and taught herself to read and write in *onmum*, Korean vernacular, and also learned a few simple Chinese characters. On her physical appearance, there is scant basis to form an intelligent opinion. Knowing that Jaisohn was one of the few who had seen her, I once asked him what she looked like. 'A cunning woman,' was his answer. Even Rose Foote, wife of the first American Minister to Korea, was one of the few to meet her and was deeply impressed by her, could only describe her as having 'an interesting face and well-shaped head.' She might not have been a beauty, but there was no question but what, if she wanted to, she could charm her way into winning anything or anyone.

Queen Min was born in 1850 in a highly aristocratic but poor family. Having been left an orphan early in her childhood, she was brought up by her uncle and his wife, who were also far from well to do. Hence, as a child, she performed all sorts of menial chores. But it was for a purpose. She had an iron will to find a husband who was not only a high *yangban*, but also rich and powerful. Since in those days marriages were arranged by the parents or guardians of eligible young men and women, she had to rely on her uncle and aunt to help realize the dream. Therefore, she did her best to ingratiate herself with them. She was ever so obedient, gentle, diligent, efficient, and kept herself immaculately neat. She conquered the hearts of her uncle and aunt. She was the most precious apple of their eyes, and they were unsparing in praising her before all their friends and relatives. One of those who heard of this 'lovely girl,' saw her and was impressed by her was Princess Min, the wife of the Taewon-gun.

Photo: Queen Min from the New York Herald reporting on her assassination. (1895)

From an Orphaned Maiden to Queen Min

In the fourth year of the reign of King Kojong, he had reached marriageable age, and his parents, the Taewon-gun and Princess Min, were deeply engrossed in the selection of a suitable consort for their son. The regent's wife, in her own mind, had already selected one. The orphaned daughter of a relative of hers. At first, the Taewon-gun objected. He had secretly promised Dowager Queen Cho that he would choose the girl among her relatives. However, after careful cogitation, he concurred with his wife's choice. Selecting a Cho girl to be his son's queen was fraught with the danger of paving way for the Cho *seido*. Whereas since his wife was a member of the Min clan and the King was already related to the Mins, his marriage to the Min girl was not likely to lead to this danger. If anything, this would serve to seal the bond between the Mins and Yis and to enhance the prestige of the House of *Yi*, of which he was the patriarch. Thus, the marriage between the King and orphaned Min was consummated, and the bride was given the royal title Queen Myong-song. Her resolve had more than paid off.

For some years, the young queen fully lived up to the Taewon-gun's expectations - ever so sweet and deferent. His continued exercise of powers after the King had reached majority did not seem to offend her in the least. Deep inside, however, she was far from sweet and deferent. She was bitter and was waiting for the right moment to strike at him. The moment to strike would not come until and unless she gave birth to a son. If she failed to do so, she would be shunted aside in favor of another woman who bore the King an heir.

Desperate, she hired sorcerers and fortune tellers to pray for her to bear a son. Twice she had become pregnant, but both pregnancies ended in miscarriages. Finally, her dream was realized when she gave birth to a baby boy in 1873. The King was so overjoyed that he preferred babysitting to attending to his royal duties. The birth of an heir to the Korean throne was also greeted with joy by the people. The position of the queen was now secure, and she decided that the time to have a showdown with her father-in-law that come.

Before her son was even a year old, she prevailed on her husband to hold an ostentatious ceremony of conferring the title of crown prince on the infant and to send a mission to Peking, headed by an enemy of Taewon-gun to obtain the sanction of the Chinese Emperor, both of which were done without consulting the 'regent.' Furthermore, on her urging, her husband countermanded all orders issued by the Taewon-gun. The 'regent' was furious. However, as none of the royal ministers, sensing the mood of the people, rose to his defense, he realized that he was through and 'left town.' His exercise of power was illegal when his son reached majority.

With lightning speed, the queen fired all the ex-regent's appointees and filled their posts with her blood relatives or their trusted allies. These new appointees proceeded to plunder the national treasury and to virtually rob the people. Min Sung-ho, a cousin of the queen's, was so preoccupied with amassing his fortune as Minister of War that he failed to pay wages to the nation's soldiers for over a year. When he finally did pay, he did it with the rice, which was mixed with sand. The irate soldiers staged a mutiny in which he was killed. Min Yong-hwi, another relative of the queen, reportedly became the wealthiest man in the country while holding governorship in *Pyongan* province. These were merely the tip of an iceberg of the corruption under the Min *seido*.

The arrival of the Min era coincided with irresistible pressures of Western expansionism. Though that immediate aggressor was not an Occidental power but Japan, the latter's actions were typically Western. She was flexing her newly acquired Western style military muscle at Korea, exactly as the United States and European powers had done to her two decades earlier. The viscerally conservative Min oligarchs fervently wished they could defy Japan. But Korea's army, tiny, neglected, poorly armed and demoralized, was utterly useless. China, on whom Korea had long relied for protection, was herself reeling under relentless pressures of the Western powers. Consequently, realizing the futility of resisting Japan, they yielded to her demand for a diplomatic and commercial treaty. This is the Korea-Japan Treaty of 1876.

Given Japan's overwhelming military superiority, her treaty demand could be considered as mild. From a broad perspective, however, her gains were sweeping.

- First, though her recognition of Korea's independence might seem almost altruistic, in reality, it constituted a tacit concession by Korea that Japan was replacing China as the suzerain of the peninsula kingdom.
- Secondly, Japan's right to send diplomatic missions to Korea was a euphemism for her political interference in Korea,
- Thirdly, the opening of two additional Korean ports, which was tantamount to Japan's right of economic penetration into the Hermit Kingdom.

From Isolation to the Crucible of Foreign Invasion

For Korea, the agonizing consequences of the treaty were far more extensive than the Mins had realized. They were just as conservative as the Taewon-gun and were fierce defenders of the ancient Confucian ideology as their vested interests lay in strict preservation of it. They agreed to the treaty, believing that Japan, in recognizing Korea's independence, would respect Korea's right to choose any political and social system she wished to. Moreover, they followed up the Korea-Japan Treaty with similar treaties with the U.S. and other Western countries, because China advised them to do so. Li Hung Chang, China's strong man, believed that, once in Korea, the 'Ocean devils' would fight among themselves and leave Korea alone. Rivals among themselves they indeed were. However, they always presented a common front in seeking special rights from Korea.

One of the unforeseen consequences of the Korean-Japanese Treaty was a crack in Korea's ancient ideological wall of isolation. Immediately after concluding the treaty, Japan reminded the Seoul government that when civilized nations agreed to maintain friendly relations, they exchanged diplomatic missions and that it was Korea's turn to send one to Japan. Reluctantly, the Mins complied with the dispatch of an 80-man mission. This was followed by two other missions during the ensuing eight years, and they served to whet the appetite of an increasing number of Koreans for a modern way which the 'Westernized Japan' represented. 'Reform movement' in Korea was thus born, and the Min *seido* was forced into a deadly, losing war against forces nurtured by Western thought, which seeped in through the crack caused by the Korea-Japan Treaty and swelled into flood-tides as a result of the subsequent treaties with Western powers.

Tong-hak Party and *Kaehwa* Party

Those forces may be grouped into two: the *Tong-hak* (Eastern-learning Party) and *Kaehwa* (Progressive Party) or *Toknip Dang* (Independence Party). Ironically, though both were bitter foes of the Min oligarchy, they were also antagonistic to each other. While the *Tong-haks* opposed all things Western as evil, the latter called for an all-out introduction of the Western system. Originally, the *Tong-haks* were adherents of a religious group. Founded in the 1850s by a Confucian scholar of a plebeian class as a counter force against Roman Catholicism, which was known as the 'Western Learning', the *Tong-hak* Party thrived on the conservative leaning of the Korean people. Though its teaching were said to be in opposition to Catholicism, in reality, it was an amalgam of Korean indigenous beliefs, Buddhism, Confucianism and Christianity. It taught that all who believed in the Heavenly Master and worshipped Him would be free of physical ailments while living, as well as assured of entrance into paradise upon death. The worship consisted of reciting the words

> "Descend now, O Master. With the Heavenly Master we shall renew creation and will be wise through eternity."
> accompanied by ritualistic dance with wooden swords.
> 至氣今至願爲大降, 侍天主造化定, 永世不忘萬事知

Because it's ritual and doctrine were simple, and its promises sweeping, the *Tong-hak* sect attracted wide following among peasants. Since the peasant class was the most oppressed, yet most numerous groups in Korea, it was natural that the *Tong-haks* would, in time, realize their potential to bring about an improvement of their social and economic lot. During the Min era, under the impact of increasing government oppression on the one hand and of the West which introduced the concept of man's natural rights on the other, the *Tong-hak* sect became, in effect, a populist political party.

Kim Ok-kiun

The *Kaehwa Dang* came into being over two decades after the rise of the *Tong-hak* movement. Its leaders, unlike those of the *Tong-haks*, belonged to the elite of Korea and their aim was limited - namely, to replace the corrupt and repressive government with one that was progressive and efficient, presumably formed by them. The group was headed by an ambitious and brilliant nobleman named Kim Ok-kiun (김옥균). Born of the once powerful Kims of *Andong* in 1850, he passed the *kwago* (government service examination) with the highest honor at the age of 15 and several years later earned an appointment as a junior official in the government then headed by the Taewon-gun. However, since the 'regent' scrupulously excluded all potential rivals, especially the Kims of *Andong*, from positions of power, Kim Ok-kiun, who was a member of that clan, was given only a minor position which carried no responsibility.

Hence, he had plenty of time to sulk, read and reflect. He wrote extensively and visited with persons of diverse backgrounds and unusual experiences. Among those he found particularly stimulating were Pak Kyu-su, Governor of *Pyongan* province at the time the American ship, General Sherman, arrived in *Pyongyang* in 1866, as well as an ex-envoy to Peking; Yu Dae-chi, who had accompanied several Korean missions to China; and O Kyung-suk, interpreter to Korean envoys to China. Kim knew that they had not reported all that they had learned while in China in their official reports to the government and wished to hear about them. Indeed, they had not because, in view of the Taewon-gun's implacable prejudice against the 'Ocean devils,' to suggest that the great and ancient Empire of China seemed certain to be vanquished by the Western powers was tantamount to committing suicide. Still, the truth needed to be told, and they consented to tell Kim what they had seen and heard in China, as they trusted him to be a young but patriotic official. The gist of what Kim learned from them was that

> the colossal but staid and complacent China was under systematic attack from the Western powers, whose dynamic social thoughts and superior military weapons born of their scientific and technological developments made them unbeatable.

According to them, China was no longer what she had been. She was steadily on the decline and for Korea to continue to rely on her for defense was to court self-destruction.

The more Kim Ok-kiun read about China and her relations with the Western powers, the more he was convinced that what Pak Kyu-su, Yu Dae-chi and O Kyong-suk told him was true. This led him to be curious about the Western powers and about how they had acquired the power to conquer such a mighty empire as China.

Buddhist Monk Lee Dong-in

The man who satisfied his curiosity was a learned Buddhist monk. This man, named Lee Dong-in, was born in *Pusan* which had long been the only port open for Japanese residence. Having grown up with Japanese children as neighbors in the city, he learned to speak Japanese. On reaching adulthood, he became a monk and entered a Buddhist monastery called *Tongdo-sa* and immersed himself in the study of Buddhism and Confucianism, in both of which he became an authority.

Under the *Yi* dynasty's discriminatory policy against the Buddhists, they suffered numerous indignities, including the loss of their freedom to even enter the capital city of Seoul, let alone preach their religion. But so long as they obeyed the rules, the government left them more or less alone, and Lee was able to visit Japan more than once, posing as a Japanese. He became the first and highly knowledgeable authority on modern, rapidly Westernizing Japan. Precisely when and how Kim first met the monk is not known. It is known that Kim, deeply impressed by the monk, had him slip into a Buddhist temple in the suburb of Seoul in order to introduce him to his trusted friends in the spring of 1879.

Kim Ok-kiun's Liberalism

As the hated Taewon-gun regency ended only to be succeeded by the Min tyranny, the people were bitterly disappointed. The *Tong-haks* on the grassroots level were no longer content with confining their activities to religious propagation. They turned increasingly toward political movement in opposition to the Min oligarchs. Their dissatisfaction was echoed by younger and bright *yangbans* in the capital who were attracted to Kim Ok-kiun's liberalism. Having extensively read books on the Western world and listened to knowledgeable persons on true conditions abroad, Kim was convinced that the road to Korea's survival lay in purging the government of the smug, ignorant and China-leaning men around Queen Min and installing to power those leaders who would emulate the architects of Japan's Meiji restoration.

To that end, he began to recruit coworkers. Soon his comrades numbered several dozens, most important of whom being Pak Yong-hyo, son-in-law of the late King Choljong; Hong Yong-sik, son of a former

Prime Minister; Soh Kwang-pom, also a son of a former Prime Minister; and Soh Jai-pil (Philip Jaisohn).

Jaisohn was by far the youngest of them. He was only in his teens. Kim Ok-kiun's selection of young Jaisohn as one of his principal colleagues is not surprising. As Jaisohn's adoptive mother was a member of the Kims of *Andong*, Kim and Jaisohn were related to each other. They also lived in the same neighborhood where powerful *yangbans*, including the Taewon-gun, had their residences. From the moment the two first met, they became close friends in spite of their disparity in age. Though Kim was Jaisohn's senior by 14 years, they had much in common. Both were adopted sons. Both were brilliant in intellect, adventurous in nature and daring. To the end, Jaisohn remained an unqualified admirer of Kim Ok-kiun. He said of Kim:

> Kim Ok-kiun was convinced that the causes of Korea's weakness were the lack of scientific and technical knowledge on the part of the rank and file of the Korean people and the ignorance and stupidity of the people of upper class. Time and time again, he reminded me of the fact that the only way to save Korea from fall lay in the education of the people, and that the task of educating them must be borne by the youth. Oldsters are utterly incapable of it, he said.

The Birth of the *Kaehwa Dang*

To the temple (*Bong-am sa*) located outside of Seoul, Kim Ok-kiun invited the four named above one day in the late 1870s. Of the secret historic gathering, Jaisohn later said as follows:

"One day, I cannot say exactly what year, in spring, I think, Kim Ok-kiun asked me to join some friends in *Bong-am* Temple for a quiet get-together. I accepted the invitation and on reaching there I found an intelligent looking Buddhist monk sitting in a room surrounded by a group of my friends and answering questions put to him by Kim. His name was Lee Dong- in. He had been to Japan, and the stories about her and Occidental countries of which he had read in Japanese books held me spellbound. Moreover, he had with him pictures of the cities, ships and railroad trains of Japan and Occidental countries. We looked at them through a kaleidoscope which he brought. We were speechless at the splendor of what we saw and at the 'magic mirror' (kaleidoscope). He also showed us a box of matches. We all took our turn in lighting a match, striking it against the rough side of the box and watching it burst into flame. We nearly shouted with delight, like little children. The monk also had a Japanese book entitled "The History of the Occidental World". Although it was written in Japanese, we could comprehend quite a bit of what was written as the author had used a great deal of Chinese characters, which we understood. We were simply flabbergasted by the speed of Japan's modernization. In little over twenty years, she had become a powerful nation by adopting Western ways."

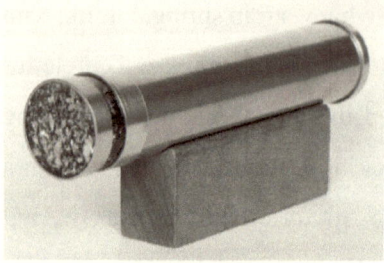

Photo: Kaleidoscope.

Anxious for more information about the Western world, Kim Ok-kiun asked the monk if he would sell the book to him. The latter declined, saying it was his only copy. However, he would gladly bring him another copy when he returned from another journey to Japan where he was planning. Kim gave him some money, telling him to bring as many books as he could. Jaisohn went on:

> Lee the monk was an impressive person: exceptionally learned, urbane and yet humble. Since in those days Buddhists were treated as social outcasts and denied privileges enjoyed by the rest of the people, they were mendicants seeking solace in meditation and monasteries. Confident that they would pose no threat to the status quo, the ruling elite did not bother to watch their movements closely, and Lee, like his fellow Buddhists, was able to slip in and out of the country without difficulty.
>
> About six months later, the monk returned, bringing with him a number of books, pictures of Western countries and a kaleidoscope and several boxes of matches. Overjoyed, we got together as often as we could in different places and read the books with absorbing interest and entertained ourselves looking

at the pictures through the kaleidoscope and lighting the matches. The books were on the history, geography, social customs and governments of leading Occidental countries. Although they were written in Japanese, we were able to comprehend their contents fairly well. We must have spent some half a year reading those books.

By the time we had finished reading them, we thought as if we had been introduced to a new and wonderful world. There was no doubt in our minds that Korea's salvation lay in the reform of the political system according to that being undergone by Japan after the pattern of the Occidental nations. We promised one another to do whatever was necessary to help introduce this Western system into Korea and revitalize her as the Japanese had done in their country. This was how Korea's first reform movement was born.

The reform movement in Korea is noteworthy in two respects.

- First, unlike that of China and Japan, it was initiated by Koreans without over external provocation.

- Secondly, in spite of Korea's stubborn refusal to enter into international intercourse till more than three decades after China was forced to, the reform movement in Korea led by Kim Ok-kiun, Pak Yong-hyo, etc. began over a decade earlier than their Chinese counterparts, Kang, Yu-wei, Liang, Chih- Chao, etc.

In these respects, Kim, Jaisohn, and their colleagues stand out as unique reformers of not only Korea, but all East Asia as well.

Kim Ok-kiun in Japan

The year 1881 was a milestone in the history of modern Korea. That year, Kim Ok-kiun's long cherished dream of a personal visit in Japan was realized. He went there as a member of the first cultural mission to be sent abroad by Korea. What the Japanese showed them were so fascinating that he decided to stay behind when the rest of the mission returned home. He remained in Japan over six months, not only observing various facets of modern westernized Japan, but also meeting and talking with the architects of the new Japan.

He met and became friends with such political leaders as K. Inoue and Okura, such financiers as E. Shibuzawa, and such educators as Y Fukuzawa and Kodo. The longer he stayed in Japan, the more he was convinced that the way to build a new Korea lay in following Japan's example. He was confident that in this he could win support of King Kojong. Had he not broken precedent by opening Korea to intercourse with Japan? Having declared that his was an independent nation through the Korea-Japan Treaty, it was in his as well as Korea's interest to build up Korea's military, economic and political power by emulating Japan to make that a reality.

Alas, an unhappy surprise awaited him. Returning to Korea in early June 1882, he found her prostrate in the aftermath of a ruinous upheaval known as the soldier's rebellion (*Imo* Military Revolt). The King had barely saved his throne. The queen saved her life by fleeing in disguise. Many of the Queen's relatives had been murdered. Government buildings and residences of the murdered ministers were burned down, and the Japanese in Seoul too suffered heavy casualties in life and property.

Japan had already demanded payment of a punitive indemnity, but the Government was bankrupt. Furthermore, the rebellion was suppressed by Chinese troops rushed in by Li Hung-Chang who, in violation of a historic tradition of non-interference in the internal affairs of each by Korea and China, sought to reduce Korea to the status of a colony of China. The Government was under the virtual control of China.

Kim Ok-kiun sighed: "There goes my dream of a new and independent Korea." However, his audience with Their Majesties somewhat mollified his despair. He found them desperately trying to resist dictations by the occupation authorities of the Chinese army. The King was greatly incensed by Yuan Shih-Kai, an aide to Admiral C.K. Wu, Commander of the Chinese troops. Yuan was not only arrogant, but he was also outright rude, and the King seemed ready to stand up to the Chinese if there was a source of help that he could rely on.

When the King expressed the hope, Kim Ok-kiun said, that 'either Japan or the United States might be willing to back him up with economic and military aid.' At the time, negotiations between Korea and the U.S. for a treaty of trade and mutual defense were in progress, and the prospects were bright. The immediate concern of Their Majesties, however, was the wherewithal to pay for urgently needed repair of the gutted buildings, pay indemnity to the Japanese and meet the soldiers' pay demands. They asked for his suggestion on how to secure it, adding:

> Some ministers suggest that we mint a half million dollars' worth of new 5 jon and 20 jon coins containing 1/2 the copper of the old ones, but to be circulated as if they were as valuable as the old coins. What do you think?

Kim firmly opposed the plan, arguing that

>it would not only drive the currency value tumbling down and force the nation into chaos, but that it was too little to meet the needs.

He advocated, instead, approaching Japan with a request for a $3,000,000 loan. Reporting that the Japanese leaders whom he had met showed an increasing interest in Korea, he expressed the belief that Japan might well respond favorably. He also offered another potential source of cash in these words;

>There are innumerable whales in our coastal waters of the Eastern Sea (Japan Sea). Whales are highly prized by the Japanese and Occidental peoples, and we may be able to realize a substantial sum of money but either catching them ourselves or selling the fishing rights to a large foreign fishing firm.

Their Majesties were so enthusiastic about Kim's suggestions that they appointed him as the King's 'Whale Catching Commissioner' right there and then. The King also offered to name him as chief of a 'Mission of Apology' to Japan for her losses in lives and property suffered during the soldiers' rebellion, which the Japanese Government had demanded. Kim suggested that Pak Yong-hyo be named in his stead. Observing that as the head of the mission he might not be free to discuss the matter of the loan, he would rather accompany Pak as adviser to the mission. Their Majesties agreed.

Photo (Left): Kim Ok-kiun at 34 years old. (Right) *Dangojun* (a type of traditional Korean coin).

The First Korean Student Group Abroad

Before leaving Their Majesty's presence, Kim brought up one matter which he believed was of great importance to Korea and to them. That was sending a group - about 50 - bright and conscientious young men to Japan to be trained in modern military and technical sciences and come back ready to pioneer in the construction of a new and viable Korea. After explaining the value of such an educational mission to them as well as Korea, he said that Japan was an ideal place to send students to, for there they could learn all the know-how which the Japanese had learned from the Occidental countries. Furthermore, it was less expensive to train students in Japan, and the Japanese language was easier to learn than the Occidental ones. He asked that in the event he succeeded in raising money through a whale-catching deal, he be allowed to apply a portion of it to sending the first batch of the student mission, numbering some 20, to Japan. He added that it was his hope to increase the number of this historic mission to 100. His Majesty approved the request.

Kim Ok-kiun immediately contacted a Japanese fishing firm in *Pusan* and secured a loan of 25,00 *won* ($12,500) in exchange for the right to catch whales in the Eastern Sea. With half of the sum in his pocket, Kim turned to Jaisohn, 'My younger brother,' and proudly told him that 'at last he was ready to put into reality his dream of sending the first student mission abroad in the history of Korea', and that he wanted it to be headed by Jaisohn. After saying that the plan had been sanctioned by the King and that the wherewithal to meet his cause had been obtained, he told Jaisohn that the initial group would be limited to no more than 20, that since Korea's most urgent need was strengthening her defense, they would be sent to a military school in Japan and therefore those selected should be bright, dedicated and physically strong youths. He concluded by saying that because he had been appointed to accompany the Pak Yong-hyo Mission of Apology to Japan, which was to leave shortly, he was entrusting to Jaisohn the responsibility of implementing the details of the mission: screening and selection of students, preparing for their travel, etc., as speedily as possible. He would be waiting for them in Tokyo.

Jaisohn accepted the appointment with alacrity. Though he was aware that it might entail risk to his future career or even physical danger to go to a country considered as an historic enemy of Korea and to learn things Western, which his people despised as diabolical, the lure of things 'new and different' was too tempting to spurn. The opportunity to see first-hand those things in Japan which Buddhist scholar Lee Dong-in's books and slides had fascinated him came his way. Even more challenging was the opportunity to help produce future leaders of Korea.

He wasted no time in recruiting suitable candidates for the student mission. But the job proved very difficult. On the one hand, most of the youths he knew were sons of *yangbans* in addition to himself. The rest were of plebeian background: Lee Kyu-won, one of Pak Yong-hyo's house servants; Im Eun-myong, Jaisohn's house servant; Yun Kyong-soon and his brother, laborers; Pak Eun-hak, Shin Jung-mok and his brother, Bok-mok, etc. In all, Jaisohn could only recruit 14, not including himself. While he was disappointed in failing to find 20 boys, he was philosophical about it. Viewed from the social milieu of the period, Jaisohn himself had found it difficult to overcome his family objections. He understood their point of view. He had been put through traditional schools to prepare himself for the *kwago*, to pass through his ordeals and to enter lucrative government service. Going to Japan as a member of the student mission might very well mean throwing away all of it and possibly ending up in disgrace in the eyes of the powers.

Toyama Military Academy

Jaisohn and his fellow students left for Tokyo in December 1882. The 'Apology Mission,' headed by Pak Yong-hyo had returned home, but Kim Ok-kiun was still in Japan. Quite understandably, the historic event went completely unnoticed by the Korean people, and their arrival in Tokyo was greeted with condescending curiosity by the Japanese. A Japanese historian wrote:

> Because the Independent Party was uninfluential, most of the student mission consisted of the children of provincial yangbans, commoners, and slaves. None of them came from the families of high government officials.

On arriving in Tokyo, led by Jaisohn, they were received by Kim Ok-kiun and Yukitsu Fuzukawa, Japan's foremost statesman-educator-philanthropist, who arranged for most of the youth to study the Japanese language under a tutor in preparation for their enrollment at school. They spent about six months studying Japanese. Their tutor, named Kaneko, who was a native of Tsushima, an island nearest to Korea, spoke Korean. He became so attached to them that he later followed them to Korea and lost his life during the 1884 coup. After a half years intensive study, which they did in a Buddhist temple, the boys were ready to enroll at the Toyama Military school.

(**Editor's Note**: Fukuzawa Yukichi's 'Outline of a Theory of Civilization', written in 1875, argued that in order to establish a new and independent nation, not only Western technology but also Western ideas and culture - most importantly, the concepts of 'freedom' and 'independence' - must be actively embraced. He wrote over 100 books in total.)

On the first day, as Jaisohn and his fellow Koreans walked into their class, their Japanese classmates were aghast. Every one of the Korean boys was a 'giant.' Subsequently, some of the Japanese boys teased the Koreans by calling them 'monsters.' This so annoyed one Korean, Im Eung-myong, that he picked up a teasing Japanese boy by the neck as if he were a chicken and threw him to the ground. After that, there were no more such incidents.

The young men found their student life in Japan enjoyable. It did not take long for them to feel at home in the Japanese language. Being athletic, they excelled in drills and gymnastics. They liked the atmosphere of orderliness and precision prevailing in the school and the purposefulness of the students as future defenders of the Empire of the Rising Sun. Remembering that they had been sent there to prepare for the role of building a modern and viable Korea, they made the most of their study.

Photo: Fukuzawa Yukichi and 'Outline of a Theory of Civilization' (1862).

Photo: The portrait of Fukuzawa Yukichi featured on the 10,000-yen banknote of Japan.(2024).

Kim Ok-kiun and the Korean Students in Japan

Though all their experiences in Japan were memorable, none was more so than their weekly visits with Kim Ok-kiun. As previously noted, Kim went to Japan as adviser to the Pak Yong-hyo Mission but stayed on in Tokyo after Pak returned to Korea. And while he posed as an observer of Japan's modernization, his real purpose was helping the King secure a $3,000,000 loan from Japan. He was in Japan till March 1883, returning briefly to Seoul in order to obtain a royal commission formally empowering him to conclude the loan arrangement. He returned to Tokyo with the commission and remained there till the end of the year, trying in vain to accomplish his mission. His enemies in Seoul, the Mins, had warned the Japanese Government that the royal commission he had with him was a 'forged one.' Thus, although its official mission ended in failure, his long sojourn in Japan proved a boon to the students he had brought there.

They visited him every Sunday at his hotel in Chiukuchi Machi. He was a delightful 'elder brother,' now exhorting them to remember that Korea looked to them for leadership and now joining them in singing and playing the ancient Korean musical instrument called *Kayakum*. Once he gave a lecture comparing the situation of Korea and Japan with that of France and Britain. As Japan was the Britain of Asia, so Korea should be the France of Asia.

On another occasion, he looked sad when describing the poverty of Korea and the apathy of the Korean people. His eyes burned with anger when he talked about what corrupt, crafty, myopic flunkies the fawning China-worshipping Mins and their cohorts in Seoul were. He hoped they would soon fade away and make way for younger, patriotic and more talented and well-trained people like "You, younger brothers." "If not," he said in a grave tone, "we will have to get rid of them."

In 1884 the educational mission had to be terminated as the Seoul Government could not and would not finance it any longer. The support for it during the previous two years had come from the $120,000 which the Japanese Government had advanced. This was to be repaid out of the indemnity which Japan had demanded of Korea. This was now exhausted. Fortunately, Jaisohn and his 14 fellow students had completed their study at Toyama, and they were impatient to return home and help defend their country. They returned to Seoul in April 1884.

CHAPTER FOUR:
A SHATTERED DREAM

In May 1884, Jaisohn and his fourteen friends graduated from the Toyama Military School in Japan and returned home ready to help renovate Korea's tiny defense force, which at this time was more a ragtag-and-bobtail than an army, and to build up its size. But they quickly realized that they had been overly optimistic. While they had not anticipated a hero's welcome, neither had they expected to be treated as 'traitors' to their country. Their acquaintances shunned them. Their relatives were bitter because they brought 'shame' to their families as well as themselves by going to a country considered as a historic enemy of Korea.

The Government, dominated by the Mins, coldly ignored them. It was understandable that their own friends and relatives, long indoctrinated in isolationism and told of Japan's repeated aggressions on Korea, would be leery of anyone who would want to learn anything from her. They could not understand, however, how the Mins, under whose *seido* Korea had been opened to Japan for intercourse, could turn against them. Granted that politicians are fickle, thought Jaisohn, they should nevertheless be sensible enough to try to get their money's worth out of the investment which the Government had made in training him and his friends in Japan by putting them to good use.

Kaehwa Party and Conservative Party

While Jaisohn and his comrades were nursing their disappointment, a ray of hope dawned on the horizon. One day, some weeks later, they were ordered to present themselves before His Majesty and give a demonstration of what they had learned in Japan. Buoyed by this, they donned their neatly pressed uniforms, put on polished boots and marched into *Kyongbok* Palace carrying wooden rifles on their shoulders. King Kojong, surrounded by an army of courtiers, was sitting on his throne.

Before the august spectators, Jaisohn led his group in a military drill, demonstrating their skill in marching and shooting. This was followed by a presentation of a series of gymnastic exercises, including fencing. His Majesty displayed his boyish delight in watching the performance the like of which he had never seen before. Jaisohn could see that he was pleased with and proud of their demonstrations, for he acted like a little circus watcher, clapping his hands and calling his ministers attention to the gymnastic stunts. This was followed by the report that the King had ordered Han Kui-jik, Minister of War, to establish a military school and staff it with Jaisohn and his fellow graduates of Toyama as instructors. Their hopes soared.

But the military school never materialized. Instead, they were ordered to report for duty as palace guards. What a disappointment after years of intensive study abroad in the history of warfare and world geography, and of backbreaking military drills and maneuvers to be employed as doorkeepers. Worse yet, the commandant of the palace guards and his aides treated them as if they were Japanese spies. Disgusted, they wanted to be released, but Kim Ok-kiun told them to be patient and stay on. He promised them better days ahead.

Jaisohn and his comrades were innocent victims of a bitter and deepening factional feud which had begun a decade earlier. As noted previously, in 1874 Queen Min and her clansmen, in collusion with their allies, ousted the Taewon-gun from power. This embittered the old prince and his supporters, leading to the emergence of two opposing factions arose: one led by the Queen, and the other by her father-in-law, the Taewon-gun. But, since both had many things in common, their mutual self-interests would have convinced them of the desirability of a modicum of cooperation. Both factions were ultra conservative, anti-Japanese and pro-Chinese. Both faced a sullen and potentially hostile populace at home. Most serious of all, they faced common external threats - China and Japan - both casting covetous eyes on strategically important Korea.

However, too myopic, too shackled by passion and prejudice, and utterly unqualified for the role they had usurped, the Queen and her aides were content to live one day at a time, suppressing the people and their enemies, and lining their pockets. The Taewon-gun and his allies were no more enlightened. With Korea's leadership so hopelessly polarized, it was inevitable that things would go from bad to worse for Korea, and that a slight incident would touch off a bloody upheaval in the country.

Imo Military Revolt (1882)

Such an incident occurred in early June 1882. As pointed out before, this was the soldiers' revolt. The Government, after falling into arrears more than a year in payment of soldiers' wages, paid them with rice heavily mixed with sand. The irate troops threw away the rice and marched to the War Ministry to protest. That they intended no violence was evident because they were unarmed. Nevertheless, War Minister, Min Kyom-ho, the culprit, not only refused to make amends, but he also ordered the arrest of the leaders of the protest.

The angry troops turned to the Taewon-gun for help. The 'old tiger,' who had been waiting for an opportunity to get even with the Mins, hastened to give secret instructions to his aides and with a lightning speed, some of his followers, disguised as soldiers, led a contingent of the mutinous troops into the palace, while his other aides and the remainder of the soldiers stormed into the residences of the leaders of the Min faction. The queen fled in disguise, and many of her supporters were either killed or driven into hiding. While the forlorn and trembling King begged his father to take the helm of the government's surviving men, surviving Min leaders sent an urgent SOS to Peking from their hideouts. The Chinese, who have been looking for a chance to reverse their country's sagging prestige as a great empire, promptly responded with the dispatch of 3,000 troops to Korea.

China's Intervention

The Chinese rushed the troops to Korea not to help quell the mutiny, for it had ended before they left China. Their aim was to take direct and firm control of the Korean Kingdom. To that end, they found it expedient to support King Kojong rather than his strong-willed father. Accordingly, the Chinese army high command kidnapped the Taewon-gun through a ruse, took him to China, and held him prisoner there, presumably for life. Their Majesties were, of course, aware of the whole sordid affair, if not directly involved. However, when the news of it became public, the King feigned surprised and sent a messenger to the Chinese commander asking for his father's release. If this was impossible, he added: 'Please take good care of him.'

To the unhappy surprise of both Peking and the Min-dominated Korean Government, China's assumption of direct control of Korea brought more problems than solutions. Internally, the elimination of the Taewon-gun from Korea brought no stability to the country. Externally, through the action, China had not only bitten off more than she could chew, but she had also openly contradicted herself regarding her relations with Korea. Though she had claimed suzerainty over Korea, China never interfered in the internal affairs of the country and at the time of the Korean-American Treaty earlier that year, she had stated that Korea was not a dependency of China. Abrasive and authoritarian, Yuan Shih Kai, China's resident-commissioner, only served to keep alive the charge of China's reckless imperialism over Korea by the powers, while stirring anti-Chinese sentiment among the Koreans, especially her intellectuals. Even Their Majesties, who firmly embraced China for protection, chafed at Yuan's vulgar ostentation.

China's intervention in the internal affairs of Korea brought more than one unsavory character to the country. Within a year after Korea's signing of the Korea-U.S. Treaty in 1882, similar treaties were concluded with other Western nations, catapulting Korea from her hermitage to the family of nations.

Treaty of Peace, Amity, and Commerce between Korea and the United States (Korea–U.S. Treaty of Amity and Commerce) (朝美修好通商條約)

1. The Great King of Korea and the President of the United States and their peoples shall forever live in peace and friendship. If there is any unfair or disrespectful act from another country, they will immediately notify each other, assist one another, and take proper actions to maintain strong ties of friendship. (Article 1: Another English translation: If Korea faces unjust aggression from a third country, the treaty partner, the United States, will immediately intervene and mediate, ensuring Korea's security. If a third country acts unjustly or oppressively toward one government, the other government will act to facilitate a peaceful resolution.)

2. The United States recognizes Korea as an independent nation and will exchange diplomatic envoys of ministerial rank.

3. Extraterritoriality is provisional.

4. The sovereignty over customs duties will be respected.

5. The citizens of both countries will be guaranteed the freedom to engage in commercial activities, as well as the right to purchase and lease land, and their territorial rights will be recognized.

6. Both countries will guarantee the fullest possible exchange of culture and scholarship.

(**Editor's Note**: It is claimed that the Treaty of Peace, Amity, and Commerce was rendered null and void by the Katsura-Taft Agreement in 1905. However, the term 'amity' (修好) in the title of the treaty does not refer to 'protection' (守護), which means guarding or defending something, but rather to fostering friendship. As can be seen from the title, it was primarily an agreement related to commerce, not a military alliance.)

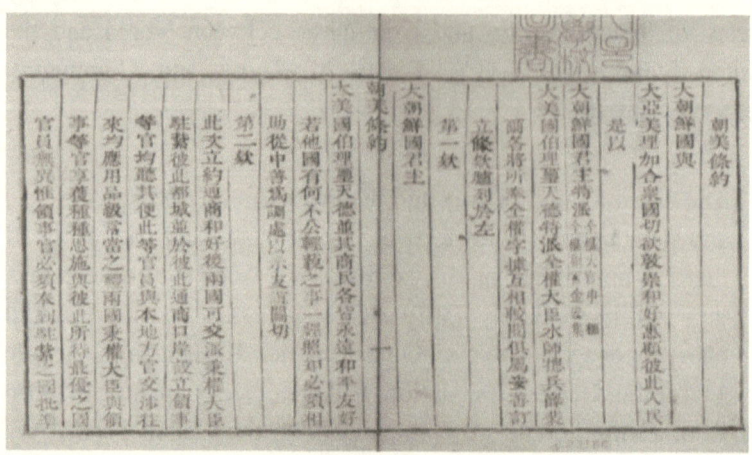

Photo: A copy of the Korea–U.S. Treaty of Peace, Amity, and Commerce (1882).

Photo: The signing ceremony of the Treaty (at *Jemulpo* Harbor), with Admiral Schufeldt representing the United States, and Shin Heon and Kim Hong-jip representing Korea. (May 22, 1882)

Paul G. von Mollendorff

The Korean Government, abysmally ignorant about diplomatic relations, requested Li Hung-chang, China's strongman, to recommend an expert on international law and finances to serve it as an adviser. The man recommended by Li was a German named Paul G. von Mollendorff. He was born in Brandenburg, Germany in 1847 and studied law and Oriental languages at the University of Halle. A born adventurer, he went to China where he found employment in the Chinese Maritime Customs Office. He learned to speak Chinese fluently and was fond of going about in Chinese costume. Later, he was hired by a German Consulate, but unable to get along with his superior, he quit the consulate and applied for employment at Li Hung-chang's viceroyalty. His engaging personality and fluency in Chinese seemed to have impressed the strongman of China.

Cho Young-ha, Seoul's mastermind of the Taewon-gun's abduction, accepted Li's recommendation and brought Mellendorff to Seoul in 1883. When the foreign adviser was presented to King Kojong, he was the first Westerner whom the monarch had met, and he too was impressed. Mollendorf was duly appointed as adviser to the Government on finances as well as international affairs. Though he was on the payroll of the Korean Government, his secret mission was to act as Li Hung-chang's agent in Seoul and to promote the interest of China.

Photo: Li Hongzhang.

Photo: Paul G. von Mollendorff.

Because Kim Ok-kiun held a position equivalent to vice Minister and served as consultant on foreign commerce, he and Mollendorff were attached to the Foreign Ministry and had ample opportunity to know each other. The more Kim knew Mollendorff, the more the foreign adviser impressed him as a man shallow in knowledge and untrustworthy in character. Unable or unwilling to give sound and truthful advice, he was only interested in ingratiating himself and telling their Majesties and their Ministers what they liked to hear. His persistent and unquestioning defense of China, too, seemed odd for a man hired by the Government of Korea.

The urgent issue on which Kim and Mollendorff differed sharply was how to meet the pressing financial needs of Korea. Leaders of the Min faction were inclined to solve it by means of coinage of cheaper (50%) copper coins, as recommended by Admiral Wu Chang-kyong, the Chinese commander. Kim Ok-kiun flatly opposed this, calling it a ruinous policy. Min Young-ik, head of the Min faction, proposed that they seek Mollendorff's opinion, and the latter was brought in. The foreign 'expert' gave unqualified support to Min. In vain did Kim give a long argument in opposition to the coinage plan and offered instead his own, which was to seek a 'sound and fundamental,' not piece meal, solution by securing a loan of $3,000,000 from Japan. Following the fruitless meeting, Kim saw the King and repeated to him that he had told Min and Mollendorff. The King, wishing to please both sides, approved the Mins' plan but also gave Kim a commission to negotiate the loan with the Japanese. With it Kim Ok-kiun went back to Japan, as he had been repeatedly assured by the Japanese Foreign Minister of Japan's willingness to make the loan, provided he had a royal commission. He was unaware that the King was 'operating on both sides of the street.'

Independence Party and China-Leaning Party

On the surface, the issue was how to solve the Government's financial problems. Deep down, however, a much larger issue was at stake: whether Korea should remain a dependency of China or whether she should break away from anachronistic and tottering China and pursue the course of independence. To Queen Min and her partisans, China, a mighty empire for thousands of years, seemed destined to remain one for a long time to come. And in spite of all the irritations caused by Yuan Shih-kai's arrogance and Chinese troops' unruliness, they preferred to live under Chinese protection.

To Kim Ok-kiun and his fellow liberals, China was not only a helpless giant, she represented everything that was outmoded and worthless. Furthermore, through her ruthless intervention in the affairs of Korea, China was dragging Korea to destruction. Anything to break loose from her was worth trying, according to Kim and his partisans. Thus, it was that two mutually exclusive parties – *Sadae Dang* (China-Leaning Party) and *Toknip Dang* (Independent Party) - came into being.

Although Kim Ok-kiun went to Japan with the royal commission empowering him to negotiate a loan, he failed to accomplish his mission due in part to obstructionist tactics of his enemies at home, such as asserting to the Japanese that Kim was carrying a forged commission and in part to Japan's decision that the time to challenge China over Korea had not arrived. In the meantime, the China-leaners at home had gone ahead with the issuance of cheap coins, which proved disastrous, just as Kim had warned. They were in deep trouble, not only because of the ruinous inflation it caused, but also because it came to light that one of their leaders had, as the head of the National Mint, enriched himself by cornering the surplus copper and silver.

Though Kim returned home empty-handed in March 1884, the King was eagerly waiting for him. Something had to be done quickly to calm the angry public, and he knew that Kim alone would offer him right advice. He told the King to order an immediate cessation of minting any more of the worthless coins and to punish the official or officials responsible for the despicable deed. The Mins knew that he was aiming at destroying them and were bitter. However, realizing that anything short of punishing the guilty might well mean revolt by the angry people, they welcomed an 'investigation.' The pro forma investigation took the form of their asking one another 'Who did it?' One after another said it was done on the advice of Mollendorff. Shortly thereafter, the King announced the punishment of the foreign adviser. He was removed from his position as the financial adviser. The next day, however, the foreigner was seen in his office at the Foreign Ministry holding the same rank as adviser to the Korean Government on international affairs.

Mollendorff was deeply hurt for being made a scapegoat. But his survival instinct told him he could not afford to lose his head. His real enemy was Kim Ok-kiun. Kim was the enemy of the Mins too. So, he told the China-leaners that both he and they would come out on top if they, the Mins and their allies, united and worked together with him in fighting Kim. He was persuasive. Furthermore, he made it clear to them that Li Hung-chang had confidence in him. Hence, it was agreed that they should work together, and during the spring and summer the Conservatives were secure in power. The fortunes of the Independents were at a low ebb.

Little wonder, therefore, that Jaisohn and his comrades suffered many indignities. But the Independents were far from finished, Kim Ok-kiun assured them. For one thing, the news that the Taewon-gun might return from his captivity in China drove Their Majesties to a frenzy of fear. The 'old tiger' was sure to seek to avenge all the humiliation and suffering to which they had put him. So, while on the one hand they exerted every effort to persuade Li Hung-chang not to set the Taewon-gun free, they appeal secretly to the Japanese Legation for asylum for themselves on the other, in case China went ahead and freed him. There was another reason for the China-leaners' nervousness. That was China's defeat by France in the Indo-China war that year. This caused them to wonder whether even China were willing to protect Korea, she was in fact capable of doing so.

Kim Ok-kiun's Assessment on China and Japan

It was against this background that Their Majesties granted Kim Ok-kiun a private audience one evening in the spring of 1884. Kim was asked to give an overview of their international situation as it looked from Japan. He responded by saying that

> in the previous decade both Britain and France had been in a race for domination of Asia but lately agreed to cooperate in establishing their spheres of interest in China and seeking commercial advantages elsewhere in Asia, and that China was no longer the mightiest Asian empire she once was. In contrast, he continued, Japan, since Perry's incursion had pursued policies entirely opposite to China's. She not only opened her door to all powers but also learned from them and adopted Western ways. Consequently, he believed that Westernized Japan would pose an even more serious and immediate danger to China.

Asked which side would win in the event of a war between Japan and China, Kim answered that

> at the moment, neither country could decisively win, but that within a decade, unless China discarded her old rotten ways and effected wholesale reform as Japan did, China would be no match for Japan.

The King, irritated by Chinese vacillation about keeping the Taewon-gun away from Korea and by Yuan Shih-kai's boorishness, was much impressed and asked

> whether, under the circumstances, the time had not come for Korea to assume an independent stance.

Kim answered that he could not agree with His Majesty more, but asked him with all his other advisers, meaning his Queen and the Mins and Chinese agent Mollendorff favoring ever firm reliance on China, would His Majesty's wish be carried out? The Queen was on the defensive. Her head told her Kim was right, but her heart was with China. Anyway, she assured him that all His Majesty's ministers had the best interest of Korea at heart and that his views would be given most careful consideration. The King felt so enlightened that in his boyish admiration for Kim's clear and incisive assessment of the world trend and of the course Korea should take, that he gave Kim Ok-kiun his commission making him a 'Permanent Adviser to His Royal Majesty,' which he wrote in his long hand in Kim's presence. This was followed by refreshments which the Queen herself served.

The King was sincere in his trustfulness of Kim Ok-kiun. They grew up in the same neighborhood, and he was always an admirer of Kim for his charm and brilliance. But he was weak-willed, and his decision on any issue was based not on its merits, but by the one closest to him. Hence, the supposedly most powerful person in this male-dominated country was under the domination of his Queen - a woman of no education, of bigotry and of blind ambition. However convincing Kim was on the relative strength of China and Japan, she was unable to wean herself from China because it never occurred to her that Korea could or should stand on her own, and her prejudice against Japan was visceral.

Though professing to be impressed by what Kim had to say, at heart she remained as firmly pro-Chinese as ever and persuaded her royal consort that Kim Ok-kiun was a peddler of a 'dangerous doctrine.' Under her prodding, the King replaced Han Kyu-jik with Min Young-ik as commander of the Seoul garrison, and with Han's dismissal the plan to found a modern military school was scrapped, causing grievous disappointment to Jaisohn and his friends.

Min Young-ik, the favorite nephew of the Queen, had no training or experience in military affairs, and no sooner had he received his appointment then he placed himself at the command of Yuan Shih-kai, the Chinese Resident-Commissioner in Korea. All officers were thoroughly pro-Chinese. There were frequent and ostentatious military drills and maneuvers, apparently as a warning to the Independents to beware. Kim Ok-kiun called on the King. The latter was aware of what was going on but was reassured by the Mins that it was a normal routine by the army. Kim told the monarch that the maneuvers were at best liable to cause alarm to the populace and at worst a threat to him and his friends. He felt it wise, therefore, for him to lie low for a while, he said, adding that he would be available whenever his service was needed.

Conflict Between Independence Party and Pro-China Faction

Kim Ok-kiun went into semi hiding. Pak Yong-hyo planned, at first, to flee abroad but later changed his mind and went underground. Hong Young-sik and Oh Kwang-pom maintained low profiles but secretly kept in touch with Kim and Pak. During July and August, they conducted a clandestine campaign of increasing and consolidating their following. Among the prominent recruits at this time where Yi Jae-won, elder brother of the King, Kim Hong-jip, former special envoy to Japan, and Yun Eung-yol, ex-Minister of War and father of Yun Chi-ho, etc.

It was also during this that Jaisohn was brought in on the Independents' secret plan to counter their enemy's anticipated move. Kim Ok-kiun told him of how conditions at home and abroad were driving the *Sadae dang* leaders to desperation.

> At home their popularity reached a new low due to their disastrous monetary policy. Abroad. China was faring very badly in the Indo-China war against France, which might force her to withdraw her troops from Korea in order to reinforce her shrinking forces in Indo-China. Hence the China-leaners were very likely to try to liquidate 'us' the Independents, before the Chinese troops were withdrawn from Korea. Min Young-ik's activities seem to indicate this, Kim said.

Statistically, Kim conceded that 'our side' was decisively inferior at that time. However, he contended that

> there were three factors which more than offset their side's inferiority. Those factors, according to him, were the time, the morale of the Independents and the international trend. The longer the China-leaners waited before striking, the stronger 'our side' would grow. The China-leaners had nothing to offer which would attract mass following while we were for an independent Korea and a better future for the Korean people.

And the trend of the world clearly showed that nations adhering to the 'status quo' were being overrun by liberal and forward-marching ones.

Jaisohn was encouraged by what Kim said. He wondered, however, whether the Independents could alone topple the China-leaners. Expressing doubt that they could, he said:

> I thought that progressive Japan might prefer a progressive Korea for mutual benefit and would support us, but judging from the flippancy of the Japanese Government, revealed in, for example, its response towards your loan approval, I doubt her reliability. If so, where can we find the support, we need?

Kim confessed that he was angered by the Japanese for playing a 'cat and mouse game' with him. Fortunately, he said, there were wise private individuals in Japan who believed as Jaisohn had supposed. Some of them were helping 'us' by smuggling in weapons. Given time, he felt confident that there would be more Japanese like them. Lately, he detected signs that the Japanese Government, too, was beginning to consider it to its advantage to come to 'our' support. However, he received no definite message to that effect, and he had no intention to initiate contact with the Japanese Legation. Then he added:

> Meanwhile, I want you to make sure that your Toyama classmates are held together on our side, as your group will have to assume a vitally important role in the coming showdown with

the China-leaners. Also do all you can to add fresh recruits. I'll talk to you more about the details of our plan later.

Prelude to *Kapsin* Coup

Jaisohn came away from this meeting with Kim Ok-kiun speechless with elation. Recalling Kim's promise of 'better days ahead' when he was about to 'quit the whole thing,' Jaisohn's admiration for him reached a new height. Kim Ok-kiun, the man of ideas for a better career, of inspiration and action and of resourcefulness, had made him a chief lieutenant for redirecting the course of Korea's history from supine dependency on reactionary China to independence and progress. His excitement gave way to a sober realization of the responsibility Kim had placed in him as a leader of the coming drama.

Jaisohn's immediate task was fence-mending among his Toyama classmates. Some of them were reportedly being bought off by the *Sadae Dangites*. Others, who were house servants of some of the Independents, were angered by ill treatment they received and were said to threaten to go their own ways. Jaisohn contacted all of them individually, appealing to their liberalism, patriotism and their vow to offer themselves for reform of Korea and promising to rectify any injustice done to them by their employers. Citing a long list of examples of the China-leaners' misdeeds to the nation which were sure to destroy Korea and reminding them that under their leadership all Koreans would become slaves forever, he told his comrades that

they were at the 'crossroads. They could either unite behind the leadership of the *Toknip Dang* in ousting the *Sadae Dang* from power and help establish a free and prosperous career, or go their separate ways, spend the rest of their lives in slavehood and stand condemned as traitors to Korea and their ideals in the eyes of history.

One of the group, Lee Kyu-won, was so moved that he offered to stand by Jaisohn through 'eternity' and volunteered to cut down the head of the *Sadae Dang* boss, Min Young-ik. From then on, Jaisohn called him 'General Lee' and gave him a sword as a symbol of Jaisohn's admiration for him. Likewise, all the rest of the 'Toyama gang' pledged their loyalty to the cause of the *Toknip Dang*.

Jaisohn frequently met his comrades clandestinely in different homes to encourage one another and to study world as well as Korean histories. Also, they occasionally visited the home of the American Minister, Lucius Foote, and listened to his and Mrs. Foote's discourse on various facets of the United States. That they were attentive and appreciative listeners was evident by the remark of the wife of Minister Foote: "They are such aspiring, daring characters, polite and refined, and of pleasing personalities thirsting for freedom."

Photo: U.S. Minister Lucius Foote and his wife.

Photo: U.S. Minister Lucius Foote riding in a *kama* (a traditional Korean sedan chair).

Photo: The U.S. Legation in *Jeong-dong* in Seoul (1887).

During September and October, Jaisohn was busy gathering new recruits and indoctrinating them into the ideals and aims of the Independence Party. In this he was greatly aided by two developments. One was China's reverses in the Indo-China war. As the French followed up their victory in Annam with a blockade of Taiwan, a dispute arose in Peking between pro-war and anti-war factions which culminated in a change of China's leadership. The anti-war faction came to power, and it was headed by the father of the boy king, Tehjung. The Independents, seizing the occasion, called for the release and return of the Taewon-gun, the father of the Korean monarch. The Korean people, who had never forgiven their King and Queen for allowing the Chinese to take the Taewon-gun as a captive, reacted favorably to the demand of the Independents.

The other development was an increasing antagonism between the Chinese troops in Korea and the Korean people. There had been numerous incidents of lawlessness by the Chinese troops - robbery, sexual assaults and murder. During the summer of that year, a Chinese merchant, with the aid of the Chinese troops, blatantly confiscated the property of a high Korean official and imprisoned him for protesting, astounding the Seoul Government. This caused a profound embarrassment to the China-leaners.

Japanese Minister Takezoye Sinichiro

The independents were definitely gaining in number as well as popularity. However, they were far too inferior in number to the China-leaners to challenge them for some time to come. Within weeks, however, Kim Ok-kiun and his partisans decided to have a showdown with the pro-Chinese as soon as possible. The main cause of the decision was the return to Seoul of Takezoye Sinichiro, Japanese Minister to Korea, on October 30. Initially, Kim Ok-kiun didn't even bother to see the mercurial and uncharacteristically pro-Chinese Japanese diplomat.

But within days, Takezoye revealed that he was a different man. He went out of his way to court the Independents and conversely, to attack the China-leaners for their servility toward China. Still suspicious of the

Japanese Minister, Kim did not wish to see him but sent Pak Yong-hyo to call on him. Pak returned from his visit with Takezoye and reported to Kim that the Japanese had indeed come with new instructions to assist in ousting the pro-Chinese party from power and help establish an independent government in Seoul.

Thereupon, Kim himself met with the Japanese, and the two had a long talk. Takezoye assured him of his seriousness in saying that he had been given a mandate by his government to support whatever action the Independents decided to take, even to the extent of a coup. Kim came away satisfied that Takezoye meant business this time. He met with Pak Yong-hyo , Soh Kwang-pom and Hong Young-sik at the latter's house and recounted the details of his talk with the Japanese Minister. They unanimously agreed that the time to take a decisive action had arrived: that a coup against the China-leaners should be staged before the Japanese Minister could back off or before the arrival of the Chitose Maru in early December. They were afraid that the indecisive Japanese Foreign Ministry might back off and send a message to Takezoye ordering him to withdraw his support. Since the Chitose Maru was expected in *Inchon* around the 10th of December 1884, the Independents decided the coup should be brought about before that date at the latest.

Photo: Japanese Minister Takezoye Sinichiro

From then on, the Independents maintained frequent and intimate contacts with the Japanese Legation in Seoul. Takezoye was himself involved in preparation for the coup and on being told that it would take place sometime before the arrival of the Chitose Maru, he asked what the ship had to do with the coup. When Kim told him with a smile: "Lest it bring you an order from your Government to withdraw support for our plan." Takezoye laughed. Although Kim answered in facetiae, he was serious. He had a premonition that the flighty Japanese diplomat might be overstepping his instructions and that the Japanese Foreign Ministry, knowing it might very likely send him a message of caution. As a matter of fact, the Japanese Government did send him such a message on the Chitose Maru, which he received only after the coup had taken place.

Several plans for the coup were considered, and the one finally adopted involved celebration of the opening of postal services in Korea. Earlier that year, Korea had joined the Universal Postal Union and preparations for postal services, including erection of a Post Office building, were nearing completion. Hong Young-sik, one of the leaders of the Independents, had been appointed Postmaster General. Thus, a celebration marking the opening of the postal services with Hong as its presider could provide an ideal screen behind which the historic drama could be conveniently enacted. Specifically, the plan was to hold the banquet on December 4th, 1884, in the new Post Office in commemoration of the opening of the postal service in Korea, to which all the nation's high dignitaries and foreign diplomats would be invited. Invitations with requests for R.S.V.P. were to be sent out by Hong in his capacity as the Postmaster General.

During the banquet, a palace building would be set on fire, and resulting fire alarms would cause a commotion throughout the city. All attending the banquet would rush out. As they did so, the ministers who were pro-Chinese would be ambushed by assassins. In the ensuing confusion, the coup leaders would hasten to *Changdok* Palace, inform the royal family of an outbreak of 'rebellion,' and persuade the King and his entourage to move with them to a smaller building, which could be better guarded. There, with the King in their custody, the Independents could issue royal decrees, which would instantly transform Korea into a modern, progressive kingdom.

During November, the Independents made careful and detailed preparations. Although this was done in strict secrecy, the inhabitants of Seoul could not help but sense an atmosphere of tenseness. Seoul was full of rumors spread by the Independents: that the China-leaners were planning to send Korean soldiers to Indo-China to help the Chinese fight the French; that more and more Chinese troops were pouring into Korea disguised as immigrants; and that the pro-Chinese were preparing to launch a preventive attack on the Independents, etc. Kim Ok-kiun realized that these rumors were counterproductive and warned Takezoye to help quash them by refraining from actions which might give rise to further rumors.

He himself was tight-lipped, refusing to divulge any hint as to whether or when a coup would occur, even to such influential sympathizer as Inouye Kakugoro, who helped the Independents by smuggling in Japanese swords, firearms and so on. To the King, who complained that he could not sleep due to the night drills by Japanese troops and wanted to know what was going on, he merely said that there was nothing to worry about.

Meanwhile, Jaisohn was given an additional duty. That was to maintain a close liaison between his own troops and the Japanese commanded by Captain Murakami. On November 6, he was invited by Murakami to attend a Japanese maneuver. The main part of it was a mock battle between two groups of soldiers - red (Japanese) and white (Chinese) - and the reds won, to Takezoye's delight. On November 9, he reported to the Japanese captain about a mysterious meeting between Min Young-ik and Yuan Shih-kai in the dead of night and of their alert orders given to their respective forces. On November 27th, Kim, Jaisohn and Murakami met for the last time to exchange latest information on the state of readiness.

Kapsin Coup – Day 1

The day arrived. It was December 4, 1884. At 7:00 p.m., the hour of the banquet in celebration of the opening of the postal service, all invited guests except the Japanese Minister, German Consulate General, and Yun Tae-jun were present. It was a colorful assemblage. A number of foreign countries were represented, and the Korean nobles were especially elaborately costumed in gorgeous robes. For a while they were stiff and quiet, but as they settled down to a delectable feast expertly prepared by a Japanese chef, everyone relaxed.

However, one of the leaders, Kim Ok-kiun, showed more and more nervousness as the evening wore on. He repeatedly whispered into the ear of the headwaiter to 'take your time.' Twice he was called outside, where he learned that things on the palace ground were not working out as planned. The building marked out for burning would not catch fire. The next house adjoining the palace could serve as a substitute, but it stood too close to the house of one of their comrades. Annoyed, Kim ordered his messenger to hurry back and set fire to any house. He returned to his seat, pretending that everything was fine and jokingly asking Shimamura, Secretary of the Japanese Legation in Japanese: "Do you know Chon (天, heaven)?" The Japanese answered: "Very well indeed." The other guests thought this was an innocent exchange of pleasantries, but it was a rehearsal of that secret code word, 'heaven'. This was the word by which the Independents could recognize one another in the darkness of the night.

While Kim and Shimamura went on chatting with an air of apparent innocence, suddenly loud cries of "Fire!" came from the direction of the royal palace. Several guests got up and looked out, but seeing no sign of fire anywhere, they returned to their seats. General Lucius Foote, American Minister, sought to calm the jittery guests with a story which was first interpreted into Japanese by his American secretary and then into Korean by Yun Tchi-ho, one of Jaisohn's fellow students in Japan. He recounted how once he had been invited to a dinner and a fire broke out in the house next door, causing a great commotion. Everyone was frightened. However, one man got up and pressed his hand against the wall nearest the house that was on fire. Finding it cool to the touch he reassured the guests. They were much relieved, and the party went on.

No sooner had the story been translated into Korean than even louder cries of "Fire!" were heard again, and Min Young-ik, leader of the China-leaners, excused himself, saying the cries sounded as if they came from the direction of his father's house and he wished to investigate. Within minutes he staggered back into the banquet hall, moaning and bleeding profusely from ghastly wounds to the head and shoulders. The hall suddenly became a pandemonium, and the Korean guests quickly shed their ornate robes and disappeared, leaving the wounded prince in the care of Minister Foote, Paul Mollendorff and Foote's secretary. Foote and Mollendorff carried Min to Mollendorff's office and called in Dr. Horace N. Allen, an American missionary, to care for him. Min recovered but most of his friends, including his father, met their violent death that night.

Photo: The appearance of the old Post Office in *Gyeonji-dong, Jongno-gu,* Seoul (2023).

Kim Ok-kiun, Pak Yong-hyo and Soh Kwang-pom slipped out of the banquet hall together and went on toward the royal palace, uttering the password '*Chon'* (heaven) in order to avoid being cut down by their colleagues in the darkness. Hong Yong-sik, host of the banquet, joined them later in the palace. As the trio approached the palace, Jaisohn was at the front gate with his fellow Toyama graduates. On Kim's order, the gate was swung open, and they all marched in and straight toward the private quarters of the royal family. Pyon Soo, the Royal Chamberlain who was a secret supporter of the Independents, met the leaders of the Independents and whispered into Kim's ear that Their Majesties were in bed unaware of what was going on. This was good news. However, Chief Eunuch Yoo Jae-hyon, who was a staunch ally of the China-leaners, suddenly emerged and tried to gain time by arguing that Their Majesties should not be disturbed at that late hour. He appeared to be trying to wake up Queen Min and take counter- measures, and a noisy argument ensued.

The King and Queen were awakened by the uproar and came out of their chambers, calling Kim by name and wanting to know what had happened. Kim informed them that a rebellion had broken out and that for their safety, they should immediately move to a smaller palace which could be more securely guarded. The Queen, seeing none of her close supporters, became suspicious and wanted to know who the rebels were. Just then, according to plan, a bomb went off at the other end of the palace ground with such shattering effect that there was no need for Kim to answer her. She was terrified and became submissive. Meekly, the royal couple and their entourage, numbering some 200, trooped over to *Kyongwu* Palace, one of the smaller buildings on the edge of the palace ground used by crown princes during their weddings.

Its size and location gave confidence to the Independents that their troops could deal with any opposition from within. However, feeling far less sure about protecting the palace against possible invaders from without, Kim Ok-kiun and his comrades suggested to the King while walking toward *Kyongwu* Palace that he sent a message to the Japanese Minister requesting help. The trembling monarch agreed and taking a piece of paper and pencil from Pak Yong-hyo, he scribbled a five word note to Takezoye. No sooner had the note been delivered than the Japanese Minister came accompanied by his troops who were deployed in front of all palace gates.

Jaisohn's aim now was maintaining strict discipline within the palace. However, on arrival at *Kyongwu* Palace, the Independents were vexed by certain members of the royal entourage who complained of overcrowding and cold. Although there were some justifications for their complaints, there were signs that the discomfort was being used as an excuse for creating trouble. The distraught Queen and Chief Eunuch Yoo were frequently seen engaged in hushed conversations behind the noisy court where ladies clamoring for more heat. Kim decided to put an end to it. He ordered Jaisohn to have his men grab Yoo and bind him up. That done, Kim recited a long list of the eunuch's crimes and ordered him punished. One of Jaisohn's men pressed his sword slowly into his chest, and as he sank to the ground in a pool of blood, terror swept through the court women. They became as gentle as lambs.

During the night those China-leaners who had attended the banquet but escaped unhurt, arrived at *Kyongwu* Palace, as they were expected to, singly or in two's, to pay their respect to His Majesty. As they arrived, they were led away by an execution squad to a secluded area where they met their death. Generals Han Kyu-jik and Lee Ju-yon, loyal allies of the Min clan, arrived together and insisted on an audience with the King to inform him perhaps, about what had happened at the banquet the night before and persuade him to turn against the Independents. As they approached the royal suite, Jaisohn, brandishing a sword, warned them that one more step forward would be their last. They turned around and began to depart when they were escorted to the outer courtyard by the same execution squad. They too met their violent death.

Kapsin Coup – The New Government

The following morning, December 5, 1884, Kim Ok-kiun and his colleagues, who had stayed up the whole night, announced the formation of a new Government, the first reform regime in the history of Korea. It was notable in several respects.

- First, all senior posts went to close relatives of the Taewon-gun, with Yi Jae-myon, his nephew, heading the cabinet.

- Second, though Pak Yong-hyo and Soh Kwang-pom held the portfolios of Commanders of Front and Rear Defenses respectively, actual operational command of all forces was entrusted to Philip Jaisohn, youngest of the reform leaders who had just turned 20.

- Third, though the leader of the Independents was unquestionably Kim Ok-kiun, he assumed a minor Vice Ministership of Finance.

- Fourth, the post of Supreme Commander of the Army was given to the Crown Prince, an 11-year-old retarded boy.

Was the cabinet composition the work of a group of sleepy, absent-minded amateurs? Although a quick glance at it does lead one to the conclusion, it represented a shrewd attempt to include all major factions except the Mins - the Taewon-gun's, the King's and neutral - in the Government, yet leave it under the control of the Independents. This was shown in the fact that Kim himself took the apparently minor but the most important post with the Vice Minister of Finance and that Pak, Soh, and Jaisohn, especially the latter, were put in charge of defense. The only exception was that Hong Yong-sik, one of the core members of the

Independents, was named Home Minister. This might have given credence to the charge by some that he was vainglorious; however, in truth, Kim might have intended that Hong might be the Prime Minister in fact, and as such enable the Independents to retain firm control of the Government.

The announcement of the cabinet make-up was followed by that of the policies the Government intended to pursue. Chief among them were:

- eradication of social inequality,
- basic freedom of the people,
- selection of government personnel according to merit,
- tax exemption to the landless,
- prosecution of illicit amassers of fortune,
- cessation of paying tribute to China,
- the return of the Taewon-gun from his captivity in China,
- reform of the police system to maintain tranquility and protect innocent people,
- release of all political prisoners and exiles,
- control of all financial matters by the Finance Ministry,
- vesting of all policy making power in the Council of Ministers and Vice Ministers,
- sending talented and patriotic youths abroad to be educated in various subjects useful in the development of the nation, and
- haircut (elimination of top knots) by all male adults.

Jaisohn later freely admitted to the contradictions and frivolities evident in the policy aims. The aim, for example, of enforcing haircut on all men was not only frivolous, but it could also not be implemented without stirring heated grassroots opposition, as a custom of wearing long hair by men was associated with Korea's ancient ancestor worship. Frivolous, too, was the announcement that the Government would push for the return of the Taewon-gun, for the Chinese Government was planning to return him to Korea anyway. Moreover, the reformers' avowed policy of eradicating social inequality was contradicted by their action - packing of the Government with *yangbans*. However, the people at large were unaware of them at the time: what doomed them to defeat were Japan's involvement in the coup and countermeasures by a remnant of the Mins in collusion with China.

Although the coup caught the people by surprise, guarding of the palace gates by the Japanese troops stirred them to indignation. Meanwhile, members of the main faction who had escaped from the Reformers spread the rumor that the 'pro-Jap traitors' inside the palace were engaged in brutal atrocities against the royal family and cabinet ministers, while appealing to the Chinese for help. Their efforts paid off. The rumors heightened the anger of the people and the swashbuckling Yuan Shih-kai, Chinese agent in Seoul, ordered his troops into the royal palace as the 'savior of Korea.'

Kapsin Coup – Day 2

During the day the American Minister and his British and German counterparts called to pay their respects to His Majesty. Their reactions to the coup varied. American Minister Lucius Foote met with Kim Ok-kiun and expressed himself as accepting the fate accompli. He asked that the safety of foreign residents in the country be assured. The British consul general showed open coolness toward the Independents, while his German counterpart was non-committal. All three foreign diplomats expressed concern for the safety of their respective nationals in Seoul. Kim promised all possible measures for their personal safety and at the same time requested their understanding and cooperation.

Much time during the day was also spent in moving from one place to another at the request of the royal entourage. First, the King and his retinue moved from *Kyongwu* Palace to the residence of Yi Jae-myon, new Prime Minister. Next, they moved back to *Changdok* Palace, their regular residence. Kim and Jaisohn did their best to dissuade the royal family from returning to the latter palace owing to its size making the palace difficult to guard. But Takezoye, whose expertise lay in anything but military strategy, thought one palace was as easy to guard as another and had already agreed to the moving. That night, Queen Min reportedly smuggled out a note to Yuan Shih-kai, asking him to bring in his troops and rescue the royal family from the Independents. The note was sent out buried in a rice bowl following her evening meal.

Kapsin Coup – Day 3

On the third day, December 6, Kim Ok-kiun planned it to devote his attention to pressing financial matters, but even more urgent was keeping his defense forces in readiness. So, he asked Pak Yong-hyo and Soh Kwang-pom to take an inventory of all available weapons. The three leaders were told by their aides that the rifles in the palace arsenal were too rusty to be of use. Thereupon all the troops under Jaisohn's command were put to cleaning them.

While the soldiers were thus occupied, Takezoye threw a bombshell at the Independents by informing them of his intention to withdraw his troops from the palace. His explanation was that guarding the palace gates by Japanese troops for many days might invite the danger of arousing anti-Japanese sentiment on the part of the Korean people. Kim Ok-kiun vehemently opposed it, arguing that to do so at that critical juncture was tantamount to throwing away all the gains made thus far.

He agreed that the Japanese troops should be withdrawn as soon as possible, but not until the new Government was in firm control.

Emphasizing that the combined strength of the Japanese and Independents' troops could beat a force twice the number of the Chinese troops, and that as soon as Jaisohn's soldiers finished greasing the weapons, there would be enough weapons and ammunition, he appealed to the Japanese Minister to be patient and to help push their common endeavor to a successful conclusion. To do less, he warned, would be an invitation of disaster for Japan as well as Korea's reform. Takezoye agreed to postpone the withdrawal of his troops for a few days. Furthermore, in response to Kim's appeal for an immediate loan of $5,000,000, he unhesitatingly answered that the loan would be granted. Kim, Pak, Hong and the two Sohs were exultant, confident that at last the coup had been assured success.

However, the coup, which had seemed so sure of success an hour earlier, took a nosedive. To begin with, although Takezoye had agreed to postpone the withdrawal of his troops from the palace, he pulled them into the palace, saying their visibility aroused the ire of Korean onlookers. This served only to further intensify the ire of the Koreans and to cause them to surge toward the gates in increasing numbers. More seriously, by midafternoon, China's Yuan Shih-kai unleashed 1,500 of his troops who were pounding at the gates leading to the palace.

Jaisohn led a group of his soldiers up the tiled roof of the *Sonin* Gate, the main gate of *Changdok* Palace and lay on their bellies with their rifles trained toward the entrance below. As the Chinese troops pressed against the gate, Jaisohn and his men gave them all they had. Since the gate was locked, the Chinese were trapped, and Jaisohn's men killed them by the scores. When their bullets had run out, they threw down tiles, wounding dozens more, but there were too many of the enemy for the handful of men under Jaisohn's command, and finally they fled down and ran toward the spot where Kim Ok-kiun, Takezoye, the panic-stricken King and all the rest were huddled together behind the rocks. The Chinese had finally broken through the *Sonin Moon* and were approaching, shooting at random and burning buildings before them. Other detachments of the enemy poured in from other gates, leaving only the North Gate for escape. Only the deepening dusk stood between them and the enemy. In the chilly darkness, the last conference between the King and the Independents took place.

First, Kim suggested that they all flee in separate directions, each trying to save himself as best as he could, and plan to reassemble at a later date and make another try. On Jaisohn's urging, he suggested instead that they flee in a group to *Incheon*, taking the King with them, and plan for a return to Seoul with Japanese reinforcements. However, the King refused. Nor did Takezoye think it feasible. Finally, they decided to escort the King to the waiting Chinese at the other end of the palace compound and then flee to *Inchon*. Hong Yong-sik, Pak Young-hyo, Yong-hyo's brother, and a group of Toyama school graduates volunteered to accompany the King. The Chinese murdered every one of the escorts. Kim Ok-kiun, Pak Yong-hyo, Soh Kwang-pom, Jaisohn and about six of their aides went with the fleeing Japanese, fighting back Korean and Chinese pursuers as they retreated.

Thus, ended Korea's first reform movement - three days and two nights after its birth. Did it have a chance of survival? What caused its fall? Much water has flowed under the bridge of history since the abortive coup, revealing the basic motive of its masterminds. Convinced that the China-leaners in control of the Government must go or the eventual fall of Korea was inevitable, Kim and his colleagues had concluded that it was their patriotic duty to eliminate them by force. It was to them, a necessary surgery in order to save their country. In this, there was no alternative to accepting help from Japan, not only because their own resources were inadequate, but also because she had those things of which Korea was badly in need: scientific and technological know-how and modern progressive ideas. They seem to have been unaware of the fact that such a serious undertaking must be preceded by an exhaustive examination of its pitfalls and feasibility, not to mention thorough preparations. They seemed to have been unaware too of the fact that 'it is a very risky thing to pin one's hope of independence from one country on the support of another.' The behavior of nations is motivated by neither justice nor charity, but their own interests.

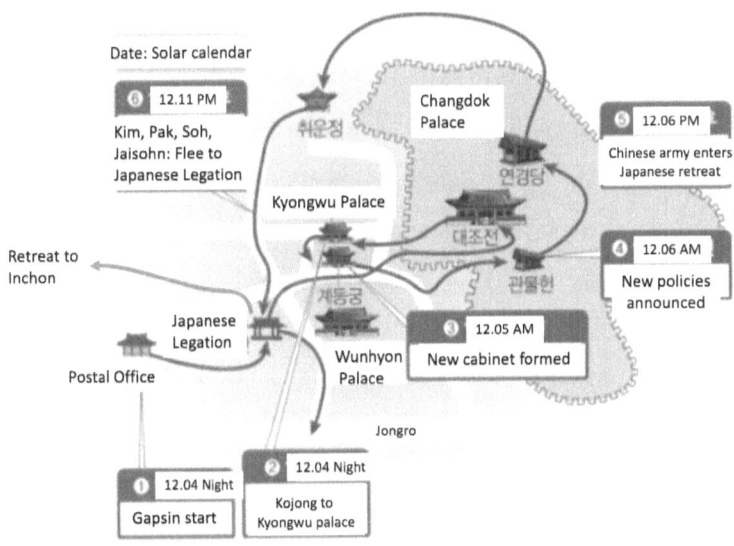

Illustration: The progress of the *Kapsin* Coup in 1884.

CHAPTER FIVE:
FIRST EXILE

With the failure of the coup, Takezoye, anything but a man of daring, had a lot to worry about: getting himself and his men out of *Changdok* Palace alive, ensuring the safety of the Japanese nationals in Korea as well as his Legation staff, and salvaging his own career.

He was in a great hurry to get away, but Kim Ok-kiun, Pak Yong-hyo, Soh Kwang-pom, Jaisohn and their followers, who had decided to flee with the Japanese, stood still, weeping and watching as the trembling King left piggyback on a Toyama Military School graduate in the direction of the Chinese to which his royal family had already fled on foot. The distraught Japanese Minister threatened to leave without them unless they followed them right away. The Koreans complied.

Under Captain Murakami's direction, the Japanese troops were divided into two sections, front and rear, and put Takezoye and the nine Koreans in the middle. By the time they began to retreat, it had gotten pitch dark, and they literally stumbled out of the palace. As they reached the streets leading to the Japanese Legation, mobsters holding sticks and stones in their hands greeted them with shouts of 'Kill the Japs! Catch the traitors!' The leader of the front section was hit by a bullet and had to be carried by his troops the rest of the way. They fought back with blank shots into the air, but the mob grew so menacing that for a while the Korean escapees thought of separating, seeking refuge in houses along the way, but decided against it, realizing that none would give shelter to the 'traitors.'

Finally, they came within sight of the Japanese Legation and heaved a sigh of relief. But they were met with a shower of bullets from the Legation. Since late afternoon, mobs had repeatedly tried to storm the Japanese Legation, and the Legation guards had, in the darkness of the night, mistaken them for Korean or Chinese mobs. Not until fifteen of them had been dead or wounded, did they succeed in establishing their identity. One of the dead in the tragic mishap was Kaneko, the Japanese language teacher to the Korean students when they were in Japan. He had followed Jaisohn to Korea and shared the Independents' shifting fortunes. The bullet that pierced his body grazed Jaisohn's hair. The Japanese guards led the Korean fugitives in reluctantly, for they feared that harboring them might cause an attack by the Koreans and Chinese.

While Jaisohn lay leaning against the wall and rested with his eyes closed in exhaustion, he overheard a muted conversation among the Japanese, suggesting that the Koreans be thrown into a nearby well. They had thought he was asleep. He opened his eyes, cleared his throat and said, "If you are so anxious for your own safety, don't take the trouble to throw us into the well. We would sooner walk out of here and be killed by our own people." The embarrassed Japanese apologized, claiming that they were merely joking.

Reassured, the Korean fugitives slumped to the floor and fell fast asleep. Waking up hours later, they saw the Japanese preparing to depart, evidently intent on leaving them behind. All the Koreans jumped up and followed the retreating Japanese party. Since this was the only way to safety and eventual political comeback, they ignored the thinly suppressed inhospitality of the Japanese.

Emerging from the Japanese Legation, they saw the cold, dark sky lit with huge flames here and there and said to themselves, "God, there go our homes up in smoke." They were right. The houses of all the leading Independents were either burned down or confiscated by their foes. Hong Yong-sik's house, one of the finest in Seoul, was converted into a torture chamber where the relatives and friends of Hong and Hong himself were tortured to death. Later, the blood-soaked house, ignored by superstitious Koreans, was taken over by Christian missionaries and converted into the first Western style hospital.

Photo: Horace Underwood and his wife, Dr. Lillias Underwood

(**Editor's Note**: The establishment of *Jejungwon* was made possible by the full trust and support of King Kojong and Queen Min toward Horace

Allen, who had saved the life of their nephew, Min Yeong-ik. This hospital was originally called *Gwanghyewon (Jejungwon)* and later renamed Severance Hospital. In 1885, the year after the *Kapsin Coup*, Allen invited William B. Scranton and Horace G. Underwood to strengthen the medical staff. Dr. Lillias Underwood worked at *Jejungwon*, where she met Horace G. Underwood, and they married. Mrs. Underwood treated female patients and was also the personal physician to Queen Min.)

The Captain of the Chitose Maru

The ill-fated Korean fugitives had more pressing things to do than indulge in such sentimental thought for the howling, rock-throwing, rifle-shooting crowds lined the streets through which they escaped. Rose Foote, wife of the first American Minister to Korea, Lucius Foote, described the scene as follows:

> Upon this amazing turn of events, the Japanese Guard and officials in quick haste secured the state papers from the Legation building, hastily gathered together many refugees, Japanese men, women and children who had congregated at the embassy and protected by their soldiers. They, as a desperate party, perilously rushed through the streets, hurled themselves against the Western Gate, beat it down and fled to *Jemulpo* (Inchon). Many were killed, and many of the wounded fell on the streets where they died. The new Japanese Legation buildings and the houses of the Liberals all over the Capital went up in flame, reddening the entire sky.

The mobs increased in size and fury as the groups fled. Only after they crossed the *Han* River at *Mapo* did the danger recede. However, a number of the escapees were killed, and many of the coup leaders sustained wounds. Kim Ok-kiun was hit in the arm. Pak Yong-hyo's leg injury was so severe that he had to be assisted by his younger companions much of the way. The injuries compounded by fatigue and hunger made their night-long trek to *Inchon* as harrowing as their flight from the Japanese Legation to the *Han* River. In vain did they stop at the roadside houses to beg for food as none dared befriend the 'traitors.' Finally, they came upon an inn keeper who threw at them pieces of dried cow-hide. They chewed on them as they limped along.

They arrived in *Inchon* at about 8:00 a.m., December 7. Even there, their ordeal was not over. Agents of the Seoul Government - Kim Yun-sik, Mollendorff and their orderlies - were already there with orders to arrest them and bring them back to Seoul. The Government followed that up with the dispatch of a delegation to Takezoye requesting him, among others, to hand them over to the Seoul authorities. So far as the Japanese Minister was concerned, he couldn't care less about what happened to Kim Ok-kiun and his fellow fugitives, and no sooner had he arrived in *Inchon* than he took only his staff with him to the Japanese consulate in *Inchon*, ignoring the Koreans. The rest of the Japanese refugees were taken to the houses of the Consular officials.

Fortunately, the head of the *Inchon* branch of the Dai Ichi Bank, an acquaintance of Kim Ok-kiun offered shelter to Kim and his comrades in his house. Evidently, it was while hiding in the house that they disguised themselves by cutting off their *sangtus* (top knots) and changing into Western suits. However, in the face of relentless efforts by the government agents to arrest them by any means whatsoever, they felt more insecure each hour. It was rumored that Takezoye had agreed to turn them into the Government. The rumor was false, but not because he wouldn't, if he could, but because he did not know where they were. By the time the government agents learned as to their whereabouts, the Korean escapees had already been spirited away from their refuge and led aboard the Chitose Maru by their Japanese friends. On learning this, the government agents ordered the police to go on board the ship and arrest them. However, the ship's captain, Tsuji Kakugoro, a stocky and powerfully built man, stopped them with a pistol in his hand and bellowed:

"On this ship I alone am the boss, and no one is allowed in here without my permission!"

Photo: Chitose Maru (千歳丸).

Free at last and tired to the bone, Jaisohn and his fleeing comrades slumped to the floor and 'died' of exhaustion in the coal bin in the ship's hold. Jaisohn could not recall ever having slept in a more comfortable place. Many hours later he was awakened by something rolling over him, and when fully awake, he realized it was coal doing that, perhaps triggered by his own motion while asleep. The ship still remained docked. Since she was not scheduled to leave *Inchon* until the 11th of December, they lay in the coal bin and waited. While they lay there, they thought of their folks at home and shuddered at what they were in all likelihood going through.

They also pondered what lay ahead of them and had mixed feelings of dread and exhilaration - dread because they knew that their enemies in Seoul would not cease their effort to bring them back or execute them or send assassins to Japan to murder them; and exhilaration because Kim Ok-kiun, their leader, assured the rest that the march of history had reached a point where the Serpent of the Eastern Sea - Japan - would strangle the sleeping Lion of China; that Japan, in order to carry out her historic mission, would need their help as much as they would need Japan's help to drive out the reactionaries in Seoul from power; and that once they were back in power, they would so speedily and thoroughly reform and revitalize Korea that Japan would have to treat them with respect.

Their dread was justified. As soon as they eluded the government dragnet and escaped to Japan, their enemies in Seoul tried strenuously to induce Japan to send the 'four arch traitors' - Kim Ok-kiun, Pak Yong-hyo, Soh Kwang-pom and Jaisohn - back to Korea. Japan refused to comply on the ground that they were political refugees. Failing in the effort, Seoul sent a special mission to Japan, ostensibly to heal the bridge between Korea and Japan, but in reality, to secure the extradition of the 'traitors.' Jaisohn recounted his own experience in these words:

> "Originally our group consisted of 43. However, some died
> during the battle, some were caught by our enemy and executed,
> and some accompanied the King to the Chinese side, leaving the

nine of us. Till five days before, we were in a position to institute reform in Korea and to help her move forward along with Japan and other progressive nations as an independent nation. But now we were fugitives, hiding in the ship's bottom, waiting to sail across the blue ocean to a foreign country and to an unknown future. I couldn't help feeling sorry for us."

Photo: The key figures of the *Kapsin* Coup of 1884 (from left to right: Park Young-hyo, Soh Kwang-pom, Soh Jai-pil, Kim Ok-kiun).

Photo: Soh Kwang-pom (age 26).

Photo: Hong Young-sik (age 30).

Photo: Park Young-hyo.

The Korean refugees, now separated from the Japanese, felt insecure even in the ship's hold as long as she was docked in *Inchon*, for unpredictable Takezoye might well weaken and agree to surrender them to the agents of the Seoul regime. Fortunately, this did not happen, and the Chitose Maru left for Japan as scheduled without their capture. At daybreak on the 13th of December, Jaisohn and his comrades were awakened by a commotion above. Staggering out of the coal bunker and

114

up to the deck, they looked at each other for the first time in five days and were astonished by their coal smeared, ghostlike faces. They had a good laugh at themselves.

From Nagasaki Harbor to Tokyo

Before their eyes lay an exotic landscape which they surmised was that of Nagasaki. For a while it made them forget their care. Then they called on Captain Tsuji to thank him for his hospitality and bid him farewell. The latter advised them to adopt Japanese names for the duration of their stay in Japan, saying it might serve to protect them. Upon his suggestion, Kim Ok-kiun chose the name Iwada, which became his until an assassin's bullet ended his life in Shanghai in 1894. Jaisohn chose to retain his own name.

On landing at Nagasaki, the Korean exiles were herded into a police station. The Japanese police were obviously taken aback by their appearance and took them for ordinary criminals. When their identity became known, a message was taken to the Foreign Office in Tokyo and the Koreans were taken to a hotel. There they washed and put on clean Japanese kimonos, which cost $0.60 each, and had a hearty meal.

And the next day they boarded a train for Tokyo. Jaisohn never found out who paid their expenses. In Tokyo, they first went to Count Fukuzawa's residence and were guests of that famous philanthropist. However, not wishing to impose on him unduly, they moved to a boarding house in Keikyo-Ku, but they could not stay there for long because they were without any means of support. So, they decided to separate, each to fend for himself.

Coincidentally, some American missionaries who were planning to go to Korea were detained in Japan by the aftermath of the December 4 coup and were looking for an opportunity to study Korean. While waiting, they got in touch with the Korean refugees, which proved beneficial to both sides. Pak Yong-hyo became a language teacher to Dr. John W. Heron, who subsequently became Dr. Allen's associate in the Presbyterian Hospital in Seoul. Jaisohn moved into the House of the Reverend Henry Loomis and remained there until he left for the United States five months later. There he enjoyed many of his new experiences, like sleeping in a bed instead of on a matted floor, having hot oatmeal for breakfast, and learning about the United States and customs of the American people from Loomis and his wife. The Loomis' were sent out by the American Bible Society and were preparing to open an office in Korea. Jaisohn taught him Korean, while Loomis taught him English. The rest of Jaisohn's comrades excepting Kim Ok-kiun, who had influential friends among the Japanese, were less fortunate. Unable to find employment, they lived from hand to mouth while waiting for the day when they might return home triumphantly.

Basically, all the refugees were restless. Their flight to Japan was intended not to just save their lives and live abroad, it was to prepare for and mount a second campaign to unseat the China-leaners in Seoul, and they believed that this was also the aim of the Japanese Government. Therefore, Kim Ok-kiun sought an interview with Foreign Minister Inouye immediately upon arrival in Tokyo. The latter, instead of granting the interview, went to Seoul and concluded a treaty of accommodation with the Government of their enemies. The only consolation for the fugitives was that he refused their extradition. Further, Inouye commenced the policy of modus vivendi with China as well.

The Korean exiles were stunned. How could the Japanese Government, which had explicitly let it be known that China and the China-leaners in Seoul were an anathema to Japan and that reforming Korea along the line advocated by the Independents was in the mutual interest of Korea and Japan, now pursue so diametrically opposite a course? They had taken the Japanese assurances so seriously that they staked on them the fortunes and lives of their families as well as their own. To be sure, they had been defeated in the first try, but they had lost only a battle, not a war. The more they pondered, the more they felt betrayed. Inouye had told Kim Ok-kiun that Japan was levying increased taxes on her people with the view to assisting reform and independence of Korea. On the third day of the coup, its representative in Seoul had promised to give the new reform Government a loan of $3,000,000. How else could these promises be interpreted except as a trick to use them as guinea pigs in Japan's dress rehearsal for her imperialistic drama?

Feeling especially betrayed and bitter was Jaisohn, the youngest and most idealistic of the four reform leaders. He was disgusted when he realized that the Japanese support for reform in the Korean Government was merely to exploit his and his comrades' patriotism. On further reflection, however, he concluded that

> he and his colleagues were to blame just as much as the Japanese leaders. It was naive of them to place such implicit trust in a foreign government. The naivety arose, he told himself, out of a lack of education. Education was essential, for, without it, one brings harm not only upon oneself, but also upon one's loved ones and nation.

Hence, he decided to go to the United States to secure an education. Having made up his mind, he informed his senior comrades. Kim Ok-kiun agreed. Pak Yong-hyo and Soh Kwang-pom not only agreed with him but wished to do likewise. Kim, too, wished to go with them but decided to remain behind as his political instinct convinced him that Japan would sooner or later reverse her policy toward China and Korea and that he might be able to help hasten the day.

Exile to the United States

It was easy for the three to decide to go to the United States. It was quite another matter to find the wherewithal for the venture, but they resolved to realize the dream and began to look for ways to make it a reality. The problem of raising the expenses of travel to the United States was compounded by the danger of being caught by agents of the Seoul Government. The Mins, now in complete control of the Government, included Mollendorff in a Mission of Apology to Tokyo, whose secret mission consisted of inducing the Japanese Government to extradite the Independents. In addition, there were rumors that Seoul had dispatched to Japan assassin squads for the elimination of Kim, Pak, Soh and Jaisohn, if they could not be extradited.

Under the circumstance, it was a miracle that Pak Yong-hyo and Soh Kwang-pom were able to raise over $90 in three months. They were accomplished calligraphers and wrote Chinese poems on silk scrolls. They peddled these among interested Japanese. Jaisohn believed that Pak and Soh were successful in raising the money by selling the scrolls because Japanese prized poems written by well-known Koreans. It is more likely that the Japanese Foreign Ministry, anxious to see them leave, inspired their friends to purchase the scrolls. At any rate, the necessary funds were raised, and in April 1885, Jaisohn, Pak Yong-hyo and Soh Kwang-pom left for America.

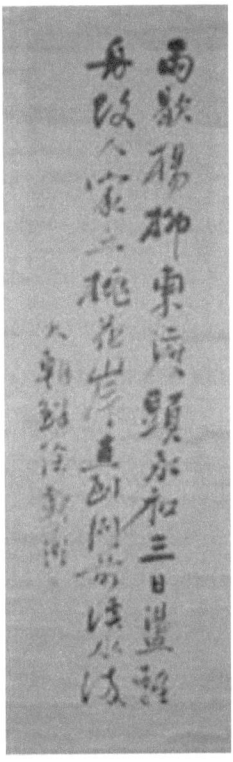

Photo: Calligraphy work Soh Jai-pil.

In late April 1885, Jaisohn and his two companions landed in America. As the five-ton United States freighter S.S. Empress of China, which Jaisohn thought the biggest ship he had ever seen, chugged toward San Francisco on the last day of her voyage, the three young Koreans stood on deck, and though their eyes were glued onto the picturesque northern California landscape on the horizon, they were too preoccupied by their own mixed feelings to appreciate its charm. On the one hand, they were glad that the long voyage was at an end. They had been seasick most of the way, and unaccustomed to the American diet, they had eaten only in order to stay alive. Having had no physical exercises during the day, they found the nights too long and lay awake in their little 'boxes,' the cheapest accommodation on the ship, for hour after monotonous hour.

They were haunted by the nightmarish sight of Seoul which they saw as they fled, of the brutal slaughter of their comrades in the palace by the Chinese soldiers and their Korean counterparts, of the shrieking mobs on the streets, threatening to bury them under piles of stones and bullets, and of the flaming mansions which no doubt belonged to them and their relatives. Even during the day, they brooded, in spite of themselves, over the mistakes in the planning and execution of the abortive coup, the treachery of the Queen, the pusillanimity and duplicity of the Japanese Government and its Minister in Seoul. There was too much time to kill and too little to do physically on the ship.

On the other hand, they regretted the end of the voyage, for it had also had its pleasant aspects. First, it was exhilarating to sit on the deck watching the blue ocean with silvery waves breaking its monotony by day and gazing up at the star-studded sky at night without the fear of assassins waiting to jump on them. Undoubtedly their enemies, in power once again in Seoul, were not satisfied with declaring the hapless exiles arch-traitors. They were determined to pursue and murder them wherever they might be. Also, for the first time in a long time, they had ample opportunity to reflect - on their omissions and commissions and on their hastes and wastes - and to dream about their future, studying in colleges and universities in America and returning to Korea to share with their fellow countrymen the knowledge they had acquired.

Challenges in San Francisco

However, as the ship slowly sailed into San Francisco Bay, their joy at having a glimpse of the 'Land of Promise' quickly turned to a fear of the life in this strange, bewildering country that lay before their eyes. The hustle and bustle of the people on the dockside seemed to confirm what they had heard and read about the United States: 'There everyone fends for himself. If you had the means and the will, it would offer you anything. Otherwise, nothing.' They had the will, but hardly the means. Among the three, they had only a few dollars left, and only Jaisohn had a smattering of English. One remote source of help might be some acquaintances of their missionary friends in Japan, to whom the latter had written letters of introduction.

Photo: An article published in the San Francisco Chronicle titled 'Exiles from the Hermit Kingdom of Korea', featuring the names of Park Young-hyo, Soh Kwang-pom, and Soh Jai-pil. (1885)

They disembarked, scared and almost wishing they had never ventured out of Japan. Pak Yong-hyo and Soh Kwang-pom were struck by the difference between the jostling crowd here and the American missionaries they had known in Japan. These people didn't seem to care that a *yangban* and a prince had arrived among them.

Somehow, the trio managed to find a boarding house in San Francisco run by a widow whom Jaisohn remembered only as Mrs. Johnson. She had a daughter named Hannah, who was a high school student. They were very kind to them. Jaisohn, Pak and Soh stayed there for about a month, calling on the people in San Francisco to whom their missionary friends in Japan had written introducing them. These Americans were friendly but did not offer any material help, which the Korean youths had hoped for but were too proud to ask. Only one of them, James B. Roberts, offered them an advice which was: 'Seek ye first God's Kingdom and His righteousness.' Back in their room, Pak and Soh grumbled that it was all very well to seek God's kingdom and his righteousness, but they also had to eat and have a roof over their heads.

With what little money they had running out fast, the three Korean exiles were desperate. Their missionary friends in Japan had spoken of America as a 'Land of Opportunity.' At the first sight of her, they had indeed exclaimed: 'Paradise on earth!' It did not take long, however, to realize that for the destitute, deaf-and-dumb exiles, even the paradise was a hell. Huddled together in a little room, they stared at each other, wondering how much longer they would remain alive. There was only one solution: to go out and find a job - any kind of job. However, Pak and Soh felt that physical labor was out of the question for *yangbans* such as themselves. Jaisohn decided to find a job. Though he, too, was a high *yangban*, he had no scruples about earning a living, whether it was through a physical or mental labor. 'A dead yangban is a mere corpse, whereas a live laborer had a chance to be an educated man', he said to himself.

He walked out of the room and combed scores of streets of the Golden Gate City for any kind of job. He found none. No one would offer a job to a person who spoke no English and had no experience at all. Soh Kwang-pom wrote to John T. Underwood in New York, the inventor and manufacturer of Underwood typewriters to ask for help. He had met the industrialist when he came to the United States in 1883 as a member of the first Korean diplomatic mission. Mr. Underwood was keenly interested in the mission and showed hospitality to the diplomatic personnel. It was natural for him to be interested in the Korean people because his younger brother was the first American missionary in Korea. Soh's intention in writing to Mr. Underwood was that the latter might send him some money which he could share with his two friends. Instead, he received an invitation to come to see him, and he left for New York immediately. Subsequently he enrolled at Rutgers University but did not remain there long.

Photo: John T. Underwood.

(**Editor's Note:** John T. Underwood, a New York businessman. He sent $50,000 to his younger brother, Horace Underwood, a missionary in

Korea, for purchasing land and constructing school buildings for the establishment of *Yonhee* College. present-day Yonsei University)

While Pak occupied himself with the study of English, Jaisohn walked the streets of San Francisco in search of a job. Occasionally he did find odd jobs and earn barely enough to feed himself and Prince Pak and to pay their rent, but no steady and satisfactory job came his way. In desperation he went, he recounted later, to a church 'on an impulse of yearning to reach something beyond the natural world.' One day Pak decided that America had no place for him and that he would be better off in Japan, where people treated a prince like one. Fortunately, a chance to return came his way. He met a Japanese friend, a nephew of Count Fukuzawa, who was on a visit in America. From him, Pak borrowed money and departed for Japan.

Now Jaisohn was left all alone. Lonely, penniless and without any hope of realizing his ambition for education, he saw no justification to go on living. He thought of drowning himself in San Francisco Bay. On further reflection, though, he convinced himself that he had not exhausted all the means at his command. He was young, healthy and intelligent. Furthermore, he had always believed that 'one's life was not something one could dispose of at one's own will. As a part of human society, one's life is as much society's as one's own. Hence, his life was Korea's as well as his.' He walked out of his room to continue his search for a job.

The Best Job

Everywhere he went, Jaisohn was asked the same question. "Can you speak English?" His stock answer, "No," ended the interview. After being turned down a dozen times, he entered a furniture store on Market Street. Again, he was asked whether he spoke English. This time he answered brokenly: "Not very well, but I am strong," holding up hands, flexing his arm muscles and pointing to his long, strong legs. The proprietor looked up and down at him in silence and offered him the job of distributing the firm's advertising circulars around town, provided he was willing to do a lot of walking. Jaisohn eagerly accepted the offer.

Jaisohn was paid two dollars a day for door-to-door delivery of the circulars covering an area of about ten square miles. At that rate, he covered nearly every street in the city of San Francisco in a week. The next week he would deliver different circulars in the like manner. Although at first his ill-fitting Japanese-made shoes caused painful blisters, and his feet were bleeding when he came home, he soon developed protective calluses on his feet. He liked his job and later recalled that 'it was one of the best he ever had.' He enjoyed it so much that sometimes he covered almost twice the assigned area without realizing it. His delighted boss praised him in front of his fellow workers as the best employee in his establishment. This led him into a minor friction with the other employees. This was a puzzle to him, but later he learned that he was guilty of an 'unfair labor practice.'

With the worry of starvation out of the way, Jaisohn decided to lick his language handicap. He enrolled in an evening class in one of the Y.M.C.A. schools. On Sundays, he attended Bible classes, worship services, and prayer meetings wherever they were held. He also learned at least one or two new words of English every day during the week with the help of a pocket dictionary, which he always carried with him. He never missed his classes. He found attendance at church services of special help in learning pronunciations and inflections, and in time he became quite familiar with the Bible. He could even recite numerous Bible passages by heart. He was learning English fast.

Photo: An English dictionary Soh Jai-pil created for his own English studies.

The Man of Faith

In time, too, he learned more than the language. He found himself embracing Christianity. Jesus, to him, was divine, not so much because he was the Son of God according to the prophets, but because he 'lived' as God would have lived, were he on this planet in the flesh. He admired Jesus not because the Bible taught him to, but, in spite of its ambiguities and seeming contradictions, his own experience confirmed that Jesus was the way. His conception of God was the product of his concern for humanity, of his urge to help promote human welfare as well as his own, and of his recognition that he could not fulfill his perceived obligation by himself. It now dawned on him that his going to a church somewhere earlier 'on an impulse to reach something beyond the natural world' was the recognition of this. When he was locked in a crucial battle between survival and suicide, his belief that his life was more than his own tipped the scale against the latter, and his exposure to the teaching by Jesus: "I am the vine, and ye are the branch. If ye abide in me, and I in ye, ye shall bear much fruit" gave him a new birth as a Christian.

For a while, Jaisohn went to a different church each Sunday, attending as many services as there were available. His purpose was in part to take free lessons in English and in part to satisfy his curiosity about Christianity. To be sure, there were religions in Korea - Confucianism, Buddhism and *Chondokyo* (Teaching of the Heavenly Way), an eclectic religion among the people. Each had temples of its own. However, only a few adherents attended them on special occasions. In contrast, Americans seemed to take church attendance seriously. He wondered whether this was responsible for their material prosperity and social progress. In time, he was persuaded that church going in America was more a custom than nurture in Jesus's teaching.

There were exceptions, of course. He thought some members of a church called 'Mason St. Presbyterian Church' took their religion very seriously and found himself attending regularly. A large and active congregation, it not only held several meetings - morning, afternoon and evening - each Sunday, all of which he enjoyed attending; there was a James B. Roberts, an elder of the church, who took a keen interest in him. Jaisohn's acquaintance with him was through the introduction of the Reverend Balagh, one of the missionaries he had met in Tokyo. Mr. Roberts, a native of Westchester, PA, had come out to California on the crest of the gold rush and settled in the Golden Gate City. He subsequently became a prosperous insurance executive and was active in civic and religious affairs in San Francisco as well as his church. Each Sunday he inquired of Jaisohn's welfare and gave him words of encouragement. Occasionally, he also invited the lonely Korean to his house for Sunday dinner.

A Fateful Encounter with Hollenback

A year had passed since Jaisohn arrived in San Francisco. One Sunday in spring, 1886, he received an invitation from Mr. Roberts to attend dinner at his house. Jaisohn accepted it. On arriving at the Roberts residence, he was surprised to see an elderly gentleman there. Mr. Roberts introduced him to the man whose name was William Hollenback. Mr. Hollenback was a wealthy coal magnate in Pennsylvania and a devout Christian. He was in San Francisco on vacation and was a guest of Mr. and Mrs. Roberts. He and Roberts were longtime friends. Though they were separated by thousands of miles, their common interests bound them together. In social philosophy, they were rugged individualists. In religious belief, they were staunch Calvinists, and as such they firmly adhered to the doctrine of predestination, of the gospel of wealth, of laissez-faire, and America's manifest destiny. Firmly convinced that they were God's trustees of earthly wealth, they conceived it their duty to accumulate wealth and invest it for the spreading of Christianity at home and abroad.

On hearing about a strange and unusual Korean youth from Roberts, Hollenback had suggested that it was perhaps providential that he came upon Jaisohn, and he wished to meet him. 'Why not invest in him by training him for the ministry and eventually sending him back to Korea as a missionary?' Roberts couldn't agree with him more, and the meeting was arranged. From the moment Jaisohn walked into the house, the coal magnate from the East was favorably impressed by him. He was a young man of dignified bearing. When he talked, he was captivating with a simple, intelligent choice of words. He was no less impressed by Mr. Hollenback, tall and austere in appearance, yet displaying gentleness when he opened his mouth, there was a lordly charm about him.

After dinner, Mr. and Mrs. Roberts excused themselves, and Mr. Hollenback and Jaisohn talked by themselves. To numerous questions posed by the Christian philanthropist from Pennsylvania - how Jaisohn happened to be a revolutionary, what led him to America, how his interest in Christianity began, what were his plans for the future, etc. – Jaisohn's answers were brief, factual and direct. When Mr. Hollenback complimented Jaisohn for his mastery of the English language in the brief period of sojourn in America, the young Korean thanked him and said he wished he could have done better, but because he was unable to attend a regular school, this was impossible. Mr. Hollenback asked whether he would like to come to Wilkes Barre, PA, his hometown. He told Jaisohn that 'if he wished, he would arrange for him to enter a preparatory school which he had helped found, that if things work out satisfactorily, he would see that Jaisohn went on to college, Lafayette, of which he was a trustee, and that if Jaisohn wished to devote his life to the service of God, he could go on to the Princeton Theological Seminary, of which he was also a trustee.'

Jaisohn was so overcome with joy that for a few moments he was speechless. How often he had dreamed of such an opportunity. Now the dream had come true. Of course he did, and he answered: "I would love to very much. Thank you very much, Mr. Hollenback." Thus, it was agreed that at the end of the summer of that year, Jaisohn would go to Wilkes Barre to begin a new chapter of his life in America.

Back in his small, bare room, Jaisohn lay in his bed, thrilled by the good fortune that had come his way. It was all so sudden and unexpected that he almost feared it might prove a dream. It was, of course, not a dream, and he was wrapped up in a happy thought of a brighter future - of at last entering an American school to prepare for college, of becoming a college student, and of returning to Korea to help reform and rejuvenate his ancient tottering native country. Grateful to God, he got up and offered a prayer of fervent thanks.

Then he sat absorbed in deep thought. He thought of his former colleagues, wondering what had become of Kim Ok-kiun, his hero; of Prince Pak after returning to Japan; of Soh Kwang-pom, who had gone to New York; and of Hong Yong-sik, who had escorted King Kojong, the night of the collapse of the 'Three-day Rule' of Korea. He, then, wondered about the fate of his family in Korea. Remembering the barbarous ancient Korean tradition of meting out capital punishment to the family of a person branded as a traitor, he felt a sudden chill running through his spine. He couldn't bear the thought of it and left his room for a walk. Later he went to a church for an evening worship.

It was fortunate for Jaisohn that he did not know of their fate. What happened to his own family has already been noted. Kim Ok-kiun's wife saved her life by disguising herself and living the life of a servant. His house was confiscated by the Government. Pak Yong-hyo's brother was killed by Chinese soldiers and his house went up in smoke. Hong Yong-sik was also killed by the Chinese, and his house was used as a torture chamber where unlucky 'Independents' met their violent death. Later, King Kojong turned the house over to Dr. Horace Allen, who converted it into a hospital - the first modern hospital in Korea.

Hillman High School

That summer, Jaisohn worked hard in order to earn his travel expenses to Wilkes Barre. He studied harder than ever before to be ready for school. September 1886, arrived, and one day early that month he bade farewell to Mr. and Mrs. Roberts, as well as other friends he had made in San Francisco and was off. Although the anticipation of becoming a bona fide student had led him to anxiously wait for the day, his leave-taking was not an unmixed joy. How could he help but feel sad as well as glad about leaving the city where he had spent his first year and a half in America of blood, sweat and tears?

Arriving in Wilkes Barre, Jaisohn found the city quite unlike the scenic, sparkling and bustling city of San Francisco. It was a dull, smoggy and rustic little city surrounded by coal-laden mountains on three sides and by a river on the fourth. Nevertheless, the expectation that there he would soon commence his long-cherished student life made him feel as though he was coming home. His delight was all the greater when a man came up to him at the railroad station and asked, "Are you Philip Jaisohn?" He was Mr. Hollenback's chauffeur. He took Jaisohn to the Hollenback residence in a sumptuous carriage, and on arrival at the stately mansion, Jaisohn's benefactor and his wife welcomed him warmly. Jaisohn stayed with the Hollenbacks for several days.

Then Mr. Hollenback took him to Mr. Scott, headmaster of Harry Hillman Academy, which was in the same city. This was to be his school. Mr. Hollenback had arranged for Jaisohn to live with Mr. and Mrs. Scott, helping them with housework, mowing the lawn in summer and tending to the furnace in winter, etc., in exchange for his room and board. On the way to the Scotts, Hollenback told Jaisohn that he would pay for Jaisohn's tuition, but that he was expected to earn his keep, saying, since

God had given Jaisohn a strong body with powerful arms and legs, it was his duty to use the asset to help pay his way through school as much as possible. Jaisohn agreed.

Photo: Mr. Hollenback.

A regular student in an American school at last, Jaisohn found his life at Harry Hillman Academy pleasant and stimulating. Though the daily schedule was full and rigorous, it was, judging from that of Toyama Military School, on the lax side. The teachers were serious about their duty, but without being overly severe. They were demanding teachers and earned the respect of their students. Though corporal punishment was not known at the school, there was no disciplinary problem. Mr. Scott's words were the law, but he was almost venerated as the father of the students and teacher of teachers. Jaisohn was particularly impressed by the method of instruction followed at Harry Hillman. It was largely that of discussions, and students were expected to participate in them, making it necessary for every student to do his homework. The homework consisted of not only learning the textbook assignments but also reading from collateral texts in the school library. All this was a novel system to Jaisohn, and he took full advantage of it.

Living with the Scotts was an additional educational experience for Jaisohn. Mrs. Scott was a tutor as well as mother to him. She was very helpful with his homework, especially during his first year when he was still under a language handicap. Even more fortunate for him was the fact that her father, a retired judge, lived with them and was always ready to help him with his study of civics and American history. Listening to him relate his experiences as a lawyer and judge was an education which no amount of money could buy. These and his earlier education in Korea and Japan pushed him so far ahead of his classmates that he was able to complete his four-year courses in two, and in early June 1888, he graduated from Harry Hillman Academy with high honors.

U.S. Citizenship

That year was a milestone in Jaisohn's life in another way. On the 19th of June, he received his United States citizenship certificate, becoming the first Korean to be naturalized as an American. In recounting it in years later, Jaisohn said that 'in spite of racial discrimination against Orientals among Americans in those days, there was no law in the United States barring citizenship for persons of Asian origin, and both Mr. Hollenback and Headmaster Scott advised him to seek it from the time of his matriculation of Harry Hillman.' Their intention was to help him prepare himself as a missionary and to send him back to Korea someday. It was their belief that his U.S. citizenship would render him immune from political persecution on his return.

Jaisohn had held off till his last year at the Academy. It seemed to him that seeking the citizenship of another country was tantamount to a betrayal of Korea. Gradually, however, he was persuaded that whether his acquisition of the U.S. citizenship constituted an unpatriotic act depended on his motive. If his motive was to pursue self-advancement, he was unpatriotic. If it was for the benefit of Korea, he should acquire it. As he looked back, the *Kapsin* (1884) Reformist coup was commendable in aim. Nevertheless, in all youthful haste to realize their aim, he and his comrades failed to win the support of the Korean masses. The masses turned against the young reformists, thinking that they were reckless power-seekers who were trying to destroy Korea with the help of Japan which was a historic enemy of Korea. Hence, he now resolved that, should another opportunity to serve Korea come his way, he would make it absolutely clear that he was not seeking his own gain.

Viewed from that standpoint, Jaisohn could see the benefit to be derived out of his American citizenship. To begin with, although at the time he felt himself in no danger of assassination by his political enemies, a potential danger did exist. Furthermore, he never gave up the hope that someday, somehow, upon completion of his education in America, he would return to Korea and share his knowledge with his fellow countrymen. The hope became a faith to him, and pondering what branch of knowledge he should lay special emphasis, he thought political science and law would be most useful to his people. He realized that the introduction into Korea of political and legal concepts and processes prevailing in the Western world was likely to stir controversy among Koreans, especially old conservatives. In such an event, he felt that his American citizenship would serve as a shield for him. So, reasoning to himself, Philip Jaisohn, now an American, having completed his preparatory school education, was confidently looking forward to going on to college.

(**Editor's Note**: Philip Jaisohn, known by his Korean name Soh Jai-pil, received U.S. citizenship on June 19, 1888. At the time, the U.S. naturalization laws were primarily governed by the 1870 Naturalization Act, which expanded the naturalization process to foreigners of African descent but excluded Asians. However, exceptions were sometimes made for specific cases, often through individual acts of Congress or by the courts interpreting the law more leniently or broadly.

It is likely that Soh Jai-pil's naturalization occurred through one of these exceptions. He was a political exile who came to the United States to receive an education and actively participated in Korea's reform movement. His arrival in the U.S. and his activities may have contributed to his naturalization despite the restrictive immigration laws of the time. Additionally, it is important to note that during this period, immigration and naturalization laws were not as strictly or consistently applied as they are today, which allowed for some flexibility in individual cases. Given the lack of detailed information about his naturalization process, it is highly probable that Philip Jaisohn obtained U.S. citizenship through his unique circumstances, the discretion of the courts, and the support of influential individuals sympathetic to or supportive of his cause, such as Hollenback.)

CHAPTER SIX:

EDUCATION IN AMERICA

Separation from Hollenback

Early in 1888, Jaisohn took his college entrance examinations and was accepted by Lafayette and Princeton. Financial help from Hollenback was expected. Things look bright for him.

Suddenly, there was an unexpected development. One day in late June, Jaisohn received a call from Mr. Hollenback's office requesting him to come to see the latter at his office. Initially he was pleased, for in spite of his seeming aloofness and idiosyncrasies, Hollenback was a warm, intelligent man, and Jaisohn had looked up to him as his father. On further thought, however, Jaisohn thought it odd that Hollenback wished to see him in his office. He had always either invited Jaisohn to his house for dinner and a visit or dropped by at the academy for a chat. At any rate, Jaisohn complied.

Hollenback looked austere, but Jaisohn did not find it unusual. He asked Jaisohn what he planned to do during the summer, how he felt about the prospect of being a college student, etc. This done, he said he had a business matter to take up with Jaisohn and went straight to the point. He referred to the first meeting in San Francisco in which Jaisohn had spoken of a deep interest in Christianity. He reminded Jaisohn of what he had said to him then, that if Jaisohn wished to offer himself to serving Christ, he would help him secure an education to that end. Accordingly, he was pleased to arrange for him to enter Hillman Academy. Jaisohn was able to graduate from the preparatory school without much help from him, but in college, Jaisohn would need much financial assistance. Now, he said, the time for a clear understanding had come. He was prepared to help 'if Jaisohn promised in writing to become a minister and return to Korea as a missionary following graduation from Lafayette College and Princeton Theological Seminary.' He wished to settle the matter then and there for the peace of mind of both. If the proposal was acceptable to Jaisohn, and if Jaisohn would sign a statement of agreement, he would underwrite the whole cost of his education as an investment in God, adding: "Mind you, this is not a charity on my part, but it's strictly a business transaction."

Jaisohn was deeply troubled. On the one hand, Mr. Hollenback had been a great benefactor and friend to him, and he did not wish to disappoint him. On the other hand, for all the love of Christ, he had never felt called to the Christian ministry, nor was it certain that even had he agreed to the proposal, he could return to Korea as a missionary seven years later. To sign the agreement now under the circumstances would be dishonesty on his part and unfair to Hollenback, so he answered:

With all due respect for you, I cannot sign the statement.
First as you are aware, the Korean Government has branded me as a traitor and will hang me the moment I return to Korea. Of

137

course, I hope it will revoke the sentence, but when and whether it will do so I do not know.

Second, I believe in God. I can guarantee you that I will remain a Christian all my life. However, I do not now feel divinely called to become a missionary. Perhaps seven years from now I shall feel called, but now I cannot foretell it. Under the circumstances, it would be unfair to you and to God for me to consent to your proposal. I am very sorry.

Hollenbeck was disappointed. He had put to Jaisohn what he believed was a sound Christian business proposition. He had no choice but to tell Jaisohn that there would be no more financial assistance to him. Jaisohn thanked him for all he had done and as he rose to take his leave, Hollenback handed him twenty dollars.

People in the Early Life of Philip Jaisohn

Jaisohn left Hollenback's office with mixed feelings: regret for having disappointed his benefactor, pride for having stuck to his conviction, and worry about how to meet his college expenses. Feeling the need of someone to talk to, he went to see Mr. Scott and his wife. They were during a visit with a guest, a Mr. Davis from Washington D.C., to whom they introduced him. The Scotts, solicitous about Jaisohn's welfare as always, noticed that he was under the weight of a worrisome problem and told him to share with them anything that was on his mind, as Mr. Davis was a friend of theirs and was interested in him as much as they were.

Jaisohn related to them about his visit with Mr. Hollenback. All three were in deep sympathy with this predicament. Davis, who was a professor of English at a college in Washington D.C., had many influential friends in the nation's capital. He advised Jaisohn to go to Washington D.C. and see Mr. Otis, Curator of the Smithsonian Institution, and gave him a letter of introduction. He thought that since the Institute's museum had numerous Oriental objects, the Curator might be able to use Jaisohn as a translator. Davis also gave Jaisohn a letter of introduction to a Mr. Hendley, who was private secretary to President Grover Cleveland.

Jaisohn thanked Professor Davis for the help and promised to do as he advised. Still hoping somehow to be able to enter Lafayette in the fall, he went to eastern Pennsylvania, where the college was located, to consult with Professor Edward Hart, who had been appointed as his freshman adviser. Professor Hart invited several of his colleagues to sit in at the meeting with Jaisohn. Told about what Mr. Hollenback had done to Jaisohn, everyone present reacted with indignation, calling him a hypocrite, tyrant, and unprintable names, but none offered a solution to Jaisohn's problem. As Jaisohn got up, feeling that the door to Lafayette was closed to him, Hart told him not to give up hope. He advised Jaisohn to find a summer job and earn his tuition money. "You needn't worry about your room and board. You can live with us and help Mrs. Hart around the house," he said.

Jaisohn was profoundly grateful. Thanking Hart for the generous offer, Jaisohn promised him to do his best to earn his tuition. He went to Philadelphia to look for a job. However hard he tried, there was nothing that paid him the wage he needed. He was forced to look for any kind of work, but even in the City of Brotherly Love (Philadelphia) one must have skill and experience or starve, let alone save money. After several weeks of try at various menial jobs, he abandoned the hope of entering Lafayette that fall and decided to try his luck in Washington D.C.

A New Life in Washington D.C.

In Washington D.C., he went to the Smithsonian Institution, as Mr. Davis had suggested, and called on Curator Otis. Mr. Otis, a very friendly man, said after reading the letter from Professor Davis, that all employees of the museum were provided by Congress, and he could not employ anybody without Congressional authorization. He said, however, 'there were many art objects from the Orient in the museum and if Jaisohn could explain them, he would personally hire him by the hour at one dollar per hour.' Jaisohn worked there for one month, identifying swords, medals, curios, etc. from China, Japan and Korea.

Meanwhile, he called on Mr. Hendley at the White House and presented to him Davis' letter. The presidential secretary wanted to know what he could do for Jaisohn. When the latter ingenuously requested an interview with President Cleveland in order to ask him for a job, Hendley was somewhat taken aback. "Young man", he said, "the President of the United States does not operate an employment agency." And he gave Jaisohn yet another letter of introduction, this time to Mr. O'Brian, who was United States Civil Service Commissioner, saying 'all employment in government must come under civil service, a new law and all applicants must take a civil service examination and pass it.'

Mr. O'Brian, an amiable man, told Jaisohn to return in a week and take the examination, and meanwhile to file with his office his citizenship papers, two or three recommendations by U.S. citizens vouching for his moral integrity, etc. These were done, and Jaisohn took the examination with twenty others. He was the assigned #3. When he returned a week later, as he had been instructed, to learn the results, O'Brian informed him regretfully that he had failed. Jaisohn thought it strange, since he had not found the examination difficult. O'Brian sent for Mr. Webster, chief examiner, and he and Jaisohn checked his paper. They found that the first two sheets bore his number #3 but that the other fifteen sheets were marked #2. There had been an administrative error. Jaisohn had actually received a mark of 97. The passing mark was 75. He was told to wait for a notice of appointment.

After two weeks, Jaisohn became impatient and went back to O'Brian to inquire about his chances of receiving an appointment. The Commissioner explained that all positions were apportioned to the states in proportion to population. Since Pennsylvania was a large state and its quota of federal employees was already filled, no appointment could be made unless a vacancy arose through either death or resignation. "Damn few die, and none resigns," O'Brien added. Jaisohn's heart sank. But refusing to give up hope, he asked if there was any possibility of bypassing the standing rule. The only way, O'Brian said, would be through a special appointment to a particular position which was vacant. In such a case, eligibility was determined by means of an examination set up expressly for that purpose.

The Smithsonian Institution

With this information, Jaisohn went back to Otis, Curator of Smithsonian Institution, for advice. The Curator promised to make inquiries and asked Jaisohn to keep in touch with him. Otis had a close friend, Dr. John H. Billings, who was in charge of the Army Surgeon General's Library. The library was only one block from the Smithsonian, and the two lunched together almost every day. Mr. Otis asked Dr.

Billings whether he knew of any government agency which could use someone with the knowledge of both Chinese and Japanese. Billings answered that "he had been looking for just such a person, for the library had thousands of medical books and periodicals from the Orient, but having no one who knew these languages, he was unable to even catalog them." Otis assured him that "he had just the man for him" and suggested that "he request the Surgeon General to ask the Secretary of War for a translator."

Within days, Jaisohn received a notice from the Office of the U.S. Civil Service Commissioner to report for a special examination in Japanese and Chinese on a certain date. On the day of examination, he showed up promptly on time and was handed papers containing two long biblical passages, one in Japanese and one in Chinese. The examiners, being totally unfamiliar with these languages, had sent for a question each to the Japanese and Chinese Legations in Washington D.C. They supplied several verses from the 15th chapter of the Gospel by John and from the 15th chapter of the Gospel by Mark to be translated to English. It so happened that he had learned them almost by heart while he was attending the Y.M.C.A. night school in San Francisco, and he had no difficulty at all in translating them. He passed the examination with a perfect mark. A week later, Jaisohn received a notice from the Surgeon General's office to report for duty the next day at the Surgeon General's Library.

Thus, it was that Jaisohn became the first native of Korea to be named a civil servant of the United States. One cannot help but deem it 'providential'. He had been made to study Chinese characters in order to qualify for a position in the fiercely anti-Western government of Korea; when he studied Japanese while a pioneering student in Japan, he had no expectation whatever that it would prepare him for a career in civil service in America; when he was grinding away at his English in San Francisco, it was to find a job and stay alive; and when he went to Washington D.C., he hoped to obtain work with the help of the President of the United States, earn his tuition money and return to Easton, P.A. to enter Lafayette College. But a far better reward than these were in store for him. His initial salary was $100 per month, which he thought fabulous.

Jaisohn's boss was Dr. Billings, Director of the Surgeon General's Library. A very learned and warm person, he was to exercise an enormous influence over Jaisohn. It was through his efforts that the library was established and had grown to become the largest medical library in the world. At first, Jaisohn was put to the task of translating the authors and titles of Oriental books. Later he wrote excerpts of the principal contents of important medical works. In the process, he became more and more interested in medicine. The financial worries behind him, he decided to pursue an education while holding his civil service job. Although he had planned, as previously pointed out, to take up government and law, his daily involvement with medical literature and his admiration for Dr. Billings as a medical scholar led him to change his mind. He wished to study medicine and entered the Corcoran Scientific School, an evening division of Columbian College which has since become George Washington University. Billings was so pleased with his decision that he not only adjusted Jaisohn's schedule at the Library but also placed the entire medical library at his disposal.

Drs. George Sternberg and Walter Reed

Deepening Jaisohn's interest in medicine, too, was Dr. George M. Sternberg, who was Surgeon General of the United States Army. A world-renowned medical authority, Dr. Sternberg was a pioneer in introducing pathology into the United States. Dr. Billings and the Surgeon General arranged for Jaisohn to divide his time between the Army Medical Library and Army Medical Museum, which were in the same building, the Medical Museum. Sternberg attached Jaisohn to Dr. Walter Reed, who was director of the museum laboratory. Dr. Reed had under him another assistant, Dr. Gray, and the three conducted experiments in microphotography and biochemistry. Dr. Gray's talent and his devotion to research greatly inspired Jaisohn. Gray designed a studio for photography, placing a generator in the basement for electricity. Sternberg's interest in pathology was inspired by a tour in Europe one summer. Noting its popularity among German medical scholars, he came home and encouraged Reed to concentrate research on it and having persuaded the Army Medical School to include bacteriology and pathology in its curriculum, he placed Reed in charge of it. Jaisohn assisted Reed, as did Gray.

(**Editor's Note**: Walter Reed Army Medical Center, a world-renowned hospital in Washington D.C., is named after Dr. Walter Reed.)

The First Korean Doctor

Evidently, Jaisohn's progress in his study, spurred by his work as assistant to Drs. Billings, Sternberg, and Reed, must have convinced the Corcoran School authorities that he was qualified to enter the Colombian Medical School the following year. With his medical study at the

Columbian College and experiments under Reed's direction at the Army Medical Laboratory complementing each other, Jaisohn's progress became phenomenal. And he received his M.D. degree in three years, 1892. On the day of his graduation, all his classmates were surrounded by throngs of admiring friends and relatives and were showered with presents and congratulations. As for him, however, there were no relatives, no presents and 'not even a cabbage to cheer him up.' But he received a unique honor: the first Western educated Korean to receive a medical degree.

Photo: Graduation photo from the Colombian Medical School. Philip Jaisohn is the third from the left in the top row (marked by an arrow). (1892).

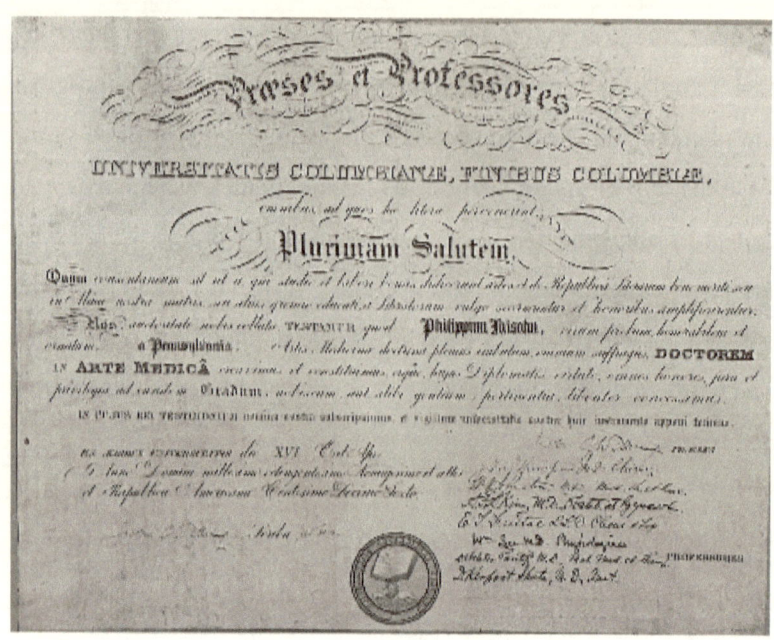

Photo: School of Medicine graduation diploma, Columbian University (now George Washington University).

Photo: Philip Jaisohn's medical license (1892).

Following his graduation from Columbian Medical College, now George Washington University, Jaisohn held an internship at Garfield Hospital, located in Washington D.C., while retaining his position as a U.S. civil servant. Meanwhile, the Army Medical Laboratory staff was over-worked, and Jaisohn was attached there for full time duty in 1893. Dr. Billings added an enlisted man named Tracy to the staff to assist Drs. Reid and Jaisohn with blood analysis and general laboratory work, thus enabling Reed and Jaisohn to travel to Baltimore in order to hear lectures by Dr. William Welch of Johns Hopkins, one of America's foremost authorities in bacteriology and pathology. They did this every week for six months. After this, Jaisohn attended weekly lectures delivered by Dr. Godding, Superintendent of Saint Elizabeth's Mental Hospital in Washington D.C., in conjunction with his duties at the Army Medical Laboratory. He never tired of learning.

However, on advice from Dr. Johnson, who had been his professor at Columbian Medical College, Jaisohn reluctantly resigned from his civil service in 1894. Johnson felt the opportunities for advancement in civil service were severely limited. Jaisohn opened his own office specializing in pathology. At first, his office consisted of the front half of a room at K and 14th streets, N.W. He curtained off the other half and used it as his bedroom. His practice steadily grew, and his patients included many out-of-towners. One day, he later recalled, a patient by the name of Morse called at his office, complaining that none of the other physicians whom he consulted could help him. Jaisohn's diagnosis revealed that the patient was diabetic. Since pathology was new in America in those days, few physicians were able to treat diabetic patients. Mr. Morse lived in a different city, but finding Dr. Jaisohn's treatment helpful, his whole family moved with him to Washington D.C. to be near Jaisohn.

Marriage to Miss Muriel Armstrong

A man of many interests, Jaisohn was not just a student of medicine, he was a keen student of world affairs. In spite of his busy schedule, he kept abreast of developments abroad, especially those of the Far East. The year, 1894, was an unforgettable one for him in many ways. It was a year of joy and pain, of hope and despair, and of warning and challenge.

That year he could not only look forward to a satisfying medical career; his courtship of a charming socialite, Muriel Armstrong of Chicago and Washington D.C., culminated in marriage. On June 20, they were married. The wedding took place at the fashionable Church of the Covenant in Washington D.C. with over 200 well-wishers, many of them prominent government officials, from Chicago, Cleveland, Pittsburgh and the nation's capital, in attendance. The event was reported in many papers in Chicago and Washington D.C.

The wedlock between Jaisohn and Muriel Armstrong, too, must be regarded as providential, since neither he nor she had anticipated it. As a Korean dedicated to the cause of Korea, he had never lost the vision of returning to his native land some day and offering his services. Marrying an American woman was likely to prove an obstacle to this. Moreover, as a young physician deeply immersed in his research and practice, he was, probably, too busy to rush into a marriage. Miss Armstrong was even less likely to have anticipated marrying a native of Korea. A pretty and well-bred daughter of a prominent Chicagoan, she undoubtedly had many admirers and suitors among eligible young men of Chicago and Washington D.C. In spite of all these, she fell in love with Jaisohn.

Their meeting was coincidental. In the hotel where he lived, there also lived Captain and Mrs. James E. White and Miss Armstrong, daughter of Mrs. White by her previous marriage. Captain White was Superintendent of the U.S. Railway Mail Service, to which he had succeeded Colonel George Armstrong, founder of the service and its head till his death. White married the latter's widow, and Muriel, the youngest daughter of Colonel and Mrs. Armstrong, was living with her mother and stepfather.

As Jaisohn later related, Miss Armstrong was an attractive and sensitive girl with an avid interest in the art and cultures of the world. Though she was shy at first, she seemed intrigued by him. Evidently, she sensed something mysterious and charismatic about him. Once they began conversing with each other, they found that they had many common interests. Though Jaisohn had not developed artistic skills, his interest in art was strong, and both had an abiding interest in learning how various peoples lived. The longer he knew her, the more pleasant he found her company. She was widely read, forthright in her expressions, yet extremely courteous.

To Muriel Armstrong, Jaisohn was not an inscrutable Oriental. He was a person, physically handsome and intellectually brilliant. Additionally, he possessed certain qualities not found in any other young men she had met, for which she thought of him as a 'man of destiny.' Though he was modest and was reticent about himself, his actions made it clear that he carried the burden of his native country on his shoulders. Though he was at times critical of certain American ways, he never ceased to marvel at the underlying causes which enabled the United States to become a rich and powerful nation, whereas the nations lying south of it remained poor and weak. He was determined to discover the secret of it as it would enable him to be more helpful to Korea someday, he often said. As a physician he was of course interested in treating the sick, but he was much more interested in finding the causes of sickness and preventing it. He was a different man from others, for which Muriel found it impossible not to admire him. So, as they got to know each other better, their bonds of mutual admiration and affection grew deeper. They remained locked in mutual love until her death in 1941.

Photo: Philip Jaisohn and Muriel Armstrong, (1894).

Another very pretty June wedding took place at 8 o'clock last night at the Church of the Covenant, the contracting parties being Dr. Philip Jaisohn, of this city, and Miss Muriel Josephine Armstrong, of Chicago, Ill. Dr. Jaisohn is a well-known physician, whose high reputation as a scientific man is not limited to this city. The bride is the daughter of the late Col. George Buchanan Armstrong, the founder of the United States Railway Mail Service, who was at the head of that bureau until the time of his death. Her eldest brother, Mr. George B. Armstrong, is the editor of the Musical Indicator of Chicago. The ceremony was per-

Photo: The Washington Post article about the marriage of Philip Jaisohn and Muriel Armstrong. (1894)

Photo: Philip Jaisohn and his wife, Muriel Armstrong (1895).

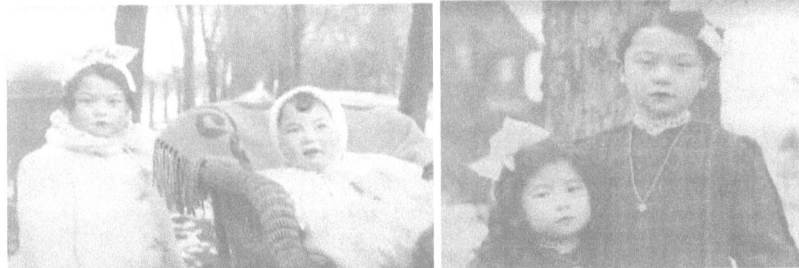

Photo: Philip Jaisohn's two daughters. The eldest, Stephanie, and the youngest, Muriel.

(**Editor's Note**: When Dr. Philip Jaisohn (Soh Jai-pil) married Muriel Armstrong in 1894, the legal and social attitudes toward interracial marriage in the late 19th-century United States varied significantly by state. Although federal law did not explicitly prohibit interracial marriages, many states had their own laws prohibiting marriage between white individuals and people of other races. These laws were primarily part of the Jim Crow laws in Southern states, which enforced racial segregation and discrimination against African Americans, and similarly affected other non-white populations. However, the enforcement and acceptance of interracial marriage varied by state and depended on the racial and ethnic background of the individuals involved.

As the first Korean to gain U.S. citizenship and a prominent advocate for Korean independence and democracy, Philip Jaisohn 's marriage to Muriel Armstrong, from a prominent American family, might have been unusual and controversial at the time. Nevertheless, unlike the legal barriers faced by marriages between white individuals and African Americans in states with strict anti-miscegenation laws, their marriage did not encounter significant legal issues. The couple's social status and Philip Jaisohn 's fame likely played a significant role in overcoming the prevailing societal norms against interracial marriage at the time. The legal and social environment surrounding interracial marriage in the U.S. began to change significantly in the mid-20th century, culminating in the landmark 1967 Supreme Court case Loving v. Virginia, which invalidated all laws prohibiting interracial marriage across the country.)

The Growing Influence of Japan in Korea

Also, that year, world-shaking incidents occurred in the Far East which caused Jaisohn profound anguish. In March, a Seoul Government's hireling in collusion with agents of China's Li Hung Chang lured Kim Ok-kiun to Shanghai and assassinated him. Before Kim's friends could reclaim his remains, Chinese authorities allowed the Korean Government to take it to Seoul. There, the Government ordered it dismembered in public as a warning to all would-be 'traitors to the King.'

That angered Kim's Japanese friends, of whom there were thousands and many of whom were highly influential. As grassroots in Japan echoed their indignation with protest demonstrations, the Tokyo Government, which had till then viewed the Korean exile as a nuisance and tried its best to drive him out of Japan, suddenly turned a defender of the dead man. It denounced the barbarity of the Korean Government and warned it to expect retribution. It attacked China's complicity in Kim

Ok-kiun's assassination as a slap in the face of Japan, pointing out that he had long been identified as a friend of Japan. It was clear that the Japanese Government's expressions of righteous indignation were not for the Korean exile, but a hint that Japan was now ready for a showdown with China for the control of Korea.

What ignited Japan's smoldering war fever into open warfare was the outbreak a few months later of another civil uprising known as *Tong-hak-nan* in Korea. The helpless Seoul regime appealed to China for help, as it had done in 1882, and Peking promptly responded with a dispatch of troops. This was a violation of the Sino-Japanese Agreement of 1885, which stated that in case a necessity to intervene in Korea arose, the two powers should first consult. This gave Japan a good excuse to launch her long prepared war on China and she rushed to Korea well-trained and well-armed troops twice the size of China's. The Sino-Japanese war was on.

The news about the outbreak of the war came as no surprise to Jaisohn, for to him the question was not whether, but when, it would occur. Not surprising also were smashing victories of the Japanese forces. He expected that. His worry was that regardless of which side won, Korea would be the loser. Though he had once relied on Japan for Korea's reform, it had been as a means to Korean independence. He had never intended to hand Korea over to Japan, and he was now fervently opposed to her taking over Korea. Jaisohn was right about Japan's decisive military superiority. As thousands of banzai-shouting Japanese soldiers swarmed ashore at *Inchon*, terror-stricken Yuan Shin-kai, China's Resident-Commissioner and bully in Korea for 12 years, fled back to China in disguise. And within weeks, the outnumbered and bedraggled Chinese troops were routed.

Jaisohn also demonstrated that he was nobody's puppet. Within months after the outbreak of the war, the Japanese Government, confident of the outcome, began to assemble Korean leaders whom it believed to be pro-Japanese. Jaisohn was also approached. He was offered the post of vice Minister for Foreign Affairs. He was not interested. Then the offer was the Ministership for Foreign Affairs. He was still not interested. Finally, the Japanese Minister in Washington D.C. reported to the Foreign Office in Tokyo: "It is positively impossible to persuade Dr. Philip Jaisohn, who has an American wife and a medical license to practice, to go to Korea."

The Japanese diplomat was wrong about Jaisohn's reasons for refusal, which had nothing to do with either his family or professional considerations. The simple fact was that Jaisohn would not sell his services to a foreign master. His longing to return to Korea and serve his people remained undiminished, for it was to that end that he had endured all kinds of hardships in America. But returning home beholden to a foreign government was not his way of serving Korea.

Physically, he went about his medical practice as usual, but mentally he was deeply preoccupied with Korea. "The Korea fever got me, and I was restless," he later recalled. Watching helplessly from abroad as his native country was tossed from China's frying pan into the consuming fire of Japanese imperialism was too painful to bear. He thought of smuggling himself into Korea and at least trying to rally his people to a struggle for independence. But that seemed as fanciful as a wish to fly to the skies to pick the stars. The Japanese Minister in Washington D.C. had informed him that King Kojong had decreed his pardon, to be sure, but would the people who had been told for a decade that he was a traitor to Korea listen to him? What chance had he, a lonely exile abroad, against the Empire of the Rising Sun?

Visit of an Old Friend, Pak Yong-hyo

In such an agitated condition, Jaisohn watched months go by. Then, one day in the late autumn of 1895, his old friend, Prince Pak Yong-hyo, surprised him with a visit. It was a poignant reunion, reminding him of the dramatic and heart-rending events of 1884, culminating in their lonely, hungry life in San Francisco. Pak had been an early recruit of the Japanese Government and had returned to Korea the previous year, assuming the powerful post of Interior Minister in the Japan-sponsored Government in Seoul. He took his position seriously and resisted the role of a mere Japanese puppet, while at the same time opposing interference by Queen Min.

The Queen, who had relied on China, now was courting Russia's support. Prince Pak came under attack from both sides. On the one hand, the Queen, suspecting his implication in the alleged plot to replace King Kojong with another member of the royal clan, was plotting to murder him. The Japanese, on the other hand, disenchanted with his failure to live up to their expectations, kicked him back to Tokyo. In the fall of 1895, fearing for his life even in Japan, Pak sneaked out of the Island Empire and came to the United States.

Jaisohn, who had been hungry for the news about Korea, was overjoyed at the opportunity to hear from his friend. However, the reports brought by Pak were disheartening. While Korea was disintegrating, nobody was capable of doing anything or even trying to do anything to help save her. Instead, the King and Queen were only interested in seeing that the King kept his throne. Politicians were interested only in seeking government positions as a means of lining their pockets at the expense of the people. The people at large were as apathetic as they were when Jaisohn and Pak fled Korea. Worse yet, a few who tried to prevent the country from falling were stopped by either Japan or other covetous powers. In the climate of despair and mutual distrust, everybody was either pro-Japanese, pro-Russian, or a traitor.

Pain by the report, Jaisohn asked: "In short, what you are saying is that Korea is beyond hope, is it not?" Pak answered: 'though the picture was anything but bright, I would not go so far as to give up hope altogether.' He attributed his failure in Korea this time to his personal vulnerability. He said that having no power base, he had to play along with either Japan or Russia. He had no support from the Koreans. Nevertheless, he believed that Jaisohn could exert a great deal more influence if he were to return. The United States commanded the respect of Korea as an uninvolved power, and his American citizenship would not only persuade Koreans that Jaisohn was not motivated by self-interest, but also those Koreans who disagreed with him would hesitate to cross swords with him.

Jaisohn gave long and serious thought to what Prince Pak said. The longer and harder he did so, the more he was led to the view that it was his duty to return to Korea. Finally, he took up the matter with his wife. He told her of how hard he had tried to forget Korea and mind his personal business as he knew she would prefer it, that nothing would please him more than to see her happy, but that he felt that his duty to share his predicament with her and reach a decision mutually satisfactory. To his relief, Mrs. Jaisohn told him that

She had known from the first day she met him that he was a man of destiny and had been proud of him for it. She had been aware that the recent events in Korea weighed on him heavily. If, therefore, he was convinced that his sense of duty called him to the land of his ancestors, she could not help but feel that it was his destiny calling him. He should go and she would go with him.

Jaisohn was profoundly grateful. The woman he loved was truly loving, understanding and unselfish. By way of warning, he pointed out that she was unfamiliar with conditions in Korea and that he himself was not sure how he would be received. But his wife was firm. She was as ready as he was.

Jaisohn closed up his office, secured passports, bought train and steamer tickets, and in early December 1895, he and his wife left for Korea.

CHAPTER 7:
THE RETURN OF THE NATIVE

At dusk on January 1, 1896. Philip and Muriel Jaisohn arrived in Seoul virtually unnoticed. Unsure of how the Korean people would react to someone who for twelve years had been branded as a traitor and had brought with him an American wife, they rode in a *riksha* to a Japanese hotel and checked in. In their room, which was heated only by a charcoal brazier, they stayed awake most of the night, shivering and wondering if this was a foretaste of what was in store for them in Korea. What kept them awake was not the intense cold alone. The depressing view of the country from *Incheon* to Seoul - denuded hills, squalid huts and ill-clad people - was in too startling contrast to that of America to forget. Though Jaisohn had been told by Pak Yong-hyo not to expect any improvement in the poverty and misery of the people in Korea, he was no less surprised than his wife. He felt sad and frustrated, too, about the necessity of seeking shelter in a foreign hotel. How he wished to go out to the street, hold a man by the hand and say: "I am your friend, I want to help you."

Minister of the Interior, Yu Kil-jun

The next morning, he dispatched the message to Yu Kil-jun, who had succeeded Pak Yong-hyo as Interior Minister. He and Yu had known each other in the days when they spent time together in secret rendezvous at a Buddhist temple, listening to monk Lee Dong-in and reading books about the Western world brought by him from Japan, with Kim Ok-kiun, Pak Yong-hyo and the other friends. Yu was the first Korean student to study in Japan. A member of the first Korean mission to the United States, he remained behind following the completion of the mission in 1883 and became also the first Korean to study in America. A staunch liberal, he would surely have participated in the 1884 abortive coup but for the fact that he was in America at the time.

Photo: Minister of the Interior, Yu Kil-jun

No sooner had he received the message then he rushed over to the hotel where the Jaisohns were staying, and the two old friends exchanged emotional greetings. Jaisohn then introduced his wife to the Interior Minister. She was pleasantly surprised to see him greet her in English. They then sat down around the charcoal brazier, and as Jaisohn

159

and Yu began to converse, Mrs. Jaisohn ordered a Japanese servant to bring them some hot tea and excused herself.

Yu began by gently chiding Jaisohn for taking so long in returning to Korea. He said that his cabinet colleagues had been anxiously waiting for him, adding: "You know, His Majesty has decreed pardon for all those connected with the *Kapsin* coup (1884) which includes you." Jaisohn replied that 'he had heard it from Pak Yong Hyo and commented that while he had never thought of himself as a traitor to Korea, he was glad that the King had seen fit to lift the stigma from him as well as his fellow traitors.'

Jaisohn said, of greater importance to him was to learn what was going on in Korea, pointing out that judging from a glimpse of the physical condition of the country he had had on the way from Incheon to Seoul, there was no improvement at all in the living condition of the people. Yu agreed that his observation was correct. Then, in a briefing which lasted over two hours, he gave a detailed report on the state of the nation. After the Chinese army led by Yuan Shih-kai had driven 'you and your fellow reformers' from power in 1884, the Mins and their allies regained control of the Government. Had they learned the lesson of the *Kapsin* challenge and instituted necessary reform, they would have set Korea on the road to political as well as economic recovery. Since China grew weaker every year, and Japan was unready to invade Korea for years to come, they could have safely pursued a policy of neutrality, as neither of the two powers could afford to upset the status quo. This would have given the Mins a golden opportunity to build up Korea's economic and military power. But the dyed-in-the-wool conservatives were unable or unwilling to seize the opportunity. They were content to rely on China for protection, to live 'high off the hog' at the expense of the people. That the once mighty empire of China had become a mere scarecrow and that the people driven to destitution would rise up in revolt sooner or later must have been obvious to them, but they remained oblivious.

The First Sino-Japanese War

The inevitable came to pass in 1894. In that year, a revolt by the populist politico-religious group known as *Tong-haks* against the corrupt, oppressive provincial governor in *Cholla* province quickly spread throughout the nation, threatening the government in Seoul. The conservatives appealed to China for help, and the equally unenlightened Chinese Government smugly obliged them. By then, however, Japan had become a formidable power, ready and impatient to flex her muscle. Though what ensued was known as the Sino-Japanese war, it was only a rout of China's rag-tag army by a well-armed, superbly trained army of Japan and the latter's replacement of China as Korea's overlord.

Japan now was a power to be reckoned with. To be sure, however, she was too ambitious and too impetuous for her own good. Instead of carrying her big stick concealed in a cloak of prudence and talking softly, she was bombastic and overbearing and provoked her adversaries into uniting against her. On the other hand, Russia had been a Far Eastern power since the middle of the 19th century and was not about to countenance Japan's predominance in East Asia without challenge. While the Czarist Empire could not restrain the Empire of the Rising Sun single handedly, a united stand by her and a few allies could. France and Germany were willing to lend their support. Thus fortified, Russia replaced China as Japan's challenger and succeeded in thwarting Japan's capture of Korea.

The Korean Government, dominated by Queen Min and her blood relatives, now sought to remain in power by throwing itself into the Russian lap. Hence, Russia, without firing a single shot, had won Korea. Yet it was for the prize of Korea that Japan had fought China, and Japan was bitter. Nevertheless, had she been shrewd and patient she could have gained the goodwill of the Korean people as well as the victory over Russia without the costly war of 1904. Unable to take on the Russian Bear yet determined to prevent Korea from slipping out of her control, Japan took a barbarously unchivalrous action. She sent a blood-thirsty general to Seoul as Minister, with plenipotentiary powers.

Under his direction, a gang of Japanese ruffians disguised as Koreans broke into *Changdok* Palace and murdered Queen Min on the night of early October 1895. This sent the anti-Japanese sentiment of the Korean people soaring to a new height, causing the Government of which Yu was a member to come under their bitter wrath. In other words, at the time of Jaisohn's return, Korea had been irreconcilably polarized into two mutually hostile camps, pro-Japanese and pro-Russian. Their antagonism was so intense that they flatly refused to recognize the existence of patriotic Koreans. All were of the one or the other camp. The King, grieving for the loss of his queen, was presumed to be pro-Russian.

Photo: *Okhoru* Pavilion at *Geoncheong-gung* Palace in *Kyongbok* Palace, where Queen Min was assassinated (photo 2023)

What was the attitude of the foreign representatives, especially those of the United States, Jaisohn asked. Yu replied that

> the American diplomats might be characterized as ambivalent, for while the State Department professed neutrality in Korean affairs, its Legation in Seoul was a refuge for anti-government Korean politicians. There was strong ground for believing that the American representatives were surreptitiously working with the Russians to take advantage of the anti-Japanese sentiment of the Korean people. The American contention was that they were not so much pro-Russian as pro-humanitarian.

Yu did concede that the Japanese brutalities perpetrated in connection with the murder of the Queen could not help but cause humanitarian concern of the American community in Seoul. However, in view of the fact that the American Minister and his secretary were openly chummy with the Korean politicians, some of whom were known murderers and torturers, one could not help wondering whether their motive was wholly honorable. Be that as in might, what Korea urgently needed was a period of peace and stability in which the Government could vigorously pursue a policy of social and political reform and of economic development. For this, an end to the polarization among Korean leaders and consolidation of governmental authority were essential. Otherwise, it was impossible to tackle the problem of poverty.

Yu was convinced that the rumor about Japan planning to get rid of the King was an exaggeration. He also believed that Russia would not fight Japan for Korea and that nor would Japan risk a war with Russia any time soon over Korea. Nevertheless, Korea's all out tilt to one side or the other was bound to trigger a Russo-Japanese war whether they liked it or not, as neither could afford to lose Korea by default. What was needed therefore, was to prevent a stampede to the Russian camp by Koreans while simultaneously putting up a polite but firm resistance against Japan's pressure. Yu's cabinet's aim was to bring in men of influence and patriotism to the Government who would help make it command such powerful support of the people that neither of the powers would find it in its interest to bring it down.

Asserting that this was at least worth trying, he invited Jaisohn to enter the Government. He believed that though the people at large were apathetic, intellectual leaders and younger people were eager for reform and independence of the nation. Hence, they would enthusiastically welcome Jaisohn's joining the Government. Furthermore, since the King wished to gain the goodwill of the United States in hopes of securing a sizable loan from that country, he was sure that the monarch would favor the participation in Government by a man of Jaisohn's position. To quote Jaisohn's own words about the invitation, Yu said,

"You can have any portfolio you choose - foreign, interior or education ministership," emphasizing that this was a consensus of the whole cabinet.

Refused to Join the Kim Hong-jip Cabinet

Jaisohn had his answer ready: "No." After thanking the Interior Minister for the generous offer, he assured the latter that his refusal in no way signified a lack of will to serve the best interests of Korea. It was because, believing he could be of better service to the country of his birth in another capacity that he felt constrained to decline the offer. He went on to tell Yu that before returning to Korea, he had decided not to take any political office, but to offer his services as a private citizen of the United States to help Korea maintain her independence in an advisory capacity. After listening to Yu, Jaisohn was ever more convinced that his decision not to accept the invitation was wise. A government which had neither the economic and military power, nor the support of the people, was a government in name only and could be toppled at any time its internal or external enemies chose to do so.

Expressing agreement with Yu's assertion that a government firmly supported by its people would discourage external enemies from undermining it at will, nevertheless, he said that the question was: "What is the best way to help the Government command unswerving support of a united people?" The answer, according to Jaisohn, was to help enlighten the rights and duties of the Government and people toward each other and to help each trust the other. He was convinced that this could be done more effectively by one who was not a part of the Government. Because he wished to be that one, he believed it advisable that he should not accept any ministerial portfolio.

He added that 'ideally, it would be preferable for him to serve without pay. Unfortunately, however, since he was without any means of self-support financially, that was out of the question. A realistic compromise seemed unavoidable if therefore, the Government saw fit to engage him as an adviser at an appropriate salary, he would perform such advisory duties as his training and experience gained in the United States enabled him to, and at the same time undertake the task mentioned above.'

Specifically, what he had in mind as to the task mentioned above had been a two-pronged campaign:

- publication of a newspaper in *onmun* (vernacular writing) in order to reach the masses and
- the establishment of an association designed to train Korea's leaders in the knowledge of democratic ideals and parliamentary procedures.

However, on being told by Yu of the polarization of Korea's leaders, he decided to postpone proposal of the leadership training activity and confined himself to suggesting the publication of the newspaper.

Yu was disappointed, as he was absolutely sure that Jaisohn's addition to the cabinet would greatly enhance its prestige. At the same time, he was impressed by the latter's analysis of Korea's needs and by his plan to help bring the Government and people closer together. He promised to lay Jaisohn's proposals before the cabinet.

Within hours after Yu Kil-jun had left, the news of the return of Jaisohn and his wife spread among official circles and high society, and as the modest Japanese hotel was turning into a Mecca of his admirers,

Mrs. Jaisohn became concerned about her husband's security. First, Soh Kwang-pom, Jaisohn's old comrade and relative, arrived to extend his greetings. He was followed by other prominent Koreans and Americans. Among the callers who subsequently became one of his closest friends was the Reverend Henry G. Appenzeller, an American Methodist missionary and founder and head of *Bae-Jae* Academy (培材學堂). When he and his wife extended an invitation to the Jaisohns to stay in their house while looking for a house of their own, they gladly accepted it. They stayed there until they took over Soh Kwang-pom's house when the latter left for the United States to take up the post of Minister to Washington.

Photo: Reverend Henry Appenzeller.

Jaisohn received a hero's welcome to the surprise of his wife and himself. On the street, he would be stopped by men who bowed to him and said: "We called you a traitor because we were ignorant." On the urging of the students of *Bae-Jae* Academy, the Reverend Appenzeller invited Jaisohn to become a special lecturer at the school. He was happy to accept. Within a few days of his first meeting with Interior Minister Yu, the Kim Hong-jip Government not only appointed him in the name of the King to the post of adviser to the Privy Council at a salary of 3,000 *won* ($1,500 per annum), equivalent to that of a cabinet member; he was granted 5,000 *won* with which to start his newspaper.

(**Editor's Note**: The *Jungchuwon* (The Privy Council) was an institution established in the late *Joseon* period, serving as an important body responsible for managing royal assets and overseeing royal ceremonies, among other duties related to the royal family.)

Photo: Students at *Bae-Jae* Academy (1896).

Korea, Gripped by Treacherous Officials and Foreign Powers

Six or seven weeks after Jaisohn's return, an ad hoc committee consisting of his friends - Yun Tchi-ho, Soh Kwang-pom, Henry Appenzeller, Homer Hulbert and many others - sponsored a 'Welcome Dr. Philip Jaisohn' meeting in the chapel of *Bae-Jae* Academy. Before the hour of meeting had arrived, the chapel was packed to capacity. By the time the welcoming program started the crowd spilled over onto the outside of the gayly decorated chapel. On being introduced by the presider, Jaisohn arose and after thanking the audience for the kind welcome, told his hearers of his experience in America, of what his 12-year exile had taught him, of how great difficulties the United States had to overcome in order to win its freedom and what the Korean people, too, were capable of accomplishing for their independence and prosperity, providing they were willing to strive for them. It was a moving and eloquent address.

Even after the meeting ended, the crowd, which consisted of Koreans and foreigners, was reluctant to leave. They wanted to look at him: a patriot through and through; but at the same time, as a Korean naturalized as a citizen of America, he symbolized the living link between Korea and the United States, which at the time was thought of as a disinterested friend of Korea.

The Privy Council

Jaisohn's role as adviser to the Privy Council was broad and imprecise. Perhaps it was intended as an honorary position to have him around and enable the Government to utilize his prestige. However, Jaisohn took his position seriously. He requested to be attached to the Department of Public Works in order, presumably, to keep an eye out for any collusion between officials and foreign concession seekers. The request was granted.

Korea was rapidly becoming a happy hunting ground for foreign concessionaries, and a major preoccupation for foreign diplomats in Seoul was to help their nationals secure concessions on as favorable terms as possible. While most foreign businessmen were honest in their dealings, Jaisohn was told that a few were unscrupulous. Since it was impossible to tell which one or ones was or were dishonest, concession agreements had to be closely scrutinized, or development of Korean resources would only benefit foreign interests and a few corrupt officials. Jaisohn was by no means a narrow-minded nationalist.

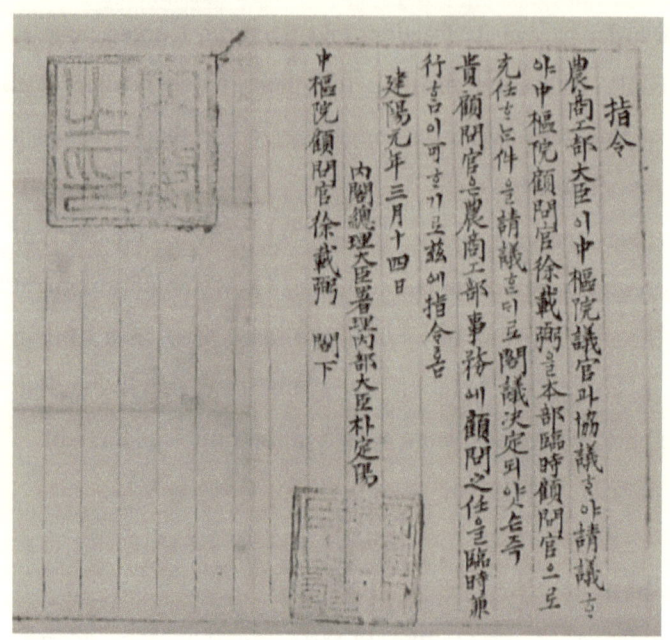

Photo: Official document appointing Soh Jai-pil (徐載弼), Adviser to the The Privy Council, as the Interim Adviser to the Ministry of Agriculture, Commerce, and Industry (1896).

Believing the introduction of foreign capital and technological know-how into Korea was necessary in order to tap the country's natural resources and to develop the economy, Jaisohn had tried to persuade prospective foreign investors to visit Korea. At the same time, he was firmly convinced that the Government should be wary of selfish exploiters, either Korean or foreign. One of the first foreigners with whom he crossed swords after taking office with Horace N. Allen, then Secretary of the American Legation. A medical missionary turned diplomat; he served mammon with as much zeal as he did God. He was always on the alert for opportunities to secure profitable concession rights for his American friends, but his motive was as much for personal gain through commissions as to help his countrymen. That this was in violation of the code of the United States State Department did not seem to bother his Christian conscience. Jaisohn caught him in the act in connection with a concession to a friend of Allen's. It was at an unfair expense to Korea, and Jaisohn advised the Public Works Minister to invalidate it. The contract was renegotiated. Allen, in a pique, called Jaisohn a 'troublesome cuss.'

Jaisohn was kept busy every day by a stream of visitors, some to discuss serious matters of the nation, some, like Syngman Rhee, to seek advice on how to go to America for an education. Others came out of plain curiosity. But those people whom he wished to see were not among them. Prominent among these were Lee Sang-jae, a member of the first Korean mission to the United States, Lee Wan-yong, Jaisohn's boyhood schoolmate, and Yun Tchi-ho, ex-Vice Minister of Education. Being hunted by the 'pro-Japanese' Kim Hong-jip regime on the suspicion that they were implicated in the abortive November (1895) *Kapsin* coup against it, they went in hiding. It grieved Jaisohn no end to see his old friends engaged in such bloody feud; both those in office and hunting and those out of office and are hunted were young liberals who had once worked together to modernize Korea. It was unthinkable that they should be locked up in the internecine struggle of their own volition. They were mere pawns in a contest with the control of Korea by the powers. However, since he was powerless to bring the warring factions together, he felt morally obligated to try to defuse the tension by means of direct contacts with the foreign representatives in Korea.

Horace Noble Allen

The first one he called on was John M.B. Sill, the American Minister. A former professor of zoology at the University of Michigan, he had obtained a diplomatic appointment with the aid of some friends who were influential supporters of President Grover Cleveland as well as his friends. They did this in order that he might have some 'fun and rest in the faraway land of Morning Calm.' Indeed, he was more interested in the collection of butterfly specimens than involvement in diplomatic intrigues, and he was content to let Horace Allen, his secretary, 'do the work' for him. So Jaisohn turned to Secretary Allen, the de facto Minister from the United States, for cooperation.

Horace Noble Allen, born in Delaware, Ohio, a graduate of Ohio Wesleyan and of Miami University Medical School, had applied for an appointment to go to China as a medical missionary and was appointed in 1883. What prompted him to become a missionary was to spread the gospel of Christ, to be sure, but love for adventure seems to have been his stronger motive. In China, restless and feeling superfluous, he moved from one place to another, dragging his pregnant wife. He longed to be in a place where he could experience the excitement of being a pioneer. On an impulse, he asked to be sent to Korea, which was known as the 'Hermit Kingdom,' and to his surprise, the request was granted. He arrived in Korea in July 1884 as the first Protestant missionary. Excitement there was aplenty in store for him in Korea. A ban on religious freedom was still on the books, and Allen's presence was illegal. However, Lucius Foote, the aging American Minister, was glad to have an American doctor in Seoul and offered to break the Korean law by naming him 'Legation physician,' to which Allen agreed with alacrity, 'for God's sake.' In 1884, Korea was undergoing a sanguinary transition from its feudal past to the modern.

Photo: Horace Allen.

(**Editor's Note**: Allen arrived in Korea in 1884 and began working as a doctor. He also played significant roles as a missionary and diplomat. He served as the U.S. Minister to Korea from 1892 to 1905, working in Korea for a total of 21 years.)

Within six months of his arrival, an abortive palace coup known as the *Kapsin* Uprising took place. One of its victims was Min Young-ik, who was the favorite nephew and right-hand man of the Queen. Though seriously wounded, he was alive and with the help of Dr. Allen, he recovered. This led Allen to become virtually palace physician, making him one of the most influential men in Korea. His close relations with the Korean King helped him win his appointment as American Legation secretary in Seoul and later promotion to the Ministership.

Jaisohn found Allen a complex person: sympathetic yet devious, austere yet affable, of progressive bent yet quite at home with some of the worst reactionaries. The American diplomat couldn't be more friendly. Jaisohn could always count on him, he asserted. Nevertheless, Allen kept Jaisohn completely in the dark about the second attempt by the anti-Japanese leaders to move the King to the Russian Legation and to liquidate the pro-Japanese team of Kim Hong-jip and Yu Kil-jun, in which the American was deeply involved. Allen suspected Jaisohn of pro-Japanese leaning, but later admitted that he had been wrong (his statement accompanying the presentation of Jaisohn's *Independent* to the New York Public Library).

Photo: *Gwanghyewon* (*Jejungwon*) (1905).

Karl Waeber

The third foreign diplomat Jaisohn contacted was Karl Waeber, the Russian Minister (from 1885 to 1897). A genial, competent man and of Estonian descent, he had a genuine personal sympathy for small countries like Korea. Though he was a faithful servant of Czarist Russia, he eschewed territorial expansionist policies, contending that Russia's interest in Korea lay in keeping her as a buffer state friendly to Russia. Jaisohn thought it fortunate for Korea to have such a person represent the Czar in Seoul. More fortunate still, his long tenure in Korea seemed indicative of the Czarist Government's confidence in him. He had arrived in Korea at about the same time as Allen. Prior to that, he had been secretary of the Russian Legation in China. He returned to Saint

Petersburg in 1890 on an extended leave but resumed his duties in Seoul in 1895.

The last foreign representative for Jaisohn to meet was Shutaro Komura, Japan's Minister in Seoul. Following the murder of the Korean queen in October 1895, he was sent to Tokyo to investigate the incident. He had been Director of Political Affairs in the Japanese Foreign Office. Subsequently, he was made Minister to Korea. A graduate of Harvard, he was fluent in English. Remembering that his government was unable to persuade Jaisohn to return to Korea under its sponsorship the previous year, the Japanese diplomat was well aware that Jaisohn was nobody's but his own man. Hence, all he could do was to warn Jaisohn 'not to cause trouble for Japan by preaching American democracy to the Korean people. Korea was not ready for it,' he said.

Six weeks after Jaisohn's returned to Korea, things took a nosedive for the Jaisohns. On the morning of February 11, Jaisohn was riding in his carriage on the *Kwangwha Mun* thoroughfare, going to his office. Suddenly, there was a great commotion, and within seconds, a huge crowd surged forward. Some shouting angry obscenities and others with terrified looks in their eyes. His driver asked the bystander what it was all about. The latter told him that the King had been either kidnapped during the night or had fled to the Russian Legation, and that a decree bearing the royal seal had been issued, declaring the incumbent Ministers traitors and ordering their punishment. No sooner had Jaisohn heard this that he caught sight of a man lying dead in front of him. It was the body of Prime Minister Kim Hon-jip. Unaware of what had happened, he was riding to his office when the police caught him, hacked him to death and dumped his body on the thoroughfare as a 'warning to all would-be pro-Japanese traitors.' Also killed elsewhere that day, where Chung Pyong-ha, Minister of Agriculture, and Oh Yun-jong, Minister of Finance. Interior Minister Yu Kil-jun and others escaped to Japan.

Jaisohn went on to his office in a state of dismay and disillusionment. He was so disgusted that his initial impulse was to go back to his house, pack and leave with his wife for the United States by the next ship. On further reflection, he felt it his duty to help, if possible, contain and resolve the crisis. First, he needed to know just what had happened and who were behind the coup.

He called at the American Legation. There he found Minister Sill and Secretary Allen in their offices, calmly attending to their duties. It was apparent that they knew what had happened to the Korean Government, and knowing well why Jaisohn came, they proceeded to supply him with such information as they felt safe while professing disapproval of the violence which accompanied the upheaval. Neither of the diplomats, however, appeared upset by the coup itself. Only later was he to learn that they were surreptitious participants in it. The feeling that these representatives of the United States were holding back some of the information from him and that it might reveal their unholy alliance with the murderers of Kim Hong-jip, Chung Pyong-ha and others made him angry. Consequently, when Sill smugly suggested to him that he pay the King a visit at the Russian Legation, supposedly to offer the monarch words of cheer, Jaisohn answered that he was certainly intending to call on the monarch, but not to do as the American Minister suggested.

On his way out of the American Legation, he saw in an adjoining room Lee Wan-yong, his brother, Lee Yun-yong, Yun Tchi-ho, Lee Sang-jae, Lee Chae-yon and Kim Ka-jin. They were hiding there. He wanted to hold each one of them by the hand and pour his heart out, but that was neither the time nor the place for that. It had to wait. With a brief exchange of greetings, he left them, but he could not forget them. They symbolized the plight of Korea: the victims of an international power struggle. Fugitives from the Japan-dominated Kim Hong-jip government, they sought refuge in the American Legation in the belief that the United States was a benign neutral. Indeed, United States policy at the time was officially one of neutrality. However, its representatives in Korea abandoned neutrality and were colluding with Russia in pursuit of their personal interests. Originally the King, hating the Japanese for having murdered his queen and fearing that they might murder him too, wished to seek refuge in the American Legation. This the State Department sternly forbade. But Allen and Sill, realizing what great bonanza doing him favor would mean, suggested that Waeber give refuge to the King in his Legation. The latter was only too happy to oblige.

King Kojong at the Russian Legation.

Upon arrival in the Russian Legation, Jaisohn was met by Minister Waeber, who greeted him warmly and escorted him upstairs to the King's suite. As he did so, he asked Jaisohn to inform His Majesty that the entire Legation staff was anxious to be at his service, and that His Majesty had only to let Waeber know his wish. Jaisohn agreed to convey the message.

In the King's reception room, Jaisohn found him sitting on a sofa with his Crown Prince at his side. Standing behind them were Lee Pom-jin, the mastermind of the coup and Kim Hong-yiuk, Russian interpreter. Jaisohn greeted the King with a bow and in response to the monarch's order, took a chair near the Crown Prince and conveyed Waeber's message. The King then said: "What should I do?"

Jaisohn replied,

> Your Majesty, this is a foreign territory. By remaining here, you are jeopardizing the independence of Korea as well as your throne. It is your duty to be with your subjects, as it is their duty to protect you and their country. If you do your duty, the people will do theirs. This is the only way to maintain your and Korea's security. Please return to your palace.

> *Keurae, keurae* (Yes, yes). But…It is too unsafe there. The King kept repeating.

Jaisohn rejoined:

> I realize so that this is a difficult thing for you to do at this time. It is the duty of all your loyal subjects to help you feel safe to return to your palace. The consequences of your continued sojourn in a foreign Legation, however friendly, is much more dangerous for you and for the country. If you let it be known that you will not desert your people, that you will return to your palace and call on them to unite in defense of the nation, it will electrify the whole population. Your Majesty will be far safer under the protection of fifteen million people than under the protection of a few hundred foreign troops. Allow me to repeat: Please return to your palace as soon as you can, Your Majesty.

> *Kulse* (Well)… The King kept repeating.

It was obvious that he had neither the courage nor sense of duty required of a true ruler. He was a pathetic figure - pale, nervous and fearful of his safety only. Unqualified and unprepared for his role, yet thrust on the throne by accident, he was nevertheless anxious to keep his throne. Instead of choosing competent and public-spirited aides to help him govern and lead the nation wisely, he was surrounded by sycophants interested only in their own benefits and who were advising him to keep his throne by relying on one foreign power or another. Even more worrisome to Jaisohn, was what would happen to the country in the event the King was either killed or pushed off his throne. Should that happen, his son was expected to succeed him, but the 22-year-old Crown Prince was far less competent than the King. He was a retarded youth. Unable to comprehend the danger his father's flight to a foreign Legation had brought to Korea, unable even to follow the conversation between his father and Jaisohn, he showed more interest in the tie pin which Jaisohn had on. Pointing to it, he asked: "What is it? How much did it cost?" As Jaisohn left, he heard Lee Pom-jin mutter: "He is still a traitor, Your Majesty."

Unquestionably, Jaisohn's advice was sound. However, at that juncture, that was a patently infeasible advice. To the people their rulers were anything but responsible or benign. How could they be expected to rally behind the present ruler, who was no exception? Even had they wished they were without any means to do so. Jaisohn was aware of that. Just the same, he offered the advice because, as he put it later, the truth had to be told.

Photo: King Kojong

The New Cabinet

If he came away from his visit with the King depressed, the announcement which followed of the new cabinet was astounding. While they included some able men, they strongly suggested that their qualifications were not the criteria of their selection. Jaisohn could not dispel the suspicion that their appointments were due to the fact that they were either Allen's or Waeber's candidates. Five ministerial posts – Premier, Interior, Foreign, Finance, and Royal Household - to the men he saw hiding in the American Legation, while the rest were distributed among those labeled as 'pro-Russian.' He was not surprised that the 'pro-Russians' should have received appointments to the cabinet posts. The King evidently thought he owed his life to them. But the choice of so many of Allen's boys for the important posts was too conspicuous to be purely coincidental. He soon learned that at Allen's behest, the powerful portfolio of Interior Minister went to Pak Jong-yang, former Minister to Washington. When Park was appointed to the post in Washington several years earlier, Allen had commented: 'Had the Government scoured the whole peninsula, they could not have found a man more unfit for the place.' However, when the Korean Government offered him the post of secretary to the Legation in Washington at a salary twice that of a missionary, he promptly turned in his resignation as a missionary and took the job, flatteringly calling Pak his 'Korean father.' While serving under his 'Korean father,' Allen discovered that his earlier characterization of Pak as the most incompetent man was correct. In spite of that, now he not only had him given the important post of Interior Minister but saw to it that Pak was made acting Premier as well, observing, "No one had thought of him for that post until I suggested it."

Neutrality Policy of The United States

So far as Jaisohn knew, the United States policy with respect to Korea at the time was one of neutrality. He knew, too, that Minister Sill, an ex-professor, was too much of a scholar and gentleman to violate the orders of his government. Therefore, the culprit had to be Horace Allen, now Secretary of the American Legation in Seoul. 'Why?' Jaisohn wondered. His quiet inquiry led him to Cho Pyong-jik, Minister of Public Works. Cho believed that Allen was a sinister influence on the King by conniving at undermining Korea's interest. He cited an example in which Allen had maneuvered Japan out of a bid for a Seoul-Inchon railroad construction concession and then arguing in favor of granting the concession to an American businessman named Morse on terms much more disadvantageous than those offered by Japan. Jaisohn urged Cho to stand firm in his opposition to Allen. Morse was forced to revise his offer. Later, it was revealed that the American Legation Secretary received kickbacks for his services on behalf of American businessmen, in violation of the law.

In view of the fact that such an unprincipled person as Allen was exercising so great an influence over the Korean Government, Jaisohn wondered whether his contract for advisership with the Kim Hong-jip Government would be honored by the new regime. Nor would he care to be associated with it should his authority be restricted. In any event, he decided to ascertain his status.

When he called on the new Foreign Minister, Lee Wan-yong, he informed Jaisohn that his contract would be honored. Jaisohn was surprised to hear the Foreign Minister, his schoolmate in the days when they were little boys, assure him that all his cabinet colleagues were eagerly looking forward to being associated with him. He found later that even Allen himself described himself as delighted to work with Jaisohn. Did the American Legation Secretary decide that it was to his advantage not to tangle with Jaisohn, whom he called a 'troublesome cuss?'

Photo: The Russian Legation in Seoul (1896).

Photo: Views of Inwangsan, Bukaksan, and Kyongbok Palace (1903).

Photo: A view of the streets of Seoul (around 1903).

CHAPTER 8:

KOREA FOR KOREANS (I):

Founding of Korea's First Newspaper

The First Newspaper in Korea

In late March 1896, Jaisohn's dream, the publication of a newspaper, began to take shape. The eagerly awaited press arrived in *Inchon* and was hauled to Seoul in an ox cart. However, starting the paper was far from a simple job. No one in the whole city of Seoul had any knowledge of the operation of the press, let alone news gathering, editing, printing and distributing. At first, he had to do everything himself and train others at the same time. Making it even more difficult was his plan to make the paper bilingual by publishing it in *onmun* (Korean phonetic alphabet) and in English. Fortunately, Homer B. Hulbert, an American teacher at the Government Foreign Language School, consented to help him edit the English section.

Photo: Homer B. Hulbert.

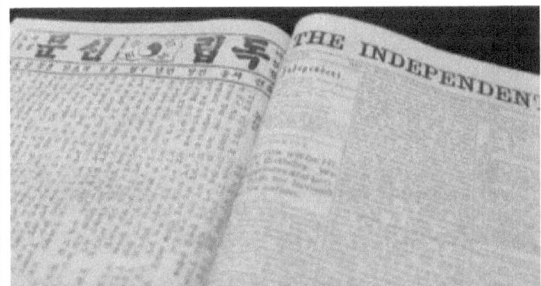

Photo: The first issue of *Independence News* (1896).

Photo: Horace Underwood.

Initially, his only paid employee was a reporter who preferred to be called *chusa* (clerk) and whom he taught how to go about interviewing government officials and the gathering of news. Other sources of news were his friends, Korean and foreign, who came from all walks of life. After gathering the news, editing it and setting the type, Jaisohn himself ran it through the press. This proved too much work for him and soon a printer was hired.

Photo: Korean-English Dictionary written by Horace Underwood (1890).

On April 7, 1896, the first issue of *The Independent (Toknip:* 독립신문*)* came off the press. There had been none like it in Korea, although the Government had officially issued an official gazette in Chinese characters which was circulated among officials. A four page, thrice weekly tabloid, the newspaper consisted of a three-page Korean and a one-page English section. Although the English section was limited to one page, it's concise writing and fine print enabled it to publish nearly all the news and comments printed in the Korean section. His rationale for making *The Independent* bilingual was twofold:

- firstly, to enlighten the Korean people on political, economic and social issues, and
- secondly, to inform foreigners about Korea and Koreans in order to help them reach an accurate understanding of the country and its people.

The contents of the paper consisted of an editorial, official notices, the latest telegrams, a digest of domestic and foreign news and communications and exchanges. In the editorial of the first issue of the newspaper, Jaisohn wrote:

> As we published the first issue of The Independent, it seems appropriate that we inform our readers what this paper stands for. First, it is a nonpartisan and independent paper. It will not be biased either in favor of or against any class, faction or party. Everyone will be treated equally and fairly.
>
> Secondly, it stands for Korea for the Koreans. By Koreans we mean not only those of Seoul, but also of the provinces. Believing that correct understanding between the people and their Government will benefit both sides, we shall endeavor to serve as a source of factual information between them.
>
> Thirdly, in order to reach a maximum number of people, we have decided to keep the price of this paper at the lowest possible level and to use the onmun instead of Chinese characters. It is regrettable that our people have so long used this alien writing system, which requires years of painstaking study just to be able to read simple writings, ignoring the onmun, which is not only easy to learn, but one of the finest of its kind

in the world. In the nations of the West, the children are first taught their native writing system. The teaching of foreign languages comes later. It is high time that Koreans learn to be proud of their heritage.

Fourthly, we shall print only the truth and all the truths that are available. We shall report the commendable deeds as well as the wrongdoings of everyone, regardless of his official position or social status. At the same time, we shall defend even the humblest of citizens if he is unjustly treated.

Also, we are adding an English section to this paper in order to help foreigners gain a true picture of Korea and Koreans. This, we believe, will be beneficial to both the Koreans and foreigners.

We conclude this editorial with a sincere wish for happiness and a long life to His Majesty. Mansei!

The Independent proved sensational. The 200 copies of the first issue were sold out the same day. Most of the buyers had never heard of a *shinmun* (newspaper) and were curious. Most of them returned a few hours later to purchase additional copies to give to their relatives. There were a number of reasons for this.

- First, it was inexpensive. 1 *jon* (0.5 cents) a copy.
- Secondly, it was written in the easy-to-read *onmun*.
- Thirdly, it was something entirely new to the people.
- Fourthly, it was published by a man who was widely hailed as a hero.

And he carried a blazing announcement at the top of the front page, which was deeply intriguing:

The Independent will publish foreign and domestic news, including that of the Government and people. They will inform the readers about politics, agriculture, commerce and health. Readers are invited to send in questions and suggestions. If they are of interest to the public, they will be either answered or printed in the paper. Caution: No communications written in Chinese characters will be accepted.

To the grassroots, who had never heard of any other country except China and Japan, the news about Occidental nations, how their people lived and governed themselves, sounded amazing. Moreover, when they read Jaisohn's editorials discussing the unalienable rights of all mankind, of the mutual obligations of the people and government, they felt as if they were awakened from their long sleep. His message was an invitation to the readers to participate in making the paper truly an organ of and for the people. In the second issue, April 9, Jaisohn reported the gratifying reaction of its readers in these words:

> At the risk of being charged with vanity, we cannot refrain from citing some of the comments which have been made apropos of the appearance of *The Independent* in the journalistic field. Among the foreigners, we hear such expressions as 'A good thing,' 'just what Korea needs,' 'an important innovation,' etc. Among the Koreans, the best praise is a rapidity with which the first issue was sold out and the number of regular subscribers enrolled.

In time, enthusiastic comments poured in from readers in *Pyongyang, Naju, Kunsan, Inchon, Taegu and Pusan,* as well as Seoul. Jaisohn saw some readers purchasing 5 or 6 copies each, saying they wanted them for their relatives and friends. Reactions came in from abroad too. Those from readers in Japan were mixed, but those of readers in Western countries were laudatory. *Japan Mail* accused *The Independent* of carelessness with truth by asserting that its report about the secret treaty between Japan and Russia regarding Korea was illustrative of it. Jaisohn's retort was that if he was an error, it was not his fault, but the fault of the *Kobe Chronicle,* a Japanese newspaper, because that was the source of his report. Likewise, comments by the press in China were not uniformly favorable. *The North China Herald* quoted its correspondent in Seoul: *The Independent's* first editorial claim of impartiality notwithstanding, like everything else here, I'm afraid it is entirely American or Russian. To this the dry comment from Jaisohn was: "The gentleman argued entirely from his fears and not at all from facts." *The Independent* also found its way to the United States. Dr. Rosetta S. Hall, who had helped establish the first modern hospital in *Pyongyang*, wrote from New York:

> At least one copy of your valuable paper does double and quadruple duty. After Dr. Mary Coulter reads her copy, she sends it to Mr. Park in Liberty, NY. He eagerly devours it and sends it to his wife in New York City, who, after reading it, gives it to me and we each enjoy it so much and feel that it is going to do great good in our dear Joseon. In fact, it already has done, and there is really a very bright and useful future before it; long may it live.

As of January 1, 1897, *The Independent* was expanded to eight pages and the Korean and English sections were separated. Its circulation grew steadily from 200 to three thousand. Although it remained stationary at around 3,000 till December 1898, when it ceased publication, Jaisohn claimed that its actual readership was many times that number. In many communities, especially in the provinces, one or two subscriptions were shared among the whole population, and the editor estimated that as many as 50 times 3,000 might have had access to the paper. In order to ensure that it reached the people of the entire country, he established branch offices in *Incheon, Wonsan, Pusan, Paju, Kaesong, Suwon, Kanghwa and Pyongyang*. As of April 16, 1896, at the request of the Interior Minister, the paper was delivered to all provincial governors' and district magistrates' offices in the country.

In his editorial, Philip Jaisohn wrote that the reason *Independence News* began using 'spacing' in *onmun* was so that 'anyone could easily read the newspaper and properly understand the words inside.' Through the first-ever newspaper layout that applied spacing, following King Sejong's creation of *onmun (Hangul)*, he made *onmun* more accessible to the public by presenting it as readable text, thereby making a significant contribution to the standardization and use of *Hangul*.

Difficulties in Newspaper Publication

Like all worthy undertakings, the publication of *The Independent* was not without problems, financial, personal, political, and so on. Although the paper carried a sizable number of advertisements, they were mostly provided gratis. Hence, at the subscription rate of 3 *won* ($1.50) per annum, 12 *jon* ($0.06) per month and 1 *jon* ($0.05) per copy, it could not break even, and Jaisohn himself had to cover the loss, which amounted to approximately 150 *won* ($75) every month.

Jaisohn was also hounded by job applicants, all of whom desired a desk job in the office. However, since all office positions were soon filled, he offered them jobs as peddlers of his paper on a commission basis in order to increase circulation as well as to provide them with jobs. They were unenthusiastic but accepted the offer and went out, each carrying a big bundle of papers under his arm. Within hours, however, they all brought back the bundle, saying that they just couldn't sell any. They thought it was demeaning and felt like beggars. They reiterated their pleas for office jobs again.

Jaisohn answered that there were no more office jobs available and added that they were missing a chance to make a good living out of selling his newspaper. Picking up a bundle he got up and asked them to follow him. He would demonstrate what he meant. They were dubious but followed him out as he led them to *Chongno* (main thoroughfare) and told them to watch him. Pulling a copy out of his bundle and holding it aloft in his hand, he cried out loudly to the passersby:

> *Toknip Shinmun* (*The Independent*)! A newspaper for everyone. It's in *onmun*, easy to read. Buy a copy and learn what's going on in Korea and in the world. Only 1 jon.

As the crowd gathered around him, he told them:

> This paper will help you discover your rights as well as duties as citizens. It will enable you to make a better living. It will help you get more out of your lives.

The paper sold like hot cakes. Some people bought several copies each, and before long, his last copy was gone. Jaisohn turned to his companions and said:

> "If you believe this paper is worth reading and its price is reasonable, you shouldn't be ashamed of selling it. It's good for those who buy it. It's good for you because you can make an honest living out of it. I know that Korea's old custom of denigrating the occupation of trade has prejudiced you against it, but I assure you that selling is as necessary and honorable an occupation as teaching or farming. Go to it, men."

Not all of those who went out with Jaisohn could muster the courage to break loose from their prejudice against being a merchant, but those who followed his advice became successful salesmen of *The Independent*. A British author travelling in Korea at the time wrote:

> The sight of newsboys passing through the streets with bundles of a newspaper in *onmun* under their arms, and of men reading them in their shops, is among the novelties of 1897.

As the paper grew in circulation and commanded respect among the people from the highest to the lowest class, Jaisohn also came under pressure from publicity seekers and ambitious officials. The wealthy and the mighty ones sent in 'news items' which in reality were their self-advertisements along with gifts of big cash. One notorious official came to his house carrying gold nuggets and asked Jaisohn not to print anything about him. He was thrown out of the house and subsequently Jaisohn exposed his crooked dealing on a number of occasions. Requests for a publication of news also came from some of the poor people, which were accompanied by coins. He was obliged to announce in his paper that no 'news' accompanied by payments of money would be accepted and advised anyone who had already sent in coins along with the 'news items' to come to the office and claim them.

A Promise to Himself

By far the greatest problem facing Jaisohn was how to fulfill the promise he made to himself when he gave up his medical career in Washington D.C. and returned to Korea - the promise to help reform and rejuvenate Korea by inculcating in the people those virtues which he believed to be responsible for making the United States and Western European nations dynamic, powerful, and prosperous. Most important among the virtues, and completely strange to Koreans, were

- nationalism,
- democracy,
- public spiritedness and
- the dignity of all kinds of productive labor.

In one way or the other, these were very sensitive issues to all strata of the people, especially the King and his trusted ministers. Monarchical authority was, in theory at least, unlimited, and in introducing these new ideas it was imperative not to provoke the opposition of the King, who was extremely jealous of his prerogatives. Also, Jaisohn was far from independent financially. After only a few years' practice as a physician, his savings were meager, and he depended on his salary as Adviser to the Privy Council for his and his family's support. Hence, he was forced to exercise caution. The following is a summary of his endeavor to help make the motto of *The Independent*, Korea for the Koreans, a reality.

A. Constitutional Monarchy

Korea at the time was in the throes of internal upheaval and external pressures. In the provinces, remnant of the *Tong-hak* rebels continued to disturb peace. In the capital, the Government was virtually in paralysis amidst the tangle of intrigues by Korean politicians and foreign interests. The queen had been murdered by killers at Japan's instigation only two months before his return. The King had saved himself by fleeing from his enemies to the Russian Legation, but his 'supporters' who had helped him escape were busy serving their own ends using his name.

Though it was obvious that some drastic measure was needed in order to save the nation, he was powerless to attempt any such a thing. In Jaisohn's view, the King, for all his shortcomings, was the only institution on which the salvation of the nation depended. Therefore, he decided to throw his support behind him and, in time, to persuade him to grant constitutional guarantees to the people. Hence his conspicuous gesture of offering the '*mansei*' wish to the King in the first issue of *The Independent*.

In the second issue of the paper, Jaisohn published the full text of the royal edict and backed it up with the lead editorial. The edict is worth quoting:

Alas, in recent days there have been some who misled their fellow men with demagoguery, as well as those who disturb tranquility, calling themselves 'righteous soldiers.' This is a shameful condition. Though I have repeatedly issued edicts and sent out messengers to persuade the wrong doers to reflect and to mend their ways, they are of no avail. Therefore, I was obliged to dispatch royal troops to the interior. The disturbers of the peace have thus become rebels. But in reality, they are my children. Because they are my children, I feel it my duty to remind them that this is spring when they should be busy plowing the fields and sowing the seeds. If the opportunity is lost, they will be the first to go hungry. It pains me to think of this.

Moreover, I am told that the lives of both foreigners and my own subjects are being sacrificed in the disturbances. This is a cause for profound regret, for whether they are Korean or foreigners, they are all human brothers to one another. Hence, to engage in mutual slaughter is to cause heaven's wrath. How can we help but tremble?

I hereby order my ministers to convey this message to all provincial magistrates and officials and to see to it that by their sincere attitudes and just deeds they win the hearts and obedience of the erring subjects of mine.

In the editorial, Jaisohn directed his appeal to the *Tong-haks*. He advised them to heed the royal edict and return to their homes for the sake of His Majesty, for he represented the nation without which all the people would become slaves. He argued that obeying the King would not only mean the saving of their lives and the happiness of their families but also help strengthen the nation. Since, too, the interests of the individual and that of the nation are interdependent, and the nation comprises all individuals within it, national interest should receive prior consideration.

Jaisohn's appeal was sound in logic. Under normal circumstances, his repeated admonitions would have been effective, but Korea was under anything but normal circumstances. Had he been able to travel in the provinces and observe under how severe privations the masses lived; he would not have made the sweeping charge that the *Tong-hak* rebellion was not the result of disaffection toward the Government but simply excesses indulged in by lawless characters.

There were lawless characters, to be sure, among the 'Righteous soldiers.' By far the main cause of the widespread uprising, however, was 'egregious governmental corruption and oppression,' the examples of which appeared in his paper as soon as communications from the interior arrived. In fact, he printed a letter from three reliable men in *Kyongsang* province in which they asserted that the people preferred the 'Righteous Army' to a Royal Inspector. It is a pity that Jaisohn was unable to acquaint himself with the truth of the *Tong-haks*. Had he done so, he, as a *yangban* who had deep sympathy for the underprivileged, could easily have reached rapport with the *Tong-haks* and exerted a constructive influence on the grassroots whom they represented.

Though constricted in the confines of Seoul where the high and the mighty were locked in a mortal game of politics, and the rank and file were concerned only about staying alive in the face of food shortages caused by the lingering disturbances in the countryside, Jaisohn's Emersonian faith in the God-given power of renewal through moral regeneration remained unshaken. Convinced that a combination of moral enlightenment with scientific and technological know-how would constitute a potent force for Korea's regeneration, he launched a mass educational campaign.

Everyone was his pupil. Foremost among his pupils was the King himself. Having assured him of his loyalty, he carefully pressed for modification of royal powers, saying it is good for him. He advocated local election of magistrates in order to insulate him from complaint by the people in the event they did not like the magistrate whom he appointed. On the other hand, should the magistrate elected by the people of the district involved prove unsatisfactory, then people had only themselves to blame. They would have no reason to blame it on the King, and when the next election time arrived, they would elect another one.

(**Editor's Note**: Emersonian faith emphasizes self-reliance, intuition, and the inherent goodness of humans.)

Other measures of limiting the powers of the King, which Jaisohn recommended as beneficial to the monarch as well as the nation, include the establishment of *Eui-jong bu* (National Council) and the adoption of new criminal laws. Fully cognizant that these were explosive issues, he exercised great tact to allay the suspicions of the King and his conservative ministers. The following editorial is one of a number of revealing his tact and caution.

Great praise is due His Majesty for sanctioning the idea of conducting the Government on a regular and systematic basis, and much credit should be given to those who helped His Majesty to make them. According to the new law, all matters of national importance will be discussed in the open Council by the members of the body, and the Ministers of State who have become ex-officio members of it. The questions that come up before the council will be debated by any member, and each will tell the world his own idea on the matter by his vote.

The trouble we found with the Korean statesmen was that one could not tell where they stood on the important questions of the nation. They all kept the diplomatic silence in all things, and so the public had no opportunity to judge them. But under the new law everybody will have a chance to express his opinion by speech and vote.

Another important point in the law is that His Majesty will attend the Council meetings and will hear the debates of the members. The difficulty which has hitherto existed in the Government was that whenever His Majesty consulted his ministers, the meeting was always a private one. Hence one minister made one representation of a case to him, and another told another story of the same case when his turn for audience came. On account of this arrangement there has been much confusion to His Majesty.

But when a new law goes into effect, His Majesty will be present at the sessions of the Council and will hear the open debate of different counselors. From these debates he will know that the facts of the case and with that knowledge he will form his opinion. On the whole, the new law is similar to the laws governing the Governments of Europe and America, and it will minimize the possible corruption of the official class.

On the adoption of the new criminal laws, he wrote as follows:

> Our readers may think that we are hard to please if they scan the columns of this paper from day to day. But the public may rest assured that whenever we do complain and criticize there are good reasons for so doing.
>
> Whenever we notice an act on the part of the Government which indicates progressive spirit, our hearts are filled with joy and hope. The latest encouraging indication is the desire on the part of the Government to readjust the criminal law. Until last spring, the so-called trials in the law courts were a farce in the true sense of the word. Influential men in the Government could arrest any citizen without making a special charge and have him punished before trial. The sentence was also decided by these men, and the judge simply carried it out without consulting his legal instincts.
>
> Consequently, many innocent persons have suffered the pang of cruel punishment, and some have lost their lives for the crime which they probably never dreamed of committing. His Majesty realizes the need of reform in the judicial administration of his government and requested General C.R. Greathouse to advise and oversee the judges and procedure of the trials of important cases that come to his notice. This reformation was most needed in Korea, and now it has begun.

Let this be extended to all courts of the land, especially to the dark corners of the Police Department, where the relics of the old barbarous system are still in evidence.

(**Editor's Note**: Mr. C.R. Greathouse was the vice-Minister of Home Affairs and Adviser to the King Kojong.)

Looked at from today's vantage point, those measures were indeed very modest. However, in view of the conditions prevailing in the country at the time, they were radical. The so-called absolute power of the King was, in reality, a shield behind which his ministers exercised real authority in their respective domains, usually with the knowledge of the King but without it at other times. In the former case the benefits accruing therefrom were shared by both; in the latter the Minister concerned was the sole beneficiary. In either case the people are the losers. An astute and strong monarch could keep his ministers from abusing the system behind his back. King Kojong was neither astute nor strong, and his ministers often used his authority for their exclusive gain. Jaisohn won Kojong's support by subtly pointing that out and by asserting that his decision to discard the rule by fiat in favor of the rule of law would win the admiration of the civilized powers, especially the United States, as well as the support of his people.

The King was an admirer of the United States. Horace Allen, Secretary of the American Legation, couldn't be nicer to him, albeit for a purpose which was less than noble. He had joined the Russian Minister in helping him escape to the Russian Legation. The American missionaries, Horace Underwood in particular, had helped protect him by forcing his way into the palace at night with a pistol in his hip, his wife and other missionary ladies preparing meals for His Majesty. No doubt humanitarian concern was one of their motives, but their ambition to gain explicit permission to engage in evangelistic work in Korea was also thought to have been their motive. The Korea-U.S. treaty was silent about the freedom of religion. Out of those relations with the Americans, he came to regard the United States as a compassionate and rich nation. He entertained the hope of obtaining from it a substantial amount of economic aid and protection from Japan, his immediate enemy, and other potential foes.

The King's hope for American aid was in vain, but it did not lessen his fondness for the missionaries, for they were careful not to offend his conservative friends. However, Jaisohn's hope that Kojong's support for the reform measures might usher in a new era for Korea proved to be unfounded. He did not hesitate to criticize the conservatives when they obstructed the path of Korea's progress. They retaliated by convincing the King that Jaisohn was out to destroy the monarchical system, and the King allowed them to undo all reforms which he had sanctioned. Chief among them which Jaisohn regarded as of crucial importance - the Royal Commission on Revision of Laws - had been set up by the King with much fanfare. However, as the conservatives' pressure forced all but one member to boycott the commission, Jaisohn observed that if its history were known to Gilbert, it would become a theme for first class farce-comedy.

B. Nationalism

Jaisohn believed nationalism to be as important to Korea as constitutionalism was to the Korean people. But he was not a blind nationalist. His fealty to his U.S. citizenship makes it clear. He stressed nationalism not as a means of aggrandizement but for the survival of Korea. As a small, undeveloped nation is thrusted into the center of great powers who were drunk with nationalistic, nay imperialistic, ambitions, Korea's sole chance of survival depended on the resort to those means which enabled the powers to become powerful. One of them was nationalism. Believing it a God-given right that Koreans as a race do not perish but contribute to the march of human civilization, Jaisohn maintained that 'they could do so only by emulating the Western powers.'

Hence, in lectures before his audience as well as through the columns of his paper, he contended that 'patriotism was next only to God's commandments in importance.' Thus, according to him, it was that everything which did not infringe on the rights of others but helped unite the Korean people was honorable. And he conceived and was instrumental in the erection of the *Independence Arch* in order that it would serve as a visible symbol of Korea's independence and inspire patriotism in the hearts of the Korean people for centuries to come. He urged all schools to display Korea's national flag and the portrait of the King and to require the students to salute them. He recommended observance of such occasions as the king's birthday and national Founder's Day. He exhorted all elementary schools to teach the history of Korea, with emphasis on the feats of great men and women of old. He wrote:

> Patriotism is the principal item in education. Therefore, in foreign countries, all public schools begin every day with a salute to the flag of the nation and to the king. Both the flag and the portrait of the king or president adorned the classroom. This enables the children to grow firmly grounded in patriotism.

Furthermore, the children are first taught their national history in order for them to learn the achievements of their forebears and to emulate them, and to discover their failings and avoiding making similar mistakes.

The people of a nation so instructed in patriotism and in the history of their nation cannot help but become a mighty force, so much so that other nations will recoil from committing aggression on their country. Besides, such people will respect one another as well as show a greater devotion to their country.

Convinced, too, that only informed and roused people can demonstrate their patriotism in a meaningful way, Jaisohn devoted a great deal of space in *The Independent* to the introduction of such Western concepts as

- the fundamental rights of man,
- equality of all persons,
- rule of law,
- contract theory of government and separation of powers and
- of such Western practices as compulsory public education and political party system, etc.

Jaisohn also sought to incorporate nationalistic sentiments in the Korean people by defending them against unfair criticism by foreigners, emphasizing positive aspects of Korea and the Koreans and closely watching and exposing exploitation of Korean resources by foreign interests. Taking strong exception to *Japan Advertisers* report on an article published in *Jiji Shinbun*. Jaisohn commented that while Koreans may not show anger when insulted, they in fact do show anger and it lasts a long time. Further, he flatly denied that Koreans are incapable of interesting themselves in achievements of other countries and asserted: 'Sometimes foreigners are annoyed at the extreme inquisitiveness of the Koreans in regard to new inventions by foreigners.' Again and again, Jaisohn stressed strong physique and mental ability of the Korean people, just as often he pointed out with pride Korea's climate and fertility of soil. He noted that 'all that was needed was the know-how and motivation in order to transform Korea into a prosperous and free nation.'

Perhaps his greatest contribution to the rise of nationalism in Korea was his campaign against Czarist Russia's encroachment on Korean sovereignty. It found an instant and enthusiastic response among the people. He helped drive the Russians out of Korea. However, as the other foreign interests entered into a conspiracy with his Korean enemies against him in order to preserve their interests, Jaisohn the victor over Russia, was also driven out of Korea.

C. Social Justice

Because Jaisohn was anxious to see the Korean people enjoy their right to live and thrive, Jaisohn was their sharpest critic as well as staunchest defender. He attacked the *yangban* class as one of social parasites. He rebuked the common people for their apathy and supineness. He bemoaned the fact that the men folk resented oppression by their rulers but smugly treated their wives as though they were slaves.

As a physician, Jaisohn was keenly interested in physical fitness of the individual as much as social reform. Members of the upper class accustomed to the diabolical notion that all forms of physical exertion are degrading, not only avoided menial labor but also neglected physical exercises. Therefore, though they were well dressed and appeared presentable, they were in reality frail and in delicate health. The commoners, on the other hand, were sturdier due to the strenuous labor they had to engage in but were badly in need of improving their physical comportment for their own satisfaction as well as to command the respect of others. Thus, he advised the people, for example,

- to take exercise,
- to let fresh air into their rooms every morning even in winter,
- to wash their bodies and hair frequently,
- to stand upright and hold their heads high when walking,
- not to expectorate loudly in the presence of people,
- not to blow the nose with bare hands in public and
- to keep their mouths closed while walking on the streets.

He also advised them to be mindful of their communities' well-being by maintaining their streets in good repair, installing public lavatories in places where large crowds gathered and employing sanitation police who would see to it that the streets were not littered, and roadsides were not used as toilets. Claiming that the level of civilization of a people is judged by the amount of water they used, he stressed the necessity of ensuring adequate, unpolluted water supply.

Jaisohn also called for abolition of such social diseases as sorcery, early marriage, and concubinage. He was especially insistent on putting to an end the noxious custom of sorcery, practiced mainly by poor peasants, but also indulged in by *yangbans*. Queen Min reportedly called in *mudang* (sorceresses) to pray for her to bear a son. People with sick relatives or wishing good fortune hired those who were said to induce spirits to do their bidding through ritualistic dances, incantations and offering of food and money. After that, the food would be given to the sick who became sicker and died as a result of eating it. The money belonged to the *mudang*. As it was claimed that the larger the sum was, the more efficacious the *goot* (sorcery) was, the hapless hirerer paid her through the nose. Since there were said to be over 1,000 *mudangs* and *pansoos* (male blind fortune tellers) in Seoul alone, Jaisohn figured that their combined income was about 180,000 *won* a year. This sum, he maintained, could go a long way toward building hospitals, schools, and a central heating system in Seoul.

Women's Treatment/Status

More significant, he was the earliest advocate of human rights in Korea, especially with respect to women's rights. Women in those days had no legal name, as they had no rights of any kind. A girl was the property of her parents when she was a child; upon marriage, which was arranged for her by her parents, she was her husband's; when or if her husband died, she had no right to remarry. On the other hand, her husband could divorce her on any one of the grounds, such as incompatibility with her parents-in-law, adultery, incurable disease, inability to bear children, theft, and a disagreeable disposition. Women of the lower classes were allowed to work in the field in addition to doing her domestic chores. Those of the *yangban* class could only go outdoors, either in curtain sedan chairs or at night. Jaisohn took the championship in their behalf:

The most pitiful humans in the world are Korean women. Today we wish to remind Korean men of one of their worst offences - injustice to women. Women are not a whit inferior to them, but they treat them like slaves. They do so because they're ignorant and uncivilized. They think they're superior to women because they are physically stronger. He who considers physical strength as the only criterion for superiority is a beast or barbarian. What distinguishes a man from a barbarian is a sense of justice, fairness, and civility. But Korean men treat their woman with utter injustice, prejudice, and rudeness. This makes them barbarians, for a man worthy of the name despises a swaggering bully, but shows courtesy, politeness, and considerateness toward physically weaker persons like women.

In all other aspects, Korean women are much superior to men, while men - most of them, if not all – indulge in adultery and concubinage. Women have the strength to suppress the sense of their outrage and put up with their men's barbarity. While men think it natural for them to remarry in the event of their wives' death, they expect their wives to forgo remarriage on their death. Korean men must change their ways, or they will remain barbarians.

In line with his support for fair treatment of women, he called for the education of women folk. However, reflecting the concept of 'Separate but equal' education then prevailing even in the United States, his demand was establishment of schools for girls as well as boys.

(**Editor's Note**: The legal principle of 'Separate but equal' education was established in the 1896 Supreme Court ruling in Plessy v. Ferguson, which allowed racial segregation under the condition of equal facilities.

This led to severe inequalities, particularly in education, where Black schools were underfunded. This principle was overturned by the 1954 Supreme Court ruling in Brown v. Board of Education, which declared that 'separate educational facilities are inherently unequal' and ruled that it violated the Equal Protection Clause.)

Another evil coming under his attack was a custom of submitting memorials to the King. Concerning it he wrote as follows:

> The custom of sending memorials to the throne is one of the oldest practices in the political institution of Korea. In olden times, it played an important and useful role in politics. Through it, the throne had an opportunity to hear the wrongs of officials and proposals for remedy.
>
> The originator of this custom had democratic ideas, for by this means the ruler of the nation could be approached by the humblest citizen of the land. It was absolutely necessary in those days when there was no public press and no representatives of the people on the Council to have such an institution. It acted as a channel through which communications between the King and the people were established.
>
> But in recent years the custom has been very much abused. It has been resorted to as a means of obtaining office and has been employed as a weapon of blackmailing officials against whom one has a grudge. These politicians, as a rule, do not do blackmailing themselves, but hire some insignificant fellows to execute their commands with the promise of an office when they succeed in procuring their rival's positions. As far as we can judge, there is not the slightest benefit to the Government by the

continuation of this custom. His Majesty has a Council of State, the duty of which is to advise him on state affairs. If His Majesty desires to receive direct representation from the people, he can give them the right of franchise so they can send their elected representatives to the Council of State.

These memorials cause more trouble in the Government than any other abused customs. The abolishment of it would be one of the most welcome reforms in Korea.

What won Jaisohn the bitterest enmity of Korea's *yangbans*, from whose ranks mighty as well as petty officials were drawn, was his persistent championship for the abused masses by means of his paper. Not only did he publish all the news of official corruptions which came to his notice, he printed as many letters of protest against oppressive and corrupt governors, magistrates and *osas* (royal inspectors) from irate commoners as space allowed. The following are typical examples of the innumerable complaints published in *The Independent*:

Yi Ho, Yi Hi-sung, Whang Yong-ku, Eun I-baek of *Yonan* district wrote:

Magistrate Hong Wu-suk has collected from the people illegal taxes for the last 16 months to the amount of 12,000 won. Besides the regular government revenue, he further broke the law by making agricultural implements with the old government guns, spears, cannons etc. from the government arsenal in the district and sent them to *Jemulpo* (Inchon), where he had them sold for his own benefit.

After lamenting the fact that while people of Turkey, Cuba, the Philippines, etc., had friends and sympathizers throughout the world, the Koreans did not have any defenders, Jaisohn cited one of many such cases as follows:

> The Government passed a law two years ago in regard to property taxes. It clearly states that the people are required to pay to the Government as stated amount annually. Lately, however, the magistrates and their underlings have collected many times in excess of the amount set by the law. At first the people resisted but were forced to pay. A leading citizen of Anak took up the case with his district magistrate. The latter was evasive. The representatives of Anak next wrote a letter of protest to The Independent. But that did not bring the desired effect.
>
> Thereupon two representatives of the district came to Seoul two weeks ago and made an appeal to the Home Department. But the reply to this appeal is like the case of the child who asked for bread and received a stone. We quote the reply of the Minister of Home Department: "Is the complaint true? If so, it is against the law. Therefore, the Governor of the province is ordered to make a report of the case to the Department after investigation. But the Department thinks that making complaints by the people against the actions of their officials is hateful. Therefore, the Governor is authorized to arrest these two complainants and punish them severely.

The following was from a citizen of *Tongnae*:

The Royal Inspector, Cho Yun-Seung, ordered the Magistrate of *Tongnae* to collect illegal taxes, and a special collector was sent to the Mayor of *Pusan*. The Mayor could not obey the order of the Inspector without first obtaining permission from the Foreign Office, which had jurisdiction over him. Upon reporting the facts to the Department of Foreign Affairs, he received a reply from the Minister that the law prohibits collection of illegal taxes. The Mayor refused to obey the Inspector. The latter ordered the Mayor's dismissal. The Mayor resisted, but the Inspector raided the Mayor's office and drove out the Mayor and other officials. The Inspector and his retinue, numbering over 100, beat local officials, imprisoned them for disobedience. Public business is at a standstill and the town is terror-stricken. It is worse than last year when the 'righteous army' (*Tong-haks*) invaded the district. The people do not know whose orders they are to obey; hence they are panic-stricken. There is a grave danger of general uprising in *Tongnae* before long. I write this to your paper hoping that this condition might be averted before the outbreaks take place.

An appeal to *The Independent* by an aggrieved soldier:

One of the *Chusas* (secretaries) in the Law Department named Chang Yung-eun, who was appointed by ex-Minister of Law Cho Pyong-sik is so ignorant that he cannot write his own name. However, he is quite well-versed in crooked matters. He enticed away my wife while I was stationed in the country and keeps her as his concubine. I heard the news and returned to Seoul on my leave of absence, and I'm trying to recover my wife. But the *Chusa* in the Law Department is so influential that a common soldier like myself cannot obtain a redress through the law courts.

Jaisohn ruefully confessed his inability to be of any help to the hapless soldier except to give publicity to his case in his paper. The outcome of the case is not known but judging from the fact that the ex-Minister became a bitter foe of Jaisohn, one may assume that the publicity of his plight in *The Independent* helped the soldier win back his wife.

The list of cases such as those cited above frightened and infuriated the officials in Seoul, and with good reason, because although many of the corrupt officials in the provinces were cheaters of the Government and plunderers of the people, just as many were sent to the provinces by their superiors, including the King, with orders to squeeze the people in their behalf as much as the traffic would bear. So, they in collusion with foreign representatives in Korea forced Jaisohn out of Korea. Jaisohn averred that some of the missionaries participated in the conspiracy. They charged that he was too serious, too self-righteous and too much in a hurry to reform a country that had been steeped in old ways for thousands of years.

If by those charges they meant that in his opinion the hour of Korea's fall was fast approaching, that he held in his hand a prescription for her salvation, and that he was being resisted, they were right. On the other hand, if they meant that he was a conceited 'sour puss,' that was an unkindly cut. There was no doubt that he was serious about Korea's ailment and about his belief that he knew its remedy. But he was not a believer in his indispensability. He was too much of a 'Franklinite' to insist that everything must be done in precisely his own way, and that therefore he alone was qualified to do it. When he was dismissed and thus forced to leave Korea before his contract had expired, he left without making a whimper.

The Independent is unique in the annals of journalism in Korea, perhaps in the world. Founded and edited by a person who had no training or experience in publishing a newspaper, lasting less than three years and with the circulation of only 3,000, it was unequaled in the influence it exerted. Virtually all the 12 million Koreans heard of it, knew what it stood for and were in hearty agreement. Those in power, who clung to the status quo, feared it. Understandably, it was a controversial paper, some attacking it as outlandishly radical, uncritically pro-American, or deficient in literary quality, especially in its Korean section. Others, an overwhelming majority, acclaimed it as phenomenal in its message and commendable in its journalistic standard. Though some of its readers' reactions have been already presented, it seems appropriate in concluding this chapter to cite a few typical and significant assessment of the paper.

1. From a citizen of *Soksan* district whose earlier letter to *The Independent* had appeared in it:

    The mention of the matter (overcharge of fees to the people by the District Magistrate, Wang Chung-sik) in your column had a wonderful effect on him. After reading the article, he called in the head citizens from each town and apologized to them for their overcharge and returned to the people all of the extra amount which he had collected.

2. From a wealthy resident of *Pungki* District:

   Kim Sok of *Pungki*, after hearing the speech of Dr. Jaisohn on Founders Day at the Independence Club, began to realize the evils of slavery. He went to his house and after consulting his family, freed the slaves belonging to him and his relatives, which numbered 32.

3. From New York Evening Post:

   The Independent, hitherto printed tri-weekly in English and Korean, edited and published by Dr. Philip Jaisohn, is now issued wholly in English. A glance at the file from April 7, 1896, to May 1, 1897, shows creditable editorial writing, admirable condensation of news and a keen sense of the needs of the once Hermit Kingdom. It is to be hoped that the freedom of the press will not be either abused or curtailed in Korea, for the good influence of this 'only English newspaper in Korea' is beyond a question.

To sum up, what Jaisohn tried to do was to implant and foster in the minds of the Korean people 'a consciousness of self-worth and self-respect.' He believed that only in this way would they achieve their true independence.

CHAPTER NINE:
KOREA FOR KOREANS (II):
The 'Yes or No' Club

Independence Club

Jaisohn, in his declining years, asserted that the concept of an organization which he later named '*Independence Club* (독립협회)' had been formed in his mind before he returned to Korea, as that of his newspaper, *The Independent*, had been. They were to function as the two legs of reform, as it were, in helping Korea achieve independence in fact as well as in name. While *The Independent* filled the role of enlightening the masses on their rights as well as duties, and on the importance of science and technology as a source of wealth and power, the *Club* would serve as a vehicle of equipping Korea's leaders with the basic knowledge of parliamentary procedures, of democratic ideals, and of welding the leaders and rank and file into one.

One wonders, therefore, why Jaisohn was so reticent about the founding of the *Club*, while being almost boastfully ostentatious about starting *The Independent*. On April 7, 1896, he began publication of the paper with the lead editorial, setting forth its aims and features, which were bold and radical. In its second issue, he proudly announced that since the first issue had been sold out in one day, he was increasing the number of the copies of future issues from 200 to 3,000. The paper's appearance was a historic event, and since then, April 7 has been widely observed as the birthday of modern journalism in Korea.

In contrast, the birth of the *Independence Club* has remained obscure to this day. Some writers, citing the July 4th issue of *The Independent*, contend that it was organized on July 2, 1896. However, it merely reported that some officials held a meeting in the new Foreign Office 'for the purpose of establishing a public park outside the Westgate,' that everyone present was enthusiastic over the project and contributed over 500 *won* toward its cost, that at the center of the park, which was to be called '*Independence Park*,' an arch bearing the name '*Independence Gate*' would be erected as a reminder to the people that

- Korea was and should be an independent nation and
- in order to plan out and supervise the work, they elected officers.

There was no mention that this was the beginning of an organization of the nature Jaisohn had envisaged before returning to Korea. Implicit in the report, however, was that the group had been in existence for some time. On June 26, *The Independent* reported: 'We are told that recently there has risen a movement to erect a new gate on the site of the old *Yongeun Mun* (Honor China Gate: 迎恩門) and name it *Independence Gate*.'

On the occasion of the cornerstone-laying ceremony November 21, 1896, Ahn Kyong-soo, President of the *Independence Club*, told his audience that the *Club* was organized about 5 months ago, June of that year, with 'a half dozen members.' Recalling Jaisohn's own statement that 'it came quietly into existence at my house sometime during the spring of 1896' and noting the club's 'Debate Rules' setting its debate schedule, I (Dr. Liem) am of the view that it had already come into existence by April 1.

Photo: *Independence Gate* (1897).

Photo: *Independence Hall* built in 1897

(**Editor's Note**: The term 'Independence' used in *Independence Gate* does not refer to liberation from Japanese colonial rule but rather means a 'sovereign state that can stand on its own.' *Independence Hall* was renamed from '*Yeongbin Hall*', which was used during the *Joseon* Dynasty for receiving and sending off Chinese envoys. In 1897, the *Independence Association* renovated it and renamed it to *Independence Hall*, where discussions were held.)

The mystery as to the birth date of the *Independence Club* is not so inscrutable. Though a young man in his early 30s, Jaisohn had learned through fiery trials that too hasty an attempt at reform would defeat his own purpose. The Government had agreed to his publication of *The Independent* for many reasons, including public relations, but a number of powerful conservative ministers expressed strong reservations about it. For him to suddenly start an organization of the elite of the nation was to invite open opposition of the conservatives who viewed him as 'still a traitor.' He was firm in the determination that in time he would establish an organization which would become the central force of reform by either absorbing all factions into it or overwhelming conservative opposition into submission.

But until the opportune moment arrived, he had to act very discreetly. Therefore, as early as March, while ostensibly going about with preparations for *The Independent* and with his duties as Adviser to the Privy Council, he held quiet meetings with a group of progressively inclined leaders, most of whom were high officials in the Government, to discuss the ways and means of establishing the *Independence Club* without stirring opposition. These men – Lee Sang-jae, Lee Wan-yong, Ahn Kyong-soo - had been planning for an organization of similar nature on their own initiative and had in fact agreed to start an informal one to be provisionally known as *Konyang Hyophoe* (1896 Consultative Association). Enthusiastic of Jaisohn's proposal, they suggested that he assume leadership in organizing the *Independence Club*. He agreed to assist them in organizing it but emphasized that it must be their organization. At his suggestion, they decided to remain for the time being as an informal group and study ways and means of serving the nation most effectively.

The group met more or less regularly, at first in Jaisohn's house, but as it grew in size, they met in the office of Privy Council. In line with Jaisohn's thinking that the *Independence Club* should evolve from a worthy activity instead of the other way around, they decided to undertake a project of unusual significance which would be of non-controversial in nature and would in their view, kindle the spirit of independence among the people. This was precisely what Jaisohn had been waiting to hear, and he said: 'why not build an arch on the ruins of the old *Yongeun Mun* (Honor China Gate) beyond the Westgate, and name it *Independence Arch*, and, funds permitting, construct a park on the land surrounding it and call it *Independence Park?*'

The group was thrilled and unanimously decided that that should be their project. They agreed, too, that since independence was the concern of 'all the people,' the cost should be borne by all, from the mightiest to the humblest, and that collection of the contributions and supervision of the construction work should be their responsibility. Thus, they had a logical reason for establishing an organization which they would call '*Independence Club*'.

An organizational meeting was duly held, and the officers and charter members were as follows: President and Treasurer, Ahn Kyong-soo; Chairman of the Executive Committee, Lee Wan-yong; Secretary,

Lee Jae-yon; Members, Kim Ka-jin, Kim Jong-han, Min Sang-ho, Kwon Jae-hyong, Lee Sang-ok, Song Hon-bin, Sim Eui-sok, Chong Hyong-chol, Pang Han-su, O Se-chang, Hyon Je-bok, Lee Kye-pil, Pak Seung-jo, Hong Wu-kan, Cho Hyong-sop. Adviser, Philip Jaisohn.

However, they decided to withhold the news of the *Club*'s formation until royal approval was received. In time. His Majesty, on learning of it, not only gave his approval; he donated 1,000 *won* in the name of his Crown Prince. Thereupon Jaisohn proudly revealed the news in his June-20 editorial, but without publishing the name of the organization which would undertake the project. The editorial was as follows:

> Today we rejoice in the fact that the King has decided to erect upon the ruins of the arch outside the Westgate a new one to be entitled *Independence Arch* (*Toknip Mun*). For centuries the arch stood there as a constant insult to the autonomy of Korea, an autonomy which China always hastened to assert when called upon to stand responsible for any trouble in the peninsula, but which she always denied when it was safe to do so. She denied once too many times, and now her suzerainty is where the old arch is, namely, *opso* (*gone*). And a new arch is to be raised on the same spot, to stand forever as a negation of Manchu dominance, to show that Korea is once and for all cut off from the blighting influence of Chinese patronage. Cut off, we hope, also from the system of fraud, corruption and trickery which today makes the most populous empire in the world the laughingstock of all. This arch means independence not from China alone, but from Japan, from Russia and from all Western powers.

The plan for the Independence Arch and Independence Park is to be one for the entire people, including the King at the top and the *jigae* laborers (지게군) at the bottom. So, it should be undertaken not by the Government, nor by a group of private individuals, but by an organization comprising everyone.

The Independent reported that on July 2, a group of men held a meeting for the purpose of establishing a public park outside the Westgate, that they raised the contribution of 500 *won* among them, and that they elected officers to supervise the work whose names were listed above. It is interesting to note that the name of the organization was still not revealed. Only on July 9, *The Independent* specifically mentioned the name:

> The projectors of the *Independence Arch* and *Independence Park* outside the Westgate have organized themselves into a society, and they will be known as the *Independence Society*. They will meet regularly every Saturday afternoon at the City Hall and will discuss and plan out the work.

The *Club* officers, after considering various models for the *Independence Arch*, selected the Arc de Triomphe from an album in Jaisohn's possession. They then turned to a Swiss amateur architect for help who was a secretary at the German Legation, and he did a good job of designing an arch modeled after the Arh de Triomphe, but a considerably smaller one. This done, they hired a Mr. Sim who was an experienced builder of Western style buildings. In August, they went with him to the site for final arrangements. Construction commenced soon thereafter. Simultaneously, they hired workers for the remodeling of the *Yongeun Kwan* (China Honor Hall) next to the *Arch*, and by November it was ready for use as *Independence Hall*.

On November 21, the ceremonies of cornerstone laying took place. The sumptuous event was reported in *The Independent* as follows:

It was a clear, warm day for November in Korea. The road leading to the park was filled with people from early morning on, and long before the ceremonies began, the place was packed with spectators, both foreign and Korean. The space reserved for the guests was separated from the rest of the grounds by a temporary fence. The entrance was decorated with the national flags of Korea. One side of the *Independence Arch*, which is under construction, served as the speaker's platform (the arch is now about 6 feet high) while on the other side stood *Bae-Jae* Academy students who at intervals sang songs. The guests were furnished with comfortable seats under a huge tent. Inside the tented area were about 4,000 people and as many outside. The whole area was guarded by a special squad of police. Behind the speaker's platform were a large Korean flag and the flag of the *Independence Club*.

At 2:30 p.m., the exercises began with the rendering of music, a song entitled 'Korea' by the *Bae-Jae* Glee Club. Then General Ahn Kyong-soo, President of the *Independence Club*, assisted by a group of members, laid the cornerstone of the arch. Following this, Reverend H.G. Appenzeller offered a prayer in Korean in which he invoked divine blessing upon Korea and asked protection for Korea's independence. President Ahn, then,

223

made an eloquent address stating the history of the *Club*, which was organized five months ago with a half dozen members, and, at present, the membership is over 2,000. The contributions came from several foreigners and even from some in the remotest districts of the land. He thanked the members for their hearty cooperation in making the *Club* grow. He hoped that the whole national affair will be managed in the same harmonious spirit as it had been with the *Club*.

The next address was made by Honorable Ye Cha Yun, the Governor of Seoul. A born orator, his arguments were full of patriotic sentiment, and he urged the people to unite their hearts in the work of maintaining Korea's sovereignty.

The *Bae-Jae* Academy students then sang a song, 'Independence.' It was an excellent performance for which Professor D.A. Bunker, the director, was thanked.

Honorable Lee Wan-yong, Minister of Foreign Affairs delivered an earnest address on the subject 'the future of our country.' He argued that if the people work a bright future, it will have great influence on making Korea's future bright. Citing the histories of the United States and Poland, he asserted that America's greatness today is due to a few people who worked for the independence of their country over a century ago, while the downfall of Poland is due to a lack of harmony on the part of the Polish people.

Dr. Jaisohn spoke on the subject 'Foreigners in Korea,' both in English and Korean. He gave the facts concerning the praiseworthy record of the foreigners in Korea and their many good deeds.

After another rendering of music by *Bae-Jae* Academy students and drill exhibition by Royal English School students, the program was concluded with loud cheers for His Majesty and the Independence Club.

After the ceremonies, the guests were invited to the *Independence Hall*, situated near the *Arch*, where they were treated to a bountiful repast. A number of foreign guests made brief informal remarks. Dr. Horace Allen, speaking on behalf of Minister Sill, expressed the hope that this was the new epoch for Korea's regeneration and assured his hearers that America would always be one of Korea's best friends.   Jaisohn's speech on that occasion was conspicuous for its brevity. One would expect him to use the memorable occasion to express his reasons for helping organize the *Club* and exhort its members to exert every effort to make it fulfill its obligations to the fullest. Why did he refrain from doing so? It seems that by saying as little as possible and staying out of the limelight, he wanted it understood that the organization was a responsibility of its members and that his enemies had no reason to fear he would use it as a weapon against them.

With the sumptuous hall ready for use and the construction of the *Arch* well under way, the popularity of the *Club* soared sky high. During the first year of its existence, its membership reached over 4,000, spurred by such incentives as the ambition for social climbing through association with the high and the mighty, desire to learn new and novel ways, passion to be a part of a crusade for a democratic and truly independent Korea, and out of sheer curiosity, people by the hundreds joined the *Club* every week. The phenomenal increase was in spite of the fact that though it is easy to secure membership, needing only to send

225

in one's name and address along with the statement of desire, it was far from easy to retain it. There was a membership fee of 10 *jon* a month. Violators of *Club* rules were fined from 10 to 30 *jon,* and repeated violators of the rules were expelled. Considering the fact that even in the final days of the *Club's* existence, December 1898, when the Government's oppression was the harshest, its membership was 4,173. It seems that Jaisohn was not exaggerating when he said it had 10,000 members when he left Korea.

The construction of the *Independence Arch* and *Independence Park* was, of course, the most conspicuous activity of the *Club* until the project was completed in November of the following year. Publication of a bimonthly magazine called *Toknip Hoebo* was another. The first issue of it came out in December. Printed in *onmun* as well as Chinese characters, it carried articles by its members, as well as various notices, together with bylaws of the *Club*. It also published an article by Jaisohn, which was entitled 'Atmosphere.' It should be pointed out that in a formal sense, the newspaper, *The Independent,* was not an organ of the *Independence Club*, although both were in effect the arms of Jaisohn's reform movement.

The most important activity of the *Club*, however, was 'debate.' To put it differently, it was discussion of the pro and con of an issue and reaching a decision in accordance with parliamentary procedures. Viewed from the vantage point of today, this may seem all too trite and trivial, but in those days, it was something entirely new. Former President Syngman Rhee, one of Jaisohn's students at *Bae-Jae* Academy, said:

There were not even words in the Korean language for the parliamentary terms. There scarcely were even thoughts in the Korean minds for such ideas as amending a motion, or referring a disputed point to a committee, or rising to a point of personal privilege, or appealing from the decision of the chair. We were deeply interested in this new method of developing democratic participation and solving problems and arriving at majority-approved agreements.

Fascinated though *Club* members were by this novel method of decision-making, putting it into practice was by no means easy. Since under the system then prevailing in Korea, one secured government position or obtained promotion by either pleasing or bribing one's superior, there was no need to win the support of the public. To all but a few who had been abroad or become Christians, the term '*Yon sol*' (public address) was utterly new. Hence, it took months for Jaisohn to convince *Club* members that public debate on the pros and cons of an issue is not rabble-rousing, but a wholesome means of arriving at a sound decision, that in order for the debate to be constructive, participants must remember that differences of opinion are not personal criticisms but are confined solely to the issues, and that the presentation of arguments should be persuasive in content and respectful in manner.

Debate

When spring (1897) came and the weather allowed him to hold meetings in the *Independence Hall*, Jaisohn called a demonstration debate there. Lest he stir the suspicion of the 'Do-nothing' conservatives, the meeting was held only after May 23rd, when the sign '*Toknip Kwan*'

(*Independence Hall*) written by the Crown Prince, was hung above its door, and *Club* members decided to meet every Sunday afternoon for the purpose of discussing scientific and economic questions. With His Majesty thus committing himself to the support of the *Club*, he was now ready to push ahead with his program of training leadership. He recalled the first debate in these words:

It was held in *Independence Hall*. Both the building and grounds were packed. Although I had heard that the news of my efforts at teaching *Club* members on how to conduct debates caused curiosity among the general public, I was not aware of the intensity of interest in it, which they called 'Yes and No Meeting.'

I began the meeting with a few remarks of explanation as to what a public forum meant. It meant, I said, presenting both sides of an issue so as to enlighten hearers on the strengths and weaknesses of the issue and to enable them to make their own judgment. I told them that in democratic countries, such educational activities are carried out by political parties that when any issue, national or international, arises, the parties take opposite sides and discuss them without emotion or prejudice and allow the public to choose sides according to their merits, and that the people need not harbor personal feelings against those who hold the opposite view. The whole intent of the forum is, I pointed out, to solve all public issues in accordance with the opinion of the majority. I concluded by saying that in order to demonstrate how it works, I would pose a question and invite some of those present to present their arguments for or against it, and that at the end of the presentation of both sides, the whole assembled audience would be asked to vote which side they favored.

The question to be debated was: 'Resolved that men should cut off their top knots (*sangtoo*).' According to tradition, Korean males did not cut their hair during minority. They wore it braided in the back. On reaching adulthood, which usually was signified by their marriage, they carried it on their heads in knots. The topknots were untied only when washing their hair or as a sign of mourning when their parents passed away. Thus, the topknot served as a symbol of filial piety.

I asked a member of the audience to address the question. For a long time no one responded. After much persuasion, however, someone got up and said he thought topknots should be maintained. His reasons were that it was an ancient custom to wear a topknot, that it served as a symbol of filial fidelity, and that it caused no inconvenience for men. This man was Lee Sang-jae, a high yangban and a man of great reputation. He was followed by Lee Jay Yon, Mayor of Seoul, who presented the opposing view. He argued that wearing long hair interferes with free bodily movement while at work, that it is unsanitary because long hair accumulates dirt and dust which must be washed frequently to keep it clean, and in this busy world one cannot afford the time to care for it properly, and that people who wear long hair are usually backward in outlook and tend to oppose a change for the better.

Following the two speeches, a vote was taken. The 'Nays' constituted an overwhelming majority. Afterward, a man came up to me and said, "On listening to one side, I agreed with it, but after listening to the other side, I agreed with it too. So which side is right?" Be that as it might, this was the first popular vote ever taken in Korea.

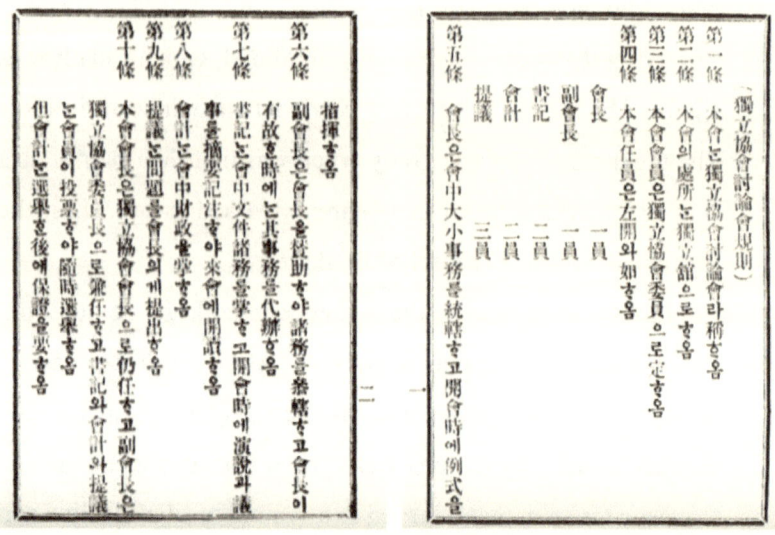

Photo: Debate Rules of *Independence Association* (1897)

The first of the regular 'Yes and No Weekly Meetings' were held on August 29, 1897. A week previously, the topic for debate had been selected. It was: 'Resolved that the education of the masses is the most urgent task for the Korean people.' Also chosen at the time were four speakers, two for the affirmative and two for the negative. At this debate, the speakers presented their prepared arguments in alternate order. Afterward, the chair invited members of the audience to express their views on the topic, adding that each speaker taking one side of this subject must be followed by another presenting the other. A number of them did, including Han Kyu-sol, Lee Wan-yong, and Lee Yun-yong, all of whom were cabinet members.

The significance of that meeting and those which followed was beyond the expectation of even Jaisohn himself. Not only did they kindle the participants desire for direct involvement in public affairs, before long they became quite adept as parliamentarians and were able, without being declared out of order, to put the Government on the defensive. Regarding some of its policies, Jaisohn in his reminiscence described his surprise in these words:

> The most remarkable thing I noticed was the quick and intelligent manner in which the Korean young men grasped and mastered the intricacies of parliamentary rule. I often noticed that some of them raised the question of the point of order in their procedure, which was well taken, worthy of expert parliamentarians of the Western countries.

The topics for the weekly debates during the remainder of the year were, on the whole, noncontroversial. For a while, most active participants were high government officials, with younger members of the *Club* not in government service sitting back and listening. With the passing of weeks, however, the latter refused to remain docile and silent. They enlivened the debates not only with eloquence and cogent arguments, but also by illustrating their points with current international events. For example, during the debate on the topic: 'Resolved that international trade is essential to the wealth of the nation,' the younger members of the *Club* nearly monopolized the arguments. Those speaking for the negative side opposed it, asserting that under international agreements unfavorable to Korea and, specifically, while the sovereign was held in a foreign Legation, it could by no means be beneficial to the country. Those taking the affirmative side maintained, pointing out the fact that the Occidental nations obtained their wealth and power through international trade, that Korea must not shirk it. At the same time, they conceded that the unfavorable conditions existing in Korea, such as the sojourn of the King in a foreign legation and unfair international treaties arising therefrom should be removed. In other words, both sides agreed on the value of international trade. Their disagreement was on the procedure. The negative side opposed any international trade while the King was in a foreign Legation and foreign interests took advantage of it, and the affirmative side favored entering into it while seeking to remove the unfavorable conditions.

The debate resulted in an implied but unmistakable criticism against not only the foreign powers but also Government ministers implicated in the King's flight to the Russian Legation. Many of them were members of the *Club* and the 'elder members' moved to confine future debate subjects to those which were of their 'proper concern.' Amidst thunderous applause from the audience, the *Club* members resoundingly defeated their motion and voted to debate on more 'relevant subjects' in the future.

What the junior *Club* members asserted was true. Under the Korea-Japan Treaty of 1876, such ports as *Wonsan* and *Chinnampo* had been opened for trade with Japan. However, even Japanese observers admitted that it was detrimental to Korea. Under the protection of Japanese authorities, unfair trade tactics of Japanese traders were so notorious that they caused severe losses to not only the people of *Wonsan*, but also the whole surrounding regions. During the King's sojourn in the Russian Legation, not only Russia but also American, French and German traders were granted concessions with little regard for Korea's interest. Since the Government ministers were, wittingly or not, a party to the notorious transactions, many of them withdrew from the *Club*, causing it to be more and more dominated by younger and more militant members. In the resultant conflict between the conservative members and the militantly liberal ones, Jaisohn did his best to be a moderating influence.

However, the tide of events which heretofore had been so favorable to his crusade began to turn against him. In September that year, Russia's urbane and respected Minister Karl Waeber was replaced by Alexis de Speyer, who was of a totally different breed. An arrogant, boisterous expansionist, he came determined to take immediate, complete and exclusive control of Korea. Allen dubbed him an 'impudent pup.' Jaisohn, after meeting him once, described him as a man 'I wouldn't want to see more than once.' The swaggering Czarist envoy once spoke derisively of his predecessor in these words: "Ah, Mr. Waeber, I do not approve of him. I like not many things he has done. You will find me a true Russian, Mr. Waeber is not."

de Speyer wasted no time in implementing the 'true Russian's plan' - control of the Korean army, Korean finances, her natural resources such as mineral and timber, and acquisition of a military base near Pusan. In October, de Speyer, having engineered the dismissal by the Korean Government of John McLeavy Brown, British adviser to the Korean Finance Ministry, brought from St. Petersburg Kir Alexeiff to take his place in spite of the fact that Brown had assumed the position only six months before and had a five-year contract. Moreover, those, including Jaisohn, who knew the British adviser believed him to be a competent and conscientious person. Koreans were alarmed, not for the sake of Brown, but de Speyer. In November, the Korean arsenal in Seoul was placed under the supervision of a Reminoff also brought in by de Speyer. In the same month, an agreement between de Speyer and Cho Pyong-sik, Korea's Foreign Minister, was signed, giving the control over Korea's customs and finance to Russia for an 'indefinite period.' And, amidst growing protests by not only Koreans but also other foreign representatives, de Speyer and Alexeiff went ahead with their scheme for Russia's takeover of Korea's finances, including tax revenues, through the establishment of the Korean-Russian Bank.

Jaisohn's initial reaction to the Russian policy was one of patience with firmness. As noted, he opposed the King's sojourn in the Russian Legation. Having done this as a matter of principle, he had no choice but to make the most of the bad situation. The King had wished it. Allen and Sill, with the tacit support of their German and French counterparts, masterminded it, and Waeber, with the collaboration of the pro-Russian Koreans, executed it. Hence, while trying to induce the King to return to his palace as soon as possible, he decided to keep a wary watch on goings-on in the Russian Legation, lest the foreign interests and Koreans around the King plundered Korea's resources at will. When the Government brought in a group of Russian officers on a one-year contract to train Korean troops to protect the King, he reluctantly supported it. On learning of the concession grants made to Russian, American, French and German businessmen, Jaisohn became angry but merely reported it in *The Independent* and advised vocal critics among *Club* members to redouble their efforts toward creating a condition under which the King could speedily leave the Russian Legation. Later, when Russia proposed to increase the size of Russian military personnel,

Jaisohn still refrained from openly criticizing it but quietly encouraged *Club* members to air their opposition. He also urged Lee Wan-yong, President of the *Club* as well as Foreign Minister, to oppose it. Thus, the latter did, for which the King, under Russian pressure, dismissed him. In February 1897, the King returned to his palace.

de Speyer's blatant attempt to turn Korea into a Russian colony led Jaisohn to resist it openly. Jaisohn began with a veiled attack on the stupidity or short-sightedness of 'certain Ministers' and an editorial in *The Independent* dated October 23, 1897:

> It is understandable that the Korean Government considers it necessary to engage foreign advisers for certain tasks when Koreans with needed knowledge or skill are not available. In order to derive benefit from the employment of foreign advisers, the Government must observe several rules.
>
> 1. It must ascertain that the person under consideration is qualified for the position.
>
> 2. Once hired, he must be given necessary support to enable him to perform his duties properly.
>
> 3. A part of his duties should be to train Korean personnel to take over the foreigner's work when his term of employment expires. Otherwise, Korea will continue to be dependent on foreign powers.
>
> We do not know whether the royal guards, now under training under Russian army officers, are ready to assume their duties, one of which is to train additional soldiers themselves. The Government must see to it that this is done, or it is derelict

in performing its duty. If, on the other hand, it had done its duty, then there is no need for us hiring foreign officers any longer.

As regards the matter of foreign adviser in the Finance Ministry, Mr. McLeavy Brown has, since commencing duties 19 months ago, not only straightened our financial mess, but he has also produced a surplus of 3,000,000 won, we are told. Nevertheless, we hear that he is being replaced with an individual of another country. We do not know whether this is true. If so, we believe it is a disservice to Korea and injustice to Mr. Brown. Maybe government authorities are acting with some special knowledge which we do not possess.

In his October 28th editorial, Jaisohn rebuked Koreans for their utter 'lack of worry,' asserting that all the powers of the world were deeply worried about any threat to their countries. He observed that Koreans alone were never worrying about the threat to their country's independence. 'They must be mighty lucky,' he added, 'their only worries are about food, clothing and about *pyosul* (government position).' He reminded his readers that people of great powers cared about their livelihoods and social advancements just as much as Koreans, but that their greater concern were 'the freedom and prosperity of their countries,' and that because of this they enjoyed more food, better clothing and better shelters. He appealed to them to be deeply worried over the foreign enemy of Korea who threatened to enslave Korea and rob them of their food, clothing and shelter. His October 30 editorial was blunt in attacking Russia, and it is worth quoting:

Recently, much confusion has arisen due to rumors concerning the advisership in the Finance Ministry. In order to help dispel the confusion, we wish to report our findings from inquiries made at the Foreign Ministry, Finance Ministry, Russian Legation and British Legation. On the 4th of this month, Mr. Alexeiff, Russian adviser to the Finance Ministry, arrived in Korea in accordance with his government's order. Thereupon Minister de Speyer notified the invitation of Minister Min Yong-hwan and requested to know when he could assume his duties. The Foreign Ministry referred the matter to the Finance Ministry. The Finance Ministry replied that it had already had a foreign adviser whose contract had not yet run out. The Foreign Ministry relayed the message to the Russian Minister. The latter rejected the answer, saying his request was when Mr. Alexeiff could begin his duties. He demanded an answer to his question.

The Foreign Ministry referred it to the Finance Ministry. The latter replied that since it is very difficult to resolve the issue of replacing the incumbent adviser with a new supervisor by the Finance Ministry, the Foreign Ministry should use its discretion in replying to the Russian Minister. Thereupon, the Foreign Ministry informed de Speyer that it considered the employment of a Russian financial supervisor for the Korean Government to be proper. The Russian Minister was still not satisfied because the Foreign Ministry's answer did not specifically say when Mr. Brown would be relieved of his duty and when the Russian supervisor could assume office. de Speyer demanded a speedy answer.

The Foreign Ministry informed British Minister Jordan of the Korean government's decision to discharge Mr. Brown and asked him to forward the message to Mr. Brown. Mr. Jordan refused to accept the message and returned it to the Foreign Office.

That is where the matter stands now. How the issue will be resolved remains to be seen. What is certain is that the Government has been forced into a mighty difficult position. What troubles us is that Mister Alexeiff is said to have been given the title of 'supervisor.' Does this mean that he is to be supervisor over the Minister of Finance? If he is the Finance Minister's boss, is he not the boss of the Korean Government?

During the ensuing weeks, Jaisohn continued his editorial attack on the Russian scheme to usurp control of Korea's Finance and Defense Ministries. In addition, he gave publicity to memorials submitted to the King by Pak Chong-yang, Ahn Kyong-soo and Min Yong-jun, urging him to defend Korea's sacred rights against foreign interests.

The *Independence Club*, dominated by younger and more militantly nationalistic members, stepped up the anti-de Speyer campaign. The weekly debates turned into rallies against Russia. Curiously, the *Club* found an ally in a foreign devil in its struggle against the 'Russian devil' - Britain. Unwilling to bow to the unceremonious dismissal of her subject, Brown, as financial adviser to the Korean government, she dispatched six 'men-of-war' to *Inchon*. Though ostensibly the fleet was on a 'routine cruise,' neither Russia nor Korea was fooled.

The *Independence Club* stepped up the anti-Russian campaign. It held a special meeting at which a petition to the King demanding expulsion of the Russians, signed by a committee of 100, was endorsed. Brown was reinstated, which signaled that de Speyer's influence was beginning to decline. Jaisohn, sensing this, gave a nod to the *Club* to further step up its pressure on him. On March 10th, the *Independence Club* called the mammoth rally called *Manmin Kongdong Hoe* (All People's Congress) in downtown Seoul. Almost 10,000 persons attended it, including foreign representatives. de Speyer was there also. Rousing speeches by *Club* members - Syngman Rhee was one of them - calling on the people to unite to rid Korea of foreign influence, especially that of Russia, moved the audience 'like boiling water.'

The significance of the rally was that this was believed to be the beginning of greater and greater show of unity among the people to rise up against foreign aggression. Alarmed, de Speyer demanded of the Korean Government to inform him 'within 24 hours' whether it was prepared to honor the Korean-Russian agreements. He threatened to take 'further action' if the Korean Government, bowing to the 'unemployed gangsters,' refused to give a satisfactory answer. When the 24-hour ultimatum expired without any response from the Korean Government, de Speyer took no further steps. Instead, a month later (April) he packed and left Korea, taking with him all Czarist advisers. Even before the blustering, blundering Czarist envoy shook the Korean dust off his feet, the *Independents* smelled the sweet perfume of victory. And on March 13, they held a big celebration to mark the 'victory' over the Czarist empire. The *Club*'s prestige reached a new height with addition of many new members. It proudly issued a club badge with the motto '*Tognip Hyop-hoe; Chungkun Aekuk*' (충군애국) (*Independence Club*; Loyalty to the King and Patriotism for the Nation), printed on a background of a flag of Korea.

The Government's eventual ouster of Jaisohn was probably intended as a means of putting the *Independence Club* to its quiet death. Indeed, it came as a severe blow to the *Club*. However, it only served to strengthen the will of its members to continue it. Under the leadership of such respected men as Yun Chi-ho and Yi Sang-jae and such strong-willed men as Chong Kyo and Yi Seung-man, the influence of the *Club* steadily grew. So much so that the King found it necessary to make concessions. Ministers hostile to the *Club* were dismissed. The long-sought change in the composition and powers of the Privy Council was granted. By the end of that year, it looked as though the *Club* had become dominant. But the concessions were merely in words.

The King, jealous of his powers, was playing a balancing act. Through these concessions, he was providing the time for the anti-*Independence Club* forces to unite as a counterbalancing block. By December, the Conservatives had not only come up with an organization known as the 'Imperial Preservation Association' to act as a rival to the *Independence Club*, but they had also activated the Peddler's Guild into an army of gangsters. The *Independence Club*, prodded by its impatient and suspicious members, pressed the King for implementation of his promises and reinforced its demand with another mass meeting of citizens. The mass meeting made clear that the *Club* had the clout. After a bloody but inconclusive confrontation between the *Independents* and the Peddler gang, the King professed to be in earnest about implementing his words. The Privy Council was allowed to elect its vice president, and Yun Chi-ho was chosen. Then the council's 29 members were told to add 11 more to its membership. Each of the 29, in accordance with the law, voted for all 11, and when the votes were tabulated, two men whom the King least liked - Pak Yong-hyo and Philip Jaisohn - were among those elected. On December 25, the King decreed the end of the *Independence Club*.

CHAPTER TEN:

A PROPHET IN HIS OWN COUNTRY

Curiously enough, the more influential the *Independence Club* became, the less secure was Jaisohn's position in Korea. As a matter of fact, his tenure had been uncertain almost from the beginning of his return. Though a segment of the population - young intellectuals - enthusiastically responded to his call for reform, the governing authority was vested exclusively in the King and his chosen aides, who were viscerally conservative. The rank and file, chained to feudalistic traditions and debilitated mentally as well as physically by grinding poverty and lack of educational opportunities, were resigned to slavehood. Having returned without any means of self-support, he was forced to be an employee of an anachronistic and corrupt government which he had vowed to transform.

Aggravating his problems was the interference of foreign representatives in the country. While they carried on intrigues against one another for the control of Korea, they were united in thwarting him, while pretending to be supportive. A regressive and weak monarchy was far preferable to them than a progressive and popular one. Yet they did not dare oppose him openly, for he was the pride of the American community in Korea, for whom he symbolized a shining gift of the United States. Was he not the product of the 'Land of Opportunity', their dear country?'

Coincidentally, the King and the American community had become close. Following the assassination of his queen the previous year (1895), His Majesty was so fearful of his life that for some time he ate only the foods prepared and brought into the palace by American missionaries and had some of the missionaries act as his personal bodyguards. This naturally helped him draw near to the United States. Unsure of Russia's reliability, with China written off as a helpless giant and bitter against Japan, he needed a powerful but benign nation to rely on. Judging from the help given by the American missionaries as well as American diplomats, he felt that the United States might be such a power. Moreover, as earlier pointed out, he was in dire need of cash and hoped to obtain a generous loan from the country.

Hence, though he remained suspicious of Jaisohn at heart, he approved the latter's appointment as adviser to his Privy Council, acquiesced in his plan to publish a newspaper, and went along with his organization of the *Independence Club*. He hoped, somehow, that Jaisohn, once a 'traitor' to him, but now an American, would help enlighten the masses into patriotic fervor by means of the proposed newspaper and train Korea's leaders through the *Independence Club* without diminishing his royal authority. His initial support for Jaisohn was, it must be admitted, generous.

American Missionaries

Before long (1898), however, powerful interest groups were covertly at work to undermine Jaisohn's activities. As noted earlier, the foreign diplomats' tongue-in-cheek praise of his work emboldened dyed-in-the-wool conservatives around the throne to warn the King of the danger of the 'still a traitor' Jaisohn's 'radical' activities. The King, pitted in the middle, chose a balancing act by appointing implacable foes of reform to high government positions. For example, Shin Ki-son, who was the first to memorialize the throne calling for Jaisohn's ouster, was named Minister of Education, while Hong Jong-wu, who was later to mastermind the destruction of the *Independence Club*, was given the Crown Prince's tutorship.

To the alliance of Korea's conservatives and foreign diplomats in Seoul a third party was added. That was the foreign community in Korea, which consisted predominantly of American missionaries. Though most of them favored Jaisohn's aim as a matter of principle, their mission was to evangelize and win Korean converts. Since most Koreans in those days were conservative, courting conservative leaders was decisively expedient. Under the circumstance, arguments of the diplomats portraying Jaisohn as a starry-eyed radical sounded convincing, and many missionaries, including very influential ones, were won over to the anti-Jaisohn point of view.

A half century later, Jaisohn recalled: "There were some Americans in Korea at the time for whom I had no respect. They were there to serve their own interests." This view was echoed by some visiting Americans (* Harrington). A visiting clergyman, after a fortnight stay with the Horace Allens criticized them for living far too well. A naval officer who visited Seoul in 1888 remarked: "If I were the King of Korea, I would cut off the head of every damn missionary in the country." Allen himself complained of the missionary's ostentatious lifestyle. A missionary's wife boasted: "Compared with the Vanderbilts, we live in a humble way. Compared with the bulk of our constituents at home, we live in the greatest comfort. Compared with those we have come to serve; we live like millionaires and princes." The missionaries served to whet the appetite of the Korean people for Western goods, and some of them engaged in business on the side. The Reverend C.C. Vinton imported sewing machines for sale; Horace Underwood sold kerosene, coal and agricultural implements; Samuel A. Moffett was involved in timber cutting near Yalu. Finding their living in Korea pleasant, many of the missionaries were willing to cater to the whims of those in authority in the kingdom and wished to either go slow on Korea's reform or leave it to God.

(**Editor's Note**: * Author: F.H. Harrington, Book Title: *God,* Mammon and the Japanese: Dr. Horace N. Allen and Korean-American Relations, 1884-1905, Publisher: University of Wisconsin Press, Madison, 1944, Available from Amazon.com)

Jaisohn was not a radical, he was a monarchist. He was for a constitutional monarchy for Korea, but that was a long-range goal. He asserted that as an American he would not be involved in Korean politics and offered to work with conservatives as well as progressives so long as they had the welfare of the nation at heart. As a matter of fact, he preferred an honest conservative to a corrupt *Kaehwaite* (reformer). He made no secret of his preference for the Western democratic system but realizing that Korea was far from ready for it, he was careful not to allow the *Independence Club* to turn into an opposition political party.

Convinced, too, that the country had been too long and too deeply steeped in virtually absolute monarchy to make a quick change from it, he scrupulously sought to help strengthen Korea without impinging on the powers of the King. However, to the diehard conservatives, any departure from old ways marked the beginning of an end to their privileges. They clung to the view that the decline of the Chinese Empire was an aberration of an historical course, that the Celestial Empire, which was founded upon the eternal foundation of Confucian wisdom, would soon return to its former might and glory, and that the safest course for Korea lay in preserving the old Confucian system and wait for China's recapture of her might.

Seen from that point of view, the reform advocated by Jaisohn was, however mild and rational, a heresy. Consequently, with subtle encouragement by the foreign diplomats, the conservatives continued to press the King to get rid of the 'traitor parading in the guise of an American citizen.' The weak-willed King was in a quandary. On the one hand, he was thoroughly compatible with the conservatives and shared their fears about Jaisohn and what he stood for. On the other, Jaisohn made his loyalty to the King explicit, and even those missionaries who were critical of him as 'too much in a hurry' for reform attested to his personal integrity. Furthermore, the King was intelligent enough to realize that China as a mighty power safe for him to rely on no longer existed, and that his conservative aides' advices were untenable and self-serving. So, he continued to straddle the lines advocated by the opposing sides.

The Increasingly Unfavorable Position

Meanwhile, Jaisohn went serenely about his job as publisher and editor of *The Independent* and adviser to the *Independence Club*. On every significant occasion such as the King's birthday and *Yi* Dynasty Founder's Day, Jaisohn never failed to conclude his editorial column with a wish for the health and happiness of His Majesty. He frequently rebuked corrupt officials or erring husbands for their misdeeds and told them to mend their ways for the 'peace of mind' of the King in his editorials. If he showed loyalty and fealty to the King in his paper, he was also fearless in exposing corruption among officials, in some cases of which the monarch's involvement was obvious. His scathing attacks on Yi Yong-ik and Cho Pyong-jik were illustrative of his muck-raking without fear or favor. The former, in particular, was widely known as the 'hatchet man' for bringing in money to the King's coffers. No less an irritant to the King was the *Independence Club*, which was founded and functioning under Jaisohn's guidance.

At first, the King had understood it as an elitist body composed of his trusted ministers through which the public could visualize his rule as a benign and caring one. Before long, however, it went out of control and became, in the view of the conservatives, a hotbed of radicalism. The more radical it became, the higher its popularity soared, and within a year of its founding, its membership mushroomed from a score to nearly 10,000, with younger men and commoners predominant in number and influence.

The King was aroused and thought of dismissing Jaisohn from his government position and expelling him from the country, but fearing violent opposition from his followers, he desisted. Instead, he requested Allen and Waeber, American and Russian Ministers respectively, to

247

warn Jaisohn that he was moving too fast for his own good. The diplomats duly conveyed the royal message to him, each acting independently of the other. Jaisohn really thanked them for bringing the message.

But through another channel, he offered the King his explanation, which, in brief, was as follows: So far as the charge of his 'reckless attacks'; on high officials in his newspaper was concerned, he had either published documented charges of official corruption by responsible citizens or rebuked official misconduct in his editorial columns. This was in line with the paper's policy announced at the outset, which was Korea for the Koreans, clean government and publishing all the news fit to print without fear or favor. Under this policy, he had also published laudatory comments on salutary deeds by any individual.

As regards the charge of 'radicalization of the *Club*,' it was a prejudicial criticism. The change in the composition of its membership was primarily due to the withdrawal of conservatives. It was true that club members at times strayed from their chosen subject in their debates. However, this was only when they believed that current issues were relevant to the debate topic. Discussions would have been calm and constructive if senior members (government officials) had refrained from attempting to shut them off. While some junior members were vociferous in their utterances, even they were loyal subjects of the King. True, they voiced deep concern about the reported concession grants to foreign interests by the government while His Majesty was residing in a foreign legation.

From a short-range point of view, this might be construed as criticism against the King. However, from a long-range point of view, this was a patriotic service and a show of loyalty to the King. For, once he was deprived of the national resources, he would be reduced to an impoverished monarch without power. To be sure, the *Independence Club* had its weaknesses, but its potential value was too great to dissolve it. It must be nurtured so that it could serve as an ideal forum through which a mutual understanding between the government and people could be reached, for here officials and civilians who reflected the will of the people could meet and talk.

Jaisohn was not sure whether he had reassured the King. Even had he succeeded in doing so, he felt that the King, whom he later dubbed 'jelly-fish' could not remain won over to his side for long. Jaisohn would just live one day at a time, paying no attention to what he would or would not do, but go on with his activities as Adviser to the Privy Council, editing his newspaper, giving behind-the-scenes guidance to the *Independence Club* and lecturing at *Bae-Jae* Academy.

As editor of the paper, he championed the cause of equality of all persons, advocated adoption of Western social and economic systems on a selective basis, encouraged public-spirited officials to go on setting good examples before the people and criticizing greedy and oppressive officials, insisting that the criticism was not personal but directed at the wrongdoing. Occasionally, he turned reporter and toured the city to observe and to talk. But soon the 'reporter Jaisohn' found himself a stump-speaker.

Once, he noticed it in front of a Chinese store a Korean being beaten up by a Chinese who was the owner of the store. The accusation was that the Korean walked into the store, picked up an article, looked at it for a moment and left it, deciding not to buy it. Jaisohn lifted up the Chinese by the collar and said: "You barbarian, since when is it a crime for a customer to examine an article and decide not to buy it?" As he threw off the Chinese, the latter cowered and apologized to the Korean whom he had beaten. Noting a large crowd quickly gathering around him, Jaisohn said: "We must show politeness to all people, especially foreigners in our midst. For they are our guests. But this man did not act like a guest of ours. He acted like a brute, which is a disgrace to the Chinese people. We must teach him a lesson. If we don't, foreigners will treat us with contempt."

On another occasion, as he was walking along on *Jongno*, a man came up to him, made a deep bow, and confessed that he was one of the crowds who threw stones at him while he was fleeing from Seoul in 1884. He apologized to Jaisohn saying: "I thought you were a traitor to the country." Jaisohn shook the man's hand and assured him that 'his ignorance, not he, was responsible for what he had done.' Then, looking at the swelling crowd surging closely around him, Jaisohn made an impromptu but eloquent speech on the importance of knowledge.

However, in spite of his strenuous efforts to avoid controversy, his enemies were determined to get rid of him. They spread their charges that he called himself a foreigner, that he held a cigarette in his hand during audience with the King, and that he returned to Korea on the tide of Japan's victory. Finally, discarding anonymity, they attacked him openly with memorials to the King.

1. Chung Song-wu

So-called progressives go in and out of the country and claim that the changes will benefit the people while in reality they want to eat up everything they can lay their hands on. They herd with foreigners and between them cook up horrible plots and crimes. Some who escaped in 1884 came back in June of

1894 and committed horrible crimes and were also connected with the murders of the Queen. Dr. Jaisohn committed a great crime in 1884 and now comes back and dabbles in politics again and calls himself a foreigner. What business has he then with Korean affairs? His newspaper is printed for the purpose of criticizing other people, and it destroys the right principle. So, it is not good for the country nor the people. Its sole purpose is to change the laws and customs of the ancient kings and aims to upset the country. Such traitors ought not to be allowed between heaven and earth. Kim Ka-jin and Ahn Kyong-su, who took a prominent part in 1894, have brought irremediable disease upon the country. Pak Chong-yang and Cho Pyong-jik simply covet office, have no principle and cause insurrections in the country. Yi Yun-yong has some commendable qualities, but they are outweighed by his evil ones, the worst being that his whole family holds Government positions.

This base crowd, having power and influence, watch within and without for opportunities to further their own selfish interests, and this resulted in the murder of the Queen. If you consider their crimes, they cannot be pardoned. Bring back the dead bodies of the former cabinet members and pulverize their bones. Discharge from the Government every employee who held office under the former cabinet. Rescind Dr. Jaisohn's pardon and punish him if you can. Reestablish the Confucian temple and teach students Chinese classics. Return to the old form of Government and do away with all that is new or foreign.

Jaisohn persuaded the other accused officials not to resign as tradition required, but to join him in suing the author of the memorial for libel. It was necessary not only to prove his innocence; he decided to use the occasion to help Korea get rid of the invidious custom of memorializing, for this was much more than blackmail. It was a poison causing governmental paralysis. Tradition held that it was a point of honor for a high official to immediately resign his position when he's attacked in a memorial, whether the attack was justified or not. It meant that a good official must step down whenever someone submits a malicious memorial to the King, while bad ones can continue in office so long as no one bothers or dares to criticize them. He sued Chung for $2,000 damage and requested that it be turned over to the *Independence Park* Fund. The trial was held. The defendant was found guilty and ordered to pay damage of $1,000. However, since he was unable to pay, he was excused. Instead, he was prosecuted as a criminal offender and was sentenced to three years' imprisonment. Jaisohn won the battle, or did he? The King later commuted Chung's imprisonment to banishment, and while he was not heard from since, it is most likely that he quietly crept back to freedom.

2.   Shin Ki-son

Two months after the appearance of *The Independent*, a militant foe of reform by the name of Shin Ki-son was appointed Minister of Education. Immediately upon assuming office, Shin memorialized to the King the gist of which was that cutting hair short and wearing western costume advocated by progressives would make people barbarians, that the use of *onmun* (Korean alphabet) instead of the Chinese characters would make people beast and that abandoning the old lunar calendar in favor of the solar calendar was a progressive scheme to destroy Korea. To this Jaisohn responded with the following caustic comment:

> For now, we wish to point out just one of his silly contradictions. The *onmun* is Korean in origin, having been invented by King Sejong, one of Korea's greatest rulers. Furthermore, it is 100 times easier to learn and much better as a medium of communication than the Chinese characters. Therefore, it is not only patriotic to use it, but also far superior means of educating the people. If the Minister of Education is so ignorant of his responsibility and so partial to things Chinese, he should go to China and Minister to the Chinese ruler.

Shin was a much tougher adversary than Chong Song-wu. As Minister of Education, he was in a strategically important position to undermine Jaisohn and destroy his reform movement. He followed the memorial with issuance of an order to schools, effective immediately, which consisted of three items, namely:

1. Students were forbidden to wear European suits,
2. During the hours of physical exercises, they should wear old Korean soldiers' uniforms, and
3. At all other times they were to wear traditional Korean costumes. Should any student be caught walking in the streets with European suits on, he would be punished and dismissed from school.

The order provoked loud protests. Critical letters were sent to *The Independent*, some of which were published in the paper. The entire student body of the Government-established English school, joined by some of the faculty, wrote to the Minister protesting the order and arguing that they should be given the freedom to at least wear either Korean or European attire. They requested an answer from him. In a show of protest, students of *Bae-Jae* Academy paraded through the streets in European clothes. One resident of Seoul wrote to the editor of *The Independent*: "I hear that Minister Shin wants, *Mencius and Analects* (Chinese classics: 孟子 – 論語) taught at the Russian and French language schools. Is he out of his mind?"

Jaisohn echoed the outcries with a series of comments of his own. After reporting the letter from a group of residents in *Inchon* in which they accused Shin of being more Chinese than Korean, he wrote:

> One would think that the Minister of Education would feel ashamed of himself and retract his statements on learning how the people feel about his view and how clearly they showed his illogic. However, in view of his obstinacy, I could only conclude that he possesses one quality in common with the statesman of America and Europe and that is he does not mind newspaper criticisms. We venture to say that he is the most thick-headed man in the Government.

Jaisohn was just as determined to force the Education Minister to either admit his error or to resign. He published as many letters of criticism against the Minister as space in his paper permitted. One of the harshest attacks on Shin, sent in by Mr. Chong of Yangju, was as follows:

After the bloody Manchu war, we have achieved our independence, but Shin Ki-son is not happy about it. He would rather see Korea dependent on China again. He is free to so desire so long as he keeps it to himself, but he is trying to force his idea on us. We will not allow it. The King is the parent of the people, including himself. There can be no greater disloyalty or crime than making one's parents a servant of another person. This is what Shin is doing to our King. His duty is to help our youth gain knowledge in subjects which will enable them to lead Korea to a new era of prosperity and power. But he is trying to keep us ignorant and chained to the past. This makes him unworthy of the title he holds. This is what the rebels around us tried to do. There are too many rebels already. We cannot afford another, especially in the Government.

Jaisohn's campaign paid off. In less than 5 months, the diehard conservative Minister of Education was fired.

3. Cho Byong-sik, Yi Yong-ik, Hong Chong-wu, et al.

These anti-reformers were of a different kind than Chong Song-wu and Shin Ki-son. Unlike Shin and Chong, the trio and their ilk were neither blind China-worshippers nor indiscriminately anti-Western. They were unabashed opportunists who served their own interests by catering to the whims of the King. For example, Hong Chong-wu's interest in Western learning had led him to become the first Korean to go to France. Son of a Seoul *yangban*, his original intention had been to go to England but went instead to Paris due to reported British hostility toward Koreans. Ambitious but lacking the wherewithal, he secured the help of French missionaries and landed in France in 1890 to study law. Unable to realize his educational ambition, he remained in France for four years, working at a museum for his support. In 1894, he left France, presumably home-bound. On arrival in Japan, however, he changed his plan. Evidently, he decided he needed to accomplish something 'great and spectacular' before returning to Korea. His adventure in France had been a failure, and he was already 40. Meanwhile, leaders of the conservative Government in Seoul, lest Kim Ok-kiun and his friends should stage a second coup against them, had sent abroad agents to get rid of them. Hong met the agents and received the assignment to assassinate Kim Ok-kiun. He lured the latter to Shanghai and shot him to death in a hotel. With the 'great and spectacular achievement,' he returned to Korea to a hero's welcome. The Government rewarded him with an official position. But determined to receive a more lucrative appointment, he bent all his energies on ingratiating himself to the King. Jaisohn dubbed him a murderer for personal gain.

Cho Byong-sik, a sheer crook posing as a conservative also paraded as a stern, uncompromising law enforcer. If, however, conservatism meant purging the nation of things Western and restoring old Chinese ways, Cho was far from one, for he was so enamored of Russia as to sit by silently while Russia and other foreign powers talked the King into granting them one concession privilege after another, at the expense of Korea. As if that were not enough, Cho later participated in a scheme to give to Russia virtual control over Korea's financial affairs. But for Jaisohn's campaign against it through the medium of *The Independent* and the *Independence Club*, the deal would have gone through. For a while after the defeat, he felt so insecure that he sought asylum in the

French Legation. Yet he paraded in the guise of a conservative - protector of Korea and of His Majesty the King against foreign influence!

As early as the summer of 1896, he had joined his fellow conservatives in memorializing to the Throne for reestablishment of the old system of Government, prohibition of the use of *onmun*, of killing the relatives of progressive 'traitors' and for requiring the wearing of traditional Korean court costume by officials. But Jaisohn refrained from direct attack on him, content to let his attacks on Shin Ki-son, Hong Chong-wu, and Yi Il-jik serve as warnings to Cho. Nevertheless, in the fall of 1896, upon learning that he had been just named Minister of Justice, Jaisohn unleashed a bitter denunciation of him in his paper:

> The newly appointed Minister of Justice, Mr. Cho Byong-sik, has had a remarkable career. The brief record of his official life is as follows: When he was Governor of *Chung-chong* province, he stole $8,000 from the people of the province, which fact was reported to His Majesty by a special inspector. So, he was dismissed from the governorship. But later on, he was promoted to Minister of Justice. He made another brilliant record as Minister of Justice. One day, while passing through a certain place in the city, he noticed his former private secretary who had served under him while he was Governor of *Chung-chong* province. (This private secretary had given rather free information to the Special Inspector in regard to the robbery the Governor committed.) Cho ordered his servants to seize him and take him to the Law Department. There, this unfortunate man was murdered by the Minister. The Minister was banished from Seoul for a few months.

He was soon appointed Governor of *Ham-kyong* province, where he ordered export of grains from the port of Wonsan stopped. The Japanese Government strongly protested against it and made the Korean Government pay a $90,000 indemnity. Cho did not mind paying the trifling sum as the Governor's service to the country was considered worth more than that amount. He was again appointed Governor of *Chung-chong* province. The consistent Governor kept up his record as a robber by taking $12,000 and killing 22 innocent people, while collecting the money. He was again arrested on charges of robbery and murder and sentenced to so many years imprisonment. But the Government could not spare him long, so after serving one year in jail, he was appointed Grand Master of Ceremonies in the Royal Household Department. What a checkered career.

Cho did not last long as Minister of Justice, but the next year he reappeared in the national limelight, first as Minister without portfolio and later as Foreign Minister, in which capacity he tried to offer Russia virtual power of domination over Korea. To Jaisohn and members of the *Independence Club*, this was high treason. In an emotional editorial, Jaisohn lamented the indifference of 80% of the people to what went on in their government. 'Some sinister, selfish Ministers had hoodwinked the King into agreeing to let Russia gain control of Korea's financial affairs,' he wrote. Asserting that a nation is comparable to a watch, he contended that just as a watch function properly only as long as all its component parts perform their functions, a nation is viable only when its citizens fulfill their obligations. He reminded the people that 'their country's sovereignty was at stake and called on all who cared about Korea to rise up to rescue their Government from the traitors and thus help save the nation.' At the same time, he quietly called aside leaders of the *Independence Club* and advised them to demonstrate a show of force by calling a massive public rally opposing the Government's action. Accordingly, a huge rally attended by nearly 10,000 was held in downtown Seoul with speaker after speaker bitterly attacking the Russians and Korean lackeys of the Russians to the thunderous applause of the audience. It was an awesome show of force, and Russia was forced to give a second thought about seeking hegemony in Korea. Jaisohn and the *Independence Club* scored a dramatic victory.

Ironically, the victory sealed Jaisohn's expulsion from Korea. The *Independence Club* was getting too powerful. To its critics this was due to Jaisohn's influence. Hence, all parties fearing the growing influence of the *Club* agreed that he had to go. The King who had been walking a tight rope trying to strike a delicate balance between the conservatives and progressives swung over to the former, fearing a possible loss of his throne. Foreign representatives - even the Japanese, Russia's arch-rival - feared the *Independents* no less. Influential missionaries, especially the Underwoods, thought 'he was a disruptive influence.' The King requested the American and Russian Ministers to have their governments remove Jaisohn from Korea. They informed him that neither the Czar nor the President of the United States had the power to remove an American citizen from any country where he had committed no crime. Just the same, they promised to investigate what might be done.

Meanwhile, the King took steps on his own to force Jaisohn out of the country. On the one hand, he offered through the American Minister to pay Jaisohn his salary for the remainder of the contract, while on the other he filled his cabinet with sworn enemies of reform, ordered all government officials who had joined the *Club* to withdraw from it and instructed the postal department to stop delivery of *The Independent*. He also issued orders to pressure employees of the paper into resigning. The *Club*, becoming more defiant than ever, stood solidly behind him. With the readership of *The Independent* estimated at hundreds of thousands spread throughout the country, he had a nationwide following.

Consequently, the King moved with caution. He never accused Jaisohn of wrongdoing or disloyalty to him but contended that the editor of *The Independent* was a radical visionary and an impatient critic of everything that he regarded as old fashioned. The King sought to isolate Jaisohn from the American community in Korea, whose influence with the U.S. Government he had overestimated. He evidently feared that the Americans might react adversely to his drive to expel Jaisohn and jeopardize the hope for a loan from the United States. There was no need for such fear on his part, as most of the American missionaries were more than willing to please him and to receive favorable treatment from him. They let it be known that Jaisohn's impetuous drive for westernization of an ancient Korea was causing undue disturbance in the country and hurting his laudable aim.

Still, the King preferred to see Jaisohn leave Korea 'voluntarily.' To that end, he unleashed the fury of the conservatives. Some of them tried to trap him with bribes. Yi Yong-ik, the convicted criminal and 'wizard of finances,' came to his house with gold nuggets. Jaisohn threw him out of the house. Others threatened him with bodily harm. Kim Hong-yiuk, a shady character who rose from obscurity to one of Korea's most powerful men as the King's Russian interpreter, was reported as planning to assassinate him during a meeting at which Kim was present. Jaisohn got up and said:

> "I hear someone wants to kill me. I wish, if he is present here, he will tell me why he wants to kill me because I will then tell him why he should not. He should not kill me because I represent an ideal for Korea which millions of Koreans have accepted as their own. If you kill me, there will still be millions like me. You cannot kill all of them. They will kill you first."

How Kim Hong-yiuk reacted to Jaisohn's words quoted above is not known. He was later charged with attempting to poison the King, was tried, convicted and hanged. Jaisohn was aware that one or another of his enemies would either kill him or drive him out of Korea. He had been aware of it for half a year. In a fleeting moment of despair, he wondered editorially why.

> Why the Government mistreats us is a mystery. What we have done in the past years is common knowledge. To the best of our ability, we have tried to impart useful knowledge to those who govern as well as those who are governed. We have attempted to strengthen Korea by informing them of how the Western nations achieved their military and economic power, how those in positions of power should conduct themselves to inspire the support of the people, and how the people should conduct themselves in order to become loyal subjects of the King. If these attempts make us offenders, we'd gladly confess to the offence, but is it an offence?

261

The fact is that we feel honored to have had an opportunity to do what we have done, and for those who malign us, we have only pity. The Independent is not without friends. As we come under attack, our supporters in the provinces as well as Seoul have rallied to our defense. To them we appeal. Do not hate those who hate us but sympathize with them and prove that you are their true friends and loyal supporters of Korea by following the advice we have given through the columns of this paper, regardless of whether or not we remain in Korea.

During the ensuing months, Jaisohn agonized over whether to quit his work and return to America or to stay and fight on. That he would be dismissed from his advisership to the Privy Council sooner or later with certain. If he decided to remain in Korea following that, he would have to either practice medicine or go into some sort of business in order to support his family. To the bottom of his heart, he wished to stay, for there was no doubt in his mind that he was needed in Korea. Members of the *Independence Club*, readers of *The Independent* from one end of the country to the other, and hosts of plain people urged him not to leave them under any circumstances.

The question, however, was whether his income from medical practice in Korea at the time or business of any kind would be sufficient to finance the newspaper as well as his personal needs. Medical practice might enable him to support his family, but not his other activities. He might be able to do both by entering a business enterprise, but that might force him into cooperating with the authorities who were most likely to be unsympathetic to his reform activities, for there was no business opportunity available without dealing with them.

In early April 1898, he received the long-expected notice of dismissal from the Government. It was from the Council of State which he had helped establish. His notice of dismissal was accompanied by payment of the reminder of his three-year contract. It was in effect a sugar-coated order of his expulsion from Korea.

CHAPTER ELEVEN

SECOND EXILE (I):

Rejected but Loving

Exiled, but His Patriotism Remains Unchanged

Though there had been rumors about the Government's dismissal of Jaisohn, the actual news of it came as a shock to the members of the *Independence Club*. Having won a victory over Russia in thwarting her control of Korea, the influence of the *Club* had reached a new height that was mainly due to the leadership provided by Jaisohn. The majority of the Council of State, including the King, were clearly relieved when the Czarist Government recalled its swaggering, domineering envoy in Seoul, but the victory was only in a skirmish. Korea's road to reform and firm independence was still long and perilous, and Jaisohn was needed more than ever. Hence, determined to fight for his reinstatement, they held an emergency meeting and appointed a committee which dispatched a letter dated April 25, 1898, to the Council of State. The letter was as follows:

The object of employing foreigners in the Government is to accomplish certain objects through the special knowledge they possess. Dr. Jaisohn, the adviser to the Privy Council, was engaged a little over two years ago by the Government, but he was never allowed to utilize his knowledge for the benefit of our country. Now we are informed that he has been relieved from government service, and that he intends to return to America. It seems to us like throwing away government money without realizing the benefit for which the money was intended to be spent, and it is entirely contrary to the motives which the Government had when it employed him. The departure of Dr. Jaisohn will have an injurious effect upon the progress and enlightenment of the nation, and we hereby request your Excellencies to reengage him for the good of the country.

Namkung Uk
Shin Yong-jin
Committee

The Council of State replied:

We acknowledge receipt of your communication dated April 25 relating to the severance of connections by Dr. Jaisohn with our Government and requesting us to reengage him. We desire to state that your charge of throwing away money by relieving him from the service is erroneous for the very reason that through his lectures and editorials in the newspaper our people have become very much enlightened. So much so that your club realizes the importance of the people's cooperation in regard to national affairs and you have obtained the knowledge of addressing the Council on the subject of national economy. This is all due to the efforts and teachings of Dr. Jaisohn, and we consider that the money was well spent by the Government considering the amount of good that people have received. It is true that he did not have an opportunity to do more in the Privy Council, but it was due to the delay in organizing the council according to the original plan. After release from the government service, his going or remaining depends upon his own free will, and the Government has no right to determine this. It is, however, our responsibility to decide whether or not he should be reengaged. If the people realize the importance of national progress and enlightenment, they must direct their efforts in that direction, and when they are successful in it, it will not be necessary for the Privy Council or any other department of the Government to have advisers.

The negative reply served only to intensify the campaign by the club members to keep Jaisohn in Korea. On April 30, a mass meeting was held outside Seoul's Southgate, and a resolution, to be presented to the Minister of Foreign Affairs urging the reinstatement of Dr. Jaisohn was adopted. Letter to the Minister read:

We, the undersigned, have been authorized by a mass meeting of the citizens of Seoul to present to Your Excellency the request that Koreans fully realizing the benefit of the instruction of former Adviser to the Privy Council, Dr. Jaisohn, wish him to continue it. They have been informed that before long he will leave this country for America. People of Korea believe that his departure from our country will be a serious loss to Korea, but they have no means of dissuading him. Therefore, they respectfully request Your Excellency to communicate with the American Minister, informing him with the unanimous desire of our people to have Dr. Jaisohn remain in our land and continue his work as the instructor of the people. We are persuaded that if the Minister realizes our desire and lends his influence, a way may be found to cause Dr. Jaisohn to reconsider his decision to leave Korea.

Choi Jongsik
Chung Hakmo
Yi Seungman (Syngman Rhee)
Committee

The mass meeting also adopted a resolution appealing to Dr. Jaisohn to remain in Korea and to continue his work. The lengthy communication contained three main points.

Firstly, his leaving the Korean people implied that he had no regard for the land where he was born. This was patently untrue, but he chose to let time reveal the truth.

Secondly, severing his connection with the Korean people might be construed as a decision not to reciprocate the kindness which the King had shown him. This was an illusion on their part as the Council of State had merely carried out the King's order.

Thirdly, if he had any sympathy for the wretched condition of the Koreans, he would not contemplate leaving them so abruptly before completing the work he so admirably commenced.

Should he, therefore, insist upon carrying out his intention of leaving them, the Korean people would be greatly disappointed, and some might think that he was placing his own interest above that of the 20 million Koreans.

Jaisohn regarded this as an emotional expression of his friends, who were overcome by their reluctance to see him go. Hence, in his reply, Jaisohn avoided lengthy comments on these points. After expressing his deep gratitude to the citizens assembled at the mass meeting for their expression of appreciation for his work, he assured them that 'his leaving was due to circumstances entirely beyond his control,' that if they knew them, they would realize that he wished to remain in Korea as much as they did, that his bowing to the inevitable in no way implied his lack of concern for 'Korea and the Koreans', and that he trusted them to carry on the work he had begun among them, adding: "If you stand united and persist in it, you are bound to succeed."

Jaisohn was amused at the naivety of his followers to think that the King was unhappy about his decision to leave and that the American Minister would lend his assistance for Jaisohn's reinstatement. Though at the time he had no evidence, he could not dispel the feeling that he had played an active part in his dismissal. Later he learned that his feeling was a fact. His followers' intimation that he had no regard for the land of his birth saddened him, for he felt that 'he had sacrificed more than anyone alive for Korea's sake.' But, treating them as sincere but overreacting friends, he deeply regretted leaving them.

After long cogitation, Jaisohn reached the reluctant decision to go. The Foreign Minister turned down the appeal by the mass meeting of citizens for his reinstatement. As has been noted, there was no other way in which he could make a living and at the same time lead the *Independence Club* as well as edit *The Independent*. His enemies were forcing his newspaper staff into resigning, while the Government withdrew permission to deliver his paper by the postal service. Threats against his life were stepped up, making his wife's life unbearable. Meanwhile, Horace Allen, the American Minister, joined some of the missionaries who advised him to return to the United States for 'your own good,' since Korea was far from ready for the reform he advocated, he was wasting his time. He thought it strange that all of those professing to offer him their advice as his 'friends' were close to the King.

What finally led him to the decision to leave was a cablegram addressed to Mrs. Jaisohn, informing her that her mother in Washington D.C. was gravely ill. He could not deny a dying woman the pleasure of seeing her daughter; since his wife would not return to the United States by herself, he had to go with her.

Once the decision had been made, Jaisohn was philosophical. Not only were there, but he also reasoned to himself, a number of able and dedicated leaders such as Yun Chi-ho, Yi Sang-jae, Namkung Uk, Chong Kyo and Yi Seung-man to carry on his work; standing behind them were 10,000 members of the *Club* as well of hundreds of thousands of readers of *The Independent*. Also ready to render help were such foreign friends as Henry Appenzeller and Homer Hulbert. Thus, reasoning to himself, he turned to his mundane affairs. His immediate worry was financial. Although the Government had paid up his salary for the remainder of his contract, it was an insignificant sum compared to his actual needs. Having accumulated no savings, he needed a considerable sum of money in order to buy passage to America and tide them over until he resumed his medical practice or became established in other ways.

It is said that at that point, Yun Chi-ho came along and asked if Jaisohn would sell *The independent*, that Yun was somewhat taken aback by Jaisohn's offer to sell it for five thousand won, and that perhaps Yun had hoped that Jaisohn would turn the paper over to him gratis. It is, further, said that since Yun did not have the money, he urged ex-Premier Sim Sang-hoon to buy it, convert it into a government newspaper and let him manage it. Be that as it might, the fact is that Jaisohn refused to let it fall into the Government's hand. Instead, he arranged the establishment of a company known as the Triangle Press, to be jointly owned by Appenzeller, Hulbert and himself, which would publish the *Independent* and presumably other publications. How much or whether he received any cash from the other two partners is not known. Yun was made its editor at a salary reportedly of seven hundred fifty dollars a year.

Jaisohn continued to edit *The Independent* till the last minute. In addition, on learning that many of the Korean students in Japan who had been sent by the Government were in dire financial straits due to the Government's failure to support them, he raised relief funds for them, which he took with him to Japan and handed over to Yi Ha-yong, Korean Minister to Japan, to be distributed among needy youths.

Shortly before takeoff, he published a farewell message in *The Independent*, which was in part as follows.

> On the eve of my departure from Korea, I may perhaps be permitted to say a few parting words to the readers of The Independent. After considerable negotiations, we have been

fortunate enough to secure for a year the services of Yu Chi-ho. The company congratulates itself on securing the services of one so well equipped for the work now devolving upon him, and I bespeak for him the same cordial support that he has so generously given to me. Mr. Yun is a staunch supporter of the progressive movement in Korea, loyal and patriotic, and enters upon his new duties with the purpose of advancing the welfare of his country.

On the Road to Exile (Down but Not Out)

At 11:00 a.m., May 14, 1898, Jaisohn, accompanied by his wife, left Seoul, Korea for the second time. His first exile had been following a violent attempt at reform of Korea. This time he was being forced out of his native land, although he tried his best to effect reform through peaceful means. He could not know that he was to have a third chance 50 years later. Hundreds of well-wishers - government officials, foreign dignitaries, members of the *Independence Club* as well as of *Hyopsong Hoe* (Mutual Encouragement Association) - turned out to bid him goodbye. To them, he bade *"Chal kesio"* (farewell) and exhorted them to continue their endeavor to strengthen the foundation of Korea's independence and sacrifice their all, if necessary, to help make Korea the land of freedom, equality and prosperity. As he spoke, tears welled up in his eyes and his voice quavered. Many in the crowd wept, while a representative of the *Independence Club* responded with words of appreciation for all he had done, assured him that his advice would not be forgotten and expressed the fervent hope that he would soon return.

In Japan, his departure for America was delayed for a few weeks due to a lack of space on the ship on which he had hoped to sail. He spent the time visiting with some of the Korean students there. He also met with a number of Japanese leaders who assured him that Japan's interest in Korea was trade and nothing else.

Upon arriving in Washington D.C., Jaisohn and his wife hurried to her mother's home expecting to find her gravely ill. On the contrary, and to their abject amazement, she was well and happy. In response to the remark that they hurried back as soon as they could following the receipt of communication telling of her illness, her mother said with understandable feelings: "Why, I am hale and hearty!"

It was then that Jaisohn realized that he had been the victim of a ruse. In the ensuing weeks, he was to learn of a frantic international scheme involving some very prominent personages to get him out of Korea. One day he was happily surprised to see Karl Waeber, former Russian Minister in Seoul. He was now stationed in Mexico City, as Russia's Minister to Mexico, and he was on a visit to Washington D.C. From him, Jaisohn learned how de Speyer, his successor in Seoul, Horace Allen, his American counterpart there, and King Kojong had worked hand in glove to force Jaisohn out of Korea.

At first, according to Waeber, Allen 'conveyed' to the State Department King Kojong's desire to have Jaisohn recalled to the United States, while de Speyer contacted Count Cassini, Czarist Minister in Washington D.C., reportedly asking him to use his influence for the same end. However, since it was impossible for the United States to recall one of its citizens from a foreign country who was innocent of any crime, President Theodore Roosevelt, was reported as advising Cassini to employ a more subtle means. According to Waeber, Cassini discussed the matter with his daughter. The latter, who had been acquainted with the president's daughter, Alice, reportedly took up the matter with the president's daughter. This decision they reached was to induce Captain White, Mrs. Jaisohn's step-father, to send her a telegram notifying her of her mother's 'grave illness' as a ruse. Also at Captain White's behest, one of Mrs. Jaisohn's relatives wrote to her advising that if she wished to see her mother alive again, she would have to return soon.

In the physical sense, Jaisohn's expulsion from Korea was a liberation. In America, he was in no danger of bodily harm. Being a licensed physician, he did not have to worry about making a living. Mentally, however, Jaisohn was still a captive of Korea. Whenever he was alone, his mind was in Korea.

- How was *The Independent* faring?
- Would his enemies who had driven him out of the country try to destroy the *Independent Club* also?
- Would the foreign powers continue their intrigues to the detriment of all?
- Or would they allow Koreans to build up their country into a viable, enlightened and constitutional nation, free from foreign domination, but friendly and cooperative with all?

Fortunately, there was something to take his mind off Korea. In April 1898, a month before Jaisohn left Korea, the Spanish-American War had broken out. An epidemic of yellow fever had spread among U.S. forces in Cuba, and Dr. Walter Reed had been appointed chairman of a committee to deal with the problem, to investigate the cause of the disease and to find its cure. On arrival in Washington D.C., Jaisohn was told that Reed, his former mentor and colleague, had been looking for him and had wanted him to join a team of bacteriologists and doctors he had set up. It was too late for Jaisohn to join the Reed team, but since the war was still in progress, he decided to enlist. Although the war was over by the time he was inducted, the Army assigned him to the S.S. Hodge, a hospital transport ship faring the wounded from Cuba to the United States. Caring for them so preoccupied him that he had no time to miss Korea.

In December that year, he became a civilian again. Before his discharge, he had his medical license renewed. However, before resuming practice, he received an offer to conduct medical research from the prestigious Wister Institute of Anatomy and Biology of the University of Pennsylvania. This was an opportunity he could not afford to miss, and so he moved to Philadelphia.

Photo: Middle-aged Philip Jaisohn working as a medical researcher at the Wistar Institute of the University of Pennsylvania (1899-1905).

His Sense of Duty Toward Korea.

In 1905 he resigned the research position and entered business in partnership with an old schoolmate of his at Harry Hillman Academy, dealing with printing and office equipment. Off-hand, one might view his apparently shifting career - from medical practice to reformist crusade to pathological research to a printing business - as illustrative of restlessness. However, looking at the course of his life from the perspective of years, this writer is persuaded that 'it was a torturous life's journey of a man of destiny.' To be sure, he was deeply interested in pathological research, and the Wister Institute offered him economic security. However, he was no less interested in the cause of his fellow men. Indeed, when his personal interests conflicted with that of his fellow men, he always placed the latter ahead of the former. When in his teens, Kim Ok-kiun invited him to go to Japan as a member of the first student group, explaining that Korea was entering upon a new era and that she would need the services of those educated in modern learning, he accepted it in spite of the fact that such a venture might well prove dangerous to his career.

Again, when in 1895, Pak Yong-hyo called on him in Washington D.C. and told him that Korea needed a man of his qualifications, Jaisohn shelved his promising medical career and returned to Korea forthwith. What led him to shift from research to business, for which he had neither training nor experience, was, it seems, a rekindling in him of 'a sense of an unfinished mission for Korea.'

Between 1898, when he returned to America, and 1905, his contact with Korea was sporadic at best. Until the end of the year of his return, Yun Chi-ho wrote him occasionally, but after their demolition of the *Independence Club* and closing of *The Independent*, Yun took the Mayoral Position of *Wonsan* and left Seoul and stopped writing. No one else wrote him either. His only sources of news about Korea were Kim Kiu-sik, one of his followers whom he had encouraged to come to

America and was enrolled at Roanoke College and Ahn Chang-ho, who was a member of the *Independence Club* and organizer of its *Pyongyang* branch. He, too, had come to United States and was in California. They wrote him occasionally, reporting that conditions in Korea were worsening, but assuring him that what he had done for Korea would surely bear fruit eventually.

The Visit of Syngman Rhee and Yun Pyong-ku

One day in 1905, two of his proteges paid him an unexpected visit. One was Yi Seung-man (Syngman Rhee) and the other was Yun Pyong-ku. Both men had been students of Jaisohn's at *Bae-Jae* Academy. While Yun went on to study for the ministry and subsequently went to Hawaii as a Methodist preacher and interpreter for Korean laborers on the islands, Rhee joined Jaisohn's *Independence Club* and soon became a leader of its radical wing. During the tumultuous final days of the *Club*'s existence, Rhee was arrested and sentenced to a life term. However, at the start of the Russo-Japanese War (1904-1905) he was released from *Hansung* Prison and with the help of his missionary friends, came to America for study.

Before leaving for America, Rhee called on two of Korea's most highly respected leaders, ex-Prime Minister Han Kyu-sol and General Min Yong-hwan. Both were close friends of Dr. Jaisohn. These men were deeply worried about the fate of Korea. They were convinced that regardless of which side won the war - and they were sure of Japan's victory - Korea would be the loser. However, since Korea was already under Japan's strangle-hole, Koreans at home were powerless to do anything to prevent Japan's seizure of their country. As soon as the war had broken out, the Government of Korea declared neutrality, but Japan poured its troops into Korea, and Japanese agents took virtual control over the Korean Government. Therefore, they told Rhee to contact Jaisohn on his arrival in the United States and enlist his help in persuading the President of the United States to invoke the Korean-American Treaty of 1882 which committed the United States to the independence of Korea.

Photo: People of *Pyongyang* watching the Japanese army enter the city during the Russo-Japanese War (Koreans are all wearing white clothes). (1904)

In late November 1904, Rhee arrived in Honolulu, partly in order to alert the Koreans in Hawaii to the imminent downfall of Korea and partly to raise money for his own use. That night he met the Reverend Yun Pyong-ku, his old friend at *Bae-Jae* Academy, and other Korean leaders in Hawaii, and during their nearly all-night session, decided that the 4,000 Koreans in Hawaii should represent their compatriots in their homeland in the struggle for Korea's independence, and to employ all possible means toward that end. The next day Rhee resumed his journey, richer by $30, which the local Koreans presented to him, and on New Year's Eve he arrived in Washington D.C. Shortly thereafter he entered George Washington University.

Meanwhile, the Koreans in Hawaii, pursuant to the decision reached at the conference with Syngman Rhee in attendance, held a mass meeting and voted to present a petition to President Theodore Roosevelt requesting him to adhere to the 1882 Korean-American Treaty commitment to preserve the independence of Korea. Simultaneously, they chose Yun and Rhee to present their petition in the name of the entire Korean people.

Now, the problem confronting them was how to go about presenting it to the President of the United States in person. They knew that unless it was delivered in person, it would be either ignored or lost in Washington's bureaucratic maze. Finally, their will showed the way. The Reverend John W. Wadman, District Superintendent of the Methodist Church in Hawaii was a personal friend of the Governor of Hawaii at the time. In late spring of 1905, it was announced that the peace conference ending the Russo-Japanese War would be held in Portsmouth, NH with the President Roosevelt as the mediator. At about the same time, the Koreans learned that Secretary of War William H. Taft, who was leaving on a tour of the Orient, would be a guest of the Governor. Yun called on the Reverend Wadman and told him that if Wadman gave him an urgent note introducing Yun to the Governor asking him to prevail upon Taft to grant the Korean pastor an audience, the Koreans in Hawaii would enthusiastically join the Methodist Church.

Wadman could not pass up the opportunity to serve his church and complied with Yun's request. The Governor, in turn, gave Yun a note of introduction to Taft, and the letter granted Yun an audience. Yun brought Korea's plight to Taft's attention and asked his help in obtaining an appointment with President Roosevelt in order that he could submit in person the petition of the Koreans in Hawaii. To Yun's surprise, Taft gave him a note of introduction to the President, asking that the bearer of his note be given a brief audience. It is a mystery why Taft, who was on his way to Japan on Roosevelt's instruction to sign the secret agreement with Katsura, Japan's Premier, handing over Korea, in effect, to Japan, saw fit to give Yun the note of introduction to his chief. Was it a sop to the Korean people?

Unaware of what the Roosevelt-Taft team was up to with respect to their country, the Koreans in Hawaii were jubilant and raised the expenses of the Rhee-Yun mission out of their meager daily wages of $1.25. With the note of introduction from Taft to the President of the United States and the travel fund in his hand, Yun hurried to Washington D.C. There he and Rhee prepared a rough draft of the petition to President Roosevelt and went on to Philadelphia to call on Jaisohn and obtain his help in finalizing the partition.

Photo: President Theodore Roosevelt

Photo: William Taft.

Photo: Katsura Taro.

The three had an emotional reunion. Rhee briefed his mentor on the developments in Korea since Jaisohn was forced out of the country. Yun gave him a report on the Korean contract laborers in Hawaii. They wished to hear about Jaisohn's life in America since his return to his country, but in view of the urgency of their mission, they explained to him the purpose of the visit and produced the draft of the petition to Roosevelt. Jaisohn was pleased to be of help in putting it in its final shape.

Rhee and Yun returned to New York and changing into their rented frock coats and silk hats, rode in a carriage to Sagamore Hill, the

Roosevelt home in Oyster Bay, NY. They were duly received by the President. He was ebulliently friendly and said: "What can I do for you?" The youthful Korean 'diplomats,' forgetting their carefully prepared and rehearsed statements, stammered a few incoherent words and presented the petition. The President refused to receive it, saying protocol required that it be first submitted to the State Department by the Korean Minister to Washington D.C. In a minute or two the meeting ended with the President bidding them "Goodbye, Gentlemen."

Photo: Yun Pyong-ku dressed in suits to meet President Theodore Roosevelt (1905).

The Koreans hurried to the Korean Legation in Washington D.C. and asked Kim Yun-jong, Korean Minister, for his cooperation. However, the latter declined on the ground that he was not authorized to present the petition to the U.S. State Department unless it was sent to him by the Korean Government in Seoul. Needless to say, Kim had already been bought off by Japan with the knowledge of the Roosevelt administration, and the buck-passing between him, the State Department and the President had been prearranged. Rhee and Yun, angry and crestfallen, argued and cajoled with Kim, but to no avail. They went back to Philadelphia to unburden their bitter disappointment to Jaisohn. Jaisohn wrote Minister Kim, reminding him of his moral duty to Korea and suggesting that he simply give Rhee and Yun a letter of introduction to the Secretary of State without mentioning the memorandum. In view of the aforementioned collusion between the Korean Minister, Secretary of State and the President, Jaisohn's letter was, of course, in vain.

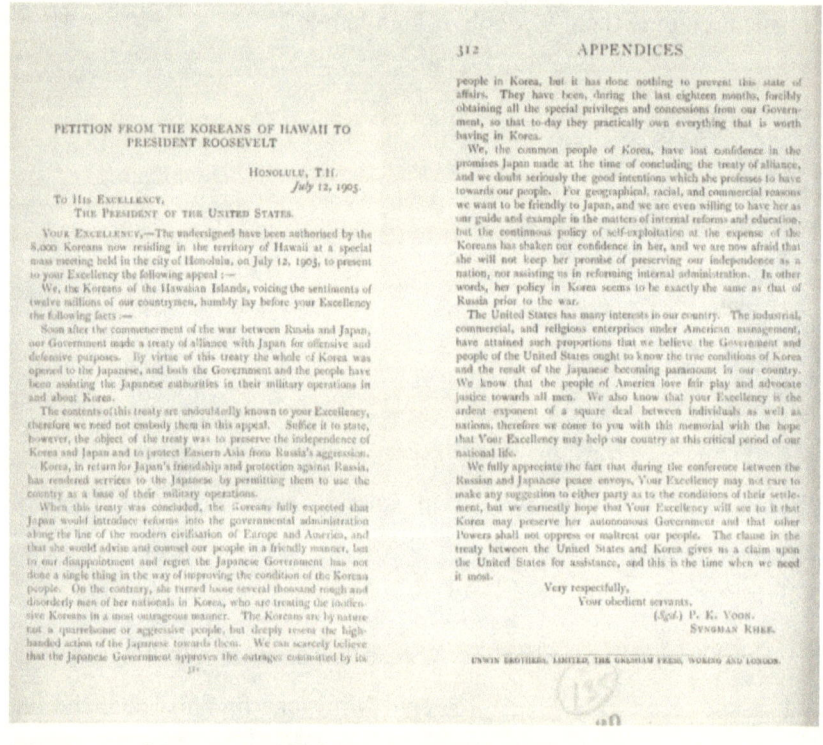

Photo: Petition to President Theodore Roosevelt, from Fred A. McKenzie's book, The Tragedy of Korea (1908).

(**Editor's Note**: Katsura-Taft Agreement between U.S. Secretary of War William Taft and Japanese Prime Minister Katsura Taro signed on July 29, 1905 mutually recognized U.S. control over the Philippines and

Japan's control over Korea. The contents of this record were not revealed to the public until 1924.)

Looking Forward to the Next Opportunity

Despite the failure of the reunion mission, Jaisohn was deeply impressed by the will and resourcefulness of the Korean people in their fight for their country's liberty. What Kim Kiu-sik and Ahn Chang-ho had told him was true; the seed of love for independence he had sown in Korea did not die out. Given encouragement and help, there was no doubt in his mind that they would eventually achieve their goal. He decided that it was his duty to give all the help he could. On pondering how best he could be of help to the land of his birth, he came to these realizations.

- First, what he called his failure in Korea a decade earlier had been mainly due to his dependence on the Korean Government financially, and he had to rely on his own resources should another opportunity to serve Korea present itself.

- Secondly, in order to be so prepared, it was necessary that he find a way in which he could make himself financially independent. The position he held at the Wister Institute brought him an income commensurate with his highly-rated qualifications and was sufficient to afford him a comfortable living.

- However, it was obvious that it would not enable him to accumulate enough savings to make him financially independent for the purpose he had in mind.

Accordingly, though he was reluctant to give up his connection with the University of Pennsylvania, he decided to enter business in partnership with a classmate, Harold Deemer, of his at Harry Hillman Academy, dealing in printing and office equipment. His business was successful from the beginning and in 10 years it grew to be in its category an important enterprise in the city of Philadelphia.

With an initial combined capital of five thousand dollars between himself and his partner, they built it up to the level of one hundred and fifty thousand dollars in value. They began with one female clerk in a small room of an office building but later employed over 50 employees and moved to a larger place, occupying an entire building on one of the best streets in the City of Brotherly Love (Philadelphia). Later still, they expanded their business to two other cities in Pennsylvania, and Jaisohn managed the Philadelphia end of it while his partner took charge of the branch establishments in Scranton and Wilkes Barre. Jaisohn said later, though commerce was not his line originally, he found buying and selling and financing very interesting.

That is not surprising. A man of versatility as well as of ability to inspire the confidence of others, he made friends with a host of people of different walks of life, both ordinary and influential. How highly he was regarded was evidenced by the fact that for years he served as Treasurer of the Business Association of Philadelphia. Among his friends were Thomas Smith, Mayor of Philadelphia, and Reverend Floyd W. Tompkins, Minister of one of the largest churches in Philadelphia, who were instrumental in helping Jaisohn make the Korean Congress of Philadelphia, April, 1919, a phenomenal success. Dr. Tompkins delivered an address of welcome before the *Congress*, enthusiastically supporting Korea's independence. Afterward, he gave support for Korea with action by heading up the Friends of Korea Association as President.

Mayor Smith, at Jaisohn's request, virtually opened the door of Philadelphia to the Koreans attending the Congress by placing the Independence Hall at their disposal and enabling them to hold a parade on one of the main streets of the city. On the third and final day of the Korean Congress two hundred Koreans, led by the Philadelphia Police Band, marched to the Independence Hall with tens of thousands of the city's residents watching. There Jaisohn, as President of the Congress, presided over the last session during which he requested Syngman Rhee to read the Korean Declaration of Independence.

Looking back, one may deem it providential that Jaisohn's change of career from pathological research to business not only led him to win such prominent and sympathetic friends as those mentioned above but also enabled him to devote years to promote the cause of Korea's liberation. Till the end of World War I, he led a busy life engaging in such activities as treasurer of the Business Association, noted above, as a member of the National (U.S.) Security League, the purpose of which was to raise funds to be loaned to the Allied Powers in order to help finance their war effort, and as a mason. Some Koreans who called on him in those days, just out of curiosity to have a glimpse of the 'legendary warrior of Korean independence,' thought he was uninterested in the Korean people. They were wrong. They expected him to sit in front of them like a museum piece, but he was too busy preparing for another hoped-for chance to serve Korea.

Philadelphia Emergency Meeting of Korean Expatriates

The news which brought to an abrupt end of Jaisohn's successful business life reached him in a fragmentary, desultory manner. One morning in late March (1919), while reading the paper, he came upon a terse report from Chefoo, China, that a revolt against Japan had broken out in Korea. Vague though the news was, he found it too intriguing to ignore and contacted the newspaper office. He was told that no further details of the news had come in, but that he would be notified should there be any. He received no call from the newspaper office that day, but the next day's paper published an article by a Canadian missionary, Percival Schofield. He gave an eye-witness account of demonstrations by the Koreans for independence from Japan, which had taken place on March 1. As ex-premier Han Kyu-sol and General Min Yong-hwan had foreseen, Japan took de facto control over Korea following her victory over Russia in 1905, and in 1910 she formally annexed the peninsular Kingdom. But the Korean people never accepted the Japanese rule and encouraged by President Woodrow Wilson's call for peace under the principle of national self-determination, they declared their intention to be free in a nationwide peaceful demonstration on March first.

Jaisohn checked the report with the State Department in Washington D.C. and found it to be true. He later described his state of mind at that moment in these words.

> It was very hard to describe my feelings at that time. I was thrilled to learn that the Korean people had the courage to defy their oppressors in the face of almost sure death. I also was proud because it demonstrated the fact that the Korean race is not of a decadent or degenerate type. I also felt the seed of the

love of freedom which I tried to sow in their minds through my newspaper and lectures during the years 1896 through 1898 might have germinated under the brutal oppression of the Japanese usurpers. If it had, I resolved to do everything in my power to help achieve their just aspirations.

He immediately got in touch with Korean leaders in the United States. Among them were Syngman Rhee and Min Chan-ho of Hawaii, who were attending a convention of the League of Small Nations in New York; Lee Dai-wi of San Francisco, who had just replaced An Chang-ho as President of the Korean National Association in America (KNA); Yu Il-han (유일환), known as the 'King of Bean Sprouts' (He had founded a bean sprouts producing company in Detroit named the La Choy Co.); and Chung Han-kyong, author of The Case of Korea. They were delighted because some of them were trying to get in touch with him.

The electrifying news of the independence movement, which was subsequently called *Samil Wundong* (March First Movement) had reached the *KNA* headquarters on March 9 and on March 15 an emergency meeting of the *KNA* representatives from the mainland United States, Hawaii and Mexico had been held in Los Angeles. One of its decisions was to appoint Jaisohn as adviser on liaison with the American people. However, due to a mix-up in communications, the notice of the appointment failed to reach Jaisohn. Later, it was discovered that Jaisohn's office staff, unable to read Korean, had thought it was prankish mail and discarded it.

At any rate, Jaisohn immediately made a proposal in order to offer the maximum support to their compatriots at home. He proposed:

- an all-people's congress of Koreans in America, Hawaii and Mexico, and
- that this congress should be convened at the soonest possible time.

All the Korean leaders concurred and asked Jaisohn if he would assume the responsibility for arranging such a congress. Jaisohn accepted it and immediately went to work on it.

He called on his friend Thomas Smith, Mayor of Philadelphia, and after informing him of the rise of an independence movement in Korea, of the decision of the Korean leaders in the United States to offer every possible support to their countrymen at home, and of their requests that he arrange a Congress of the Korean people in America, Hawaii and Mexico, he asked the Mayor if he would help convene it in Philadelphia. The Mayor of the historic city opened it to him.

The conference, officially named the First Korean Congress, was held in 'the Little Theater' at 17th and Delancey Streets in Philadelphia on April 14-16, 1919, with 200 Koreans from various parts of America, Hawaii and Mexico in attendance. The modes of travel then, which were primitive compared with those of today, in view of the short notice (only 10 days), and remembering that most Koreans were laborers, the turnout was little short of a miracle. One out of four of the entire Korean population, or virtually all the male adults, were present. All the leading personages participated in the Congress, except Ahn Chang-ho, who had just left for Shanghai, seat of the Korean Provisional Government in exile. The delegates unanimously elected Jaisohn President of the

Congress, and he immediately set its tone: Korea's liberation was in the best interest of the United States, and the latter would support it, if the American people were but informed of the will and ability of the Koreans to be free. In a brief but eloquent acceptance speech he said, which was in part as follows:

> You all know that I am a naturalized citizen of this country. While my heart and my soul are with you, and while I will do anything within my capacity to help you and counsel with you, there is one point where I have to stop. Having taken the oath of allegiance to the Constitution of the United States, if there should be any occasion during the sessions of this Congress in words or acts, either intentional or unintentional, which in the slightest degree would be in conflict with interest or laws of the United States, I will step down. With that understanding, if you keep me as your presiding officer, I will discharge the duties to the best of my ability.

To those words, Syngman Rhee, who had been notified of his election as the head of the Provisional Government of the Republic of Korea only days before his arrival at the Congress, responded:

> That is understood. In fact, we don't want any man to preside over this Congress unless he is above all a 100% loyal American. It is indeed of peculiar interest that the aims and aspirations of the Korean people are identical with those of the President of the United States in seeking to form with our allies a League of Nations. Therefore, Mr. President, on behalf of all the delegates

assembled here, I assure you that we understand the situation clearly and have elected you as our presiding officer, to discharge the duties of your high position with the understanding that you are first of all, an American citizen, and that you will help us to espouse our cause.

The Congress was notable in several respects.

First, it clearly identified its chief interest, the independence of Korea, with the interest of the United States. To be sure, the concept of national self-determination evident in the Fourteen Points of President Wilson placed the United States squarely BEHIND Korean aspiration for independence. However, national interests born of the higher moral laws are dependent on 'political animals' for their implementation and under their influence they usually result in ones that are at best 'amoral.' The participants at the Congress were soon to realize this. As Wilson decided that Japan's cooperation was more important for the establishment of the League of Nations than Korean independence, he ignored a personal letter from Rhee appealing his help for Korea and instructed the State Department not to issue Rhee's visa application to attend the Peace Conference in Paris.

Secondly, the Congress was highly religious. It was opened with a prayer for divine guidance. All the speakers were either laymen with strong religious convictions or clergymen, and the man on whom Jaisohn relied for assistance the most was the Reverend Dr. Floyd Tompkins, a prominent Episcopal Minister in Philadelphia. Yet, in spite of all the display of religious fervor, the Congress was boycotted by representatives of every denomination which had missionaries in Korea. They had sent out missionaries to preach the heathens not to fear the devil, but they feared the Japanese. Jaisohn and his aides were bitterly disappointed as they had done their best to secure their moral support. Later, to his missionary friends who came to visit him on their furlough in America and counseled patience with the reminder that God knew the trials of the Korean people, he said: "God is too slow."

Thirdly, the Congress was boycotted by not only church leaders but also representatives of the U.S. Government. Not even a message of good wishes by any official of the State Department arrived. Although President Wilson had prevented the Korean Delegation from attending the Peace Conference in Paris, the leaders of the Philadelphia Congress were confident that the administration, headed by the man who had not only electrified the world with the call for national self-determination by all, but had denounced Japan's oppression of Korea, would at least show a gesture of support.

In spite of the lack of support from Washington and the religious establishments, the participants in the Congress were cheered by the genuine hospitality showered on them by the City of Philadelphia, the press, and civic leaders of the historic city. The Mayor gave the Koreans permission to hold their concluding session in the Independence Hall. On the 16th of April, as the delegates marched in procession to Independence Hall, a torrential April shower burst upon them, but the city's police band and escort of the mounted police more than offset the disheartening effect of the freakish downpour. As the flag-waving delegates marched on braving the heavy shower, tens of thousands of Philadelphians lining the streets applauded.

In fact, the results of the Congress were far-reaching. A number of U.S. Senators were moved to register their support for Korea's cause in the Congressional Record. The Federal (now National) Council of the Churches of Christ in America launched an inquiry into Japanese atrocities against the Korean people, and the establishments of religious bodies sought to reassure the Korean people that their apparent neutral stance was only to avoid jeopardizing their missionary work in Korea.

If the Congress succeeded to a remarkable degree in winning Philadelphia support for Korea's cause, the Koreans attending it were far less successful in forging unity among themselves. For a while it appeared that they would leave the Congress with their old feud intensified. In brief, the dispute was between the partisans of Syngman Rhee and those of Ahn Chang-ho, with the rest leaning to one side or the other. Ahn supporters accused Rhee of avarice, opportunism and dictatorial tendencies. Rhee and his followers charged that the Ahn faction with factionalism and jealousy. Adding to their dispute were two recent developments.

A month before the rise of the independence movement in Korea, Syngman Rhee, on his own, had submitted to President Wilson a memorandum proposing a trusteeship for Korea by the League of Nations. His critics, contending that it was anachronistic to take such a position at a time when a tide of nationalist movement was sweeping the world, called for his apology to the people. The other incident was Ahn Chang-ho's precipitate departure for the Far East upon receipt of the news of the uprising from Korea. Rheeites asserted that Ahn's intention was to go to China ahead of others and grab the leadership of the provisional government, which was being organized in Shanghai. Actually, Ahn had left for China with a strong doubt about the timeliness of establishing a formal provisional regime, although he accepted the ministership of labor in the government and gave financial support to it. His main interest was in a stepped-up preparation for independence through education of the children of the emigre Koreans in China and Siberia and the encouragement of industrialization by emigres.

Photo: In front of Independence Hall in Philadelphia. To the left of Philip Jaisohn stand Syngman Rhee and Yun Pyong-ku. (April 16, 1919)

Photo: In front of Independence Hall in Philadelphia. (April 1919)

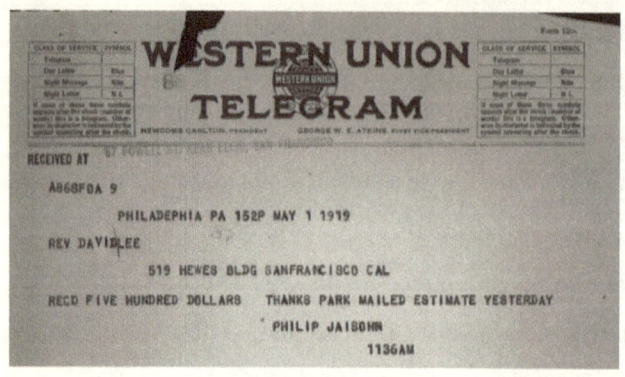

Photo: Telegram confirming David Lee sent $500 to Philip Jaisohn (1919)

Adviser to the Provisional Government

Jaisohn, in a lengthy session with Rhee, Lee Dae-wi and other leaders, warned that unless they worked together in cooperation, Korea's cause was doomed, and they would be held responsible by the people of Korea. Finally, a compromise was reached whereby the Korean National Association would undertake the sole responsibility to raise funds for all activities in connection with the independence movement. The *KNA* in turn would support Rhee's premiership, and a bureau of information on Korea would be set up in Philadelphia with Jaisohn as its director. In the name of the *KNA* Lee Dae-wi pledged eight hundred dollars per month for support of the bureau's activities and the same amount for the Provisional Government.

Jaisohn immediately established an office in the Weightman Building, Philadelphia, calling it the Bureau of Information for the Republic of Korea, and assumed the publication of the Korea Review, which had been started some months earlier by a group of Korean students in Ohio. Simultaneously, Jaisohn launched a campaign to organize the League of Friends of Korea, beginning with its Philadelphia chapter, which came into being on May 16, at the City Club, to which Dr. Tompkins had invited interested Philadelphians. The attendants chose the Reverend Dr. Floyd W. Tompkins to serve as President. This was followed by a big rally in support of Korea held in Philadelphia under the League's sponsorship. At Jaisohn's invitation, Senator William E. Borah, a powerful critic of Japan, was the main speaker at the rally. Present also was a silent observer - Ransford Miller, director of the Korea Division of the State Department. Personally, he found Jaisohn's argument too persuasive not to be sympathetic. However, the U.S. policy was to appease Japan in order to win her support for the League of Nations. Miller had accepted Jaisohn's invitation to the rally on the condition that he would not be asked to speak. The League of Nations was Wilson's answer to how he would 'end all wars.' But he did not answer how the League, participated in as an important member by an expansionist power, could ensure world peace.

Jaisohn traveled from coast to coast, addressing scores of meetings on Japan's menace to the entire Far East, writing articles on it and buttonholing Senators, Congressmen and State Department officials. Within a year, ten chapters of the League of Friends of Korea were organized in various parts of the United States and in England. Among the supporters of Korea's Independence were Senators Borah, G.W. Norris, H. Cabot Lodge, chairman of the Senate Foreign Relations Committee, and Charles S. Thomas.

For the remainder of the year following the Philadelphia Congress, things moved along smoothly. The *KNA* fulfilled its promise of financial support for the Information Bureau. Jaisohn, in a spirit of cooperation with Rhee, served concurrently as adviser to the Korean Commission in Washington D.C., which Rhee had established, and the latter promised to support the Bureau in Philadelphia. Below the surface, however, the unity reached in Philadelphia gradually eroded.

The *KNA*, without the dynamic leadership of Ahn Chang-ho, was unable to secure sustained support of rank and file Koreans. To compound its difficulty, Rhee on his own initiative and without the approval of the legislature of the Provisional Government in Shanghai, issued Korean 'Independence' bonds in the amount of $5,000,000 and ordered all Koreans in the United States to purchase them. Under the Philadelphia agreement, the *KNA* had been empowered to act as the sole agent to raise funds for all activities in connection with Korea's independence movement. Furthermore, in August, 1919, Choe Jae-yong, Finance Minister of the Provisional Government, had commissioned the *KNA* to take charge of raising independence funds among Koreans in America. In the face of the competition between the *KNA* and the Korean Commission, some sent in their contributions to the *KNA*, some bought the bonds issued by the Commission, and others were disgusted and refused to do either.

Consequently, the *KNA* support for the Bureau of Information had decreased steadily during 1920. By the following year, the *KNA* was all but unable to meet its commitment, and Jaisohn was in trouble. Fortunately, in 1919, Jaisohn was appointed as the Provisional Government's adviser on Foreign Affairs, and Rhee was obliged to fill the gap in the Bureau's budget left by the *KNA* with income from the sale of Independence Bonds. Even so, the total amounts sent in by the two organizations were barely enough to pay the office rent, salaries of the clerical staff, and the cost of publishing Korea Review. Jaisohn served gratis and paid for his own travel expenses. Moreover, he had to hire help to take his place at his firm at his own expense. Gradually, the

Commission, too, failed to fulfill its pledge of support, and by April, 1921, he either had to cover most of the expenses of the Bureau out of his own pocket or close up shop. In a letter to a friend dated April 13, he wrote:

> As for our plans, they are at sea at the present time. Dr. Rhee cables from Shanghai that I must continue this work for the sake of the country, and all the people asked me to do the same, yet the Commission in Washington has cut off our financial support. It is very unfortunate that we should have this destructive influence working on us at this critical moment. The work in London is equally important. We have been doing certain work there in regard to the renewal of the Anglo-Japanese alliance question. If that work is cut off, the effect will be very serious.

The Korean Commission was from the beginning in anomaly at best. Now it was degenerating into a tool of private gain in the guise of patriotic services set up by Syngman Rhee after his election to the provisional Presidency. It was intended to function as the de facto diplomatic agency of the Korean Provisional Government in exile. Its title was the 'Korean Commission to America and Europe.' Since, as President, Rhee could not be his own diplomatic agent, he appointed Kim Kiu-sik to the Chairmanship of the Commission. Dr. Kim was an admirable choice, widely known and respected as a scholar and statesman. He had just arrived from Paris, where he represented Korea at the Peace Conference. In reality, however, the Commission was Rhee's personal property and its staff, beholden to him, all but ignored Dr. Kim.

Matters grew worse when Hyon Soon arrived on the scene from Shanghai in April 1920, styling himself as a representative of the Provisional Government. He wormed into Dr. Rhee's favor by pandering to the latter's vanity, and before long Rhee named him treasurer of the Commission. That summer, more than a year after Rhee was elected to the Provisional Presidency, he left for Shanghai, seat of the Provisional Government, and Hyon acted as though he were Rhee's deputy. Chairman Kim Kiu-sik could not take it any longer and left for the Far East. Hyon was made acting Chairman of the Commission, and in that capacity, he commenced his intrigue to make himself chairman in fact as well as in name, taking complete charge of the Commission's affairs - personnel, financial and diplomatic. Through flattery and promises of reward he won over Chung Han-kyong (Henry Chung), secretary of the Commission, to his side. There left two men whom he had either to conquer or get rid of: Fred A. Dolph, counselor, and Philip Jaisohn, Adviser to the Commission. Dolph was as good as 'dead' because he did not understand Korean. But Jaisohn was a problem. Hyon could not cross swords with this widely respected man openly. He could fool him as he did to Chung. But he found one weakness in Jaisohn. That was that Jaisohn was a foreigner. Hyon decided to eliminate him on the ground that Koreans should be self-reliant. That's what independence is all about, he told himself gleefully.

He stopped payment to the Bureau of Information and to its branch in London, through which Jaisohn was endeavoring to persuade the British government to terminate the Anglo-Japanese Alliance. He followed this with an announcement to Koreans through a circular to the effect that the Commission was closing the Bureau of Information in Philadelphia and its London office, that publication of Korea Review would be assumed by the Commission, and that Koreans who were fighting for their independence from Japan should learn to manage their affairs without relying on foreigners. While preaching self-reliance, he himself relied on a foreigner to help him gain absolute control of the Commission. Prior to the receipt of the circular, Lee Pyong-du had received the letter from Hyon in which the acting chairman of the Commission informed him of the Commission's takeover of Korea Review and asked him to come to Washington D.C. and work for the Commission at least for the summer.

Surprised by the news, Lee wrote Jaisohn inquiring what it was all about. Jaisohn immediately answered, saying he was vaguely aware of some 'funny stunts' being perpetrated at the Commission and advised Lee not to go to Washington D.C. 'until you hear from me.' The same day Lee received Jaisohn's letter, the Hyon circular arrived. Lee was so agitated by the circular that he dashed off a post-midnight letter of protest and warning to Hyon, pointing out that although Jaisohn was an American citizen, his love for Korea surpassed that of 'any of us.' He reminded him that he was committing a gross error by impugning Dr. Jaisohn's patriotism for Korea. He asked: "Who will edit Korea Review? Henry Chung?" He warned that if Chung became its editor, Koreans would have nothing to do with it because he and Rhee had committed an unpardonable mistake in 1919 by proposing that Korea be placed under the League of Nations trusteeship. And he went on: "Obviously you cannot edit it as you do not understand English." Advising Hyon not to go ahead with this scheme, he wrote: "I know what it takes to publish a magazine. Korea Review was started by four of us students in Ohio, and I served as its manager and secretary for five months until we turned it over to Dr. Jaisohn."

Hyon wrote an acerbic answer to Lee's letter. It began in Korean with: "Hyon Soon, who does not understand English, replies to Lee Pyong-du, the great doctor of English" and, after excoriating Lee for having lost the soul of Korea in a rambling style, ended with the warning: "If you write me again in English, I will tear it to pieces and throw it away."

Meanwhile, Jaisohn hurried down to Washington D.C. and made an investigation of the whole situation in the Commission. He revealed his finding in the letter to Lee dated April 18, 1921. It is worth quoting in whole:

I have yours of the 12th inst., together with the copy of your letter to Hyon. I found out the cause of the whole trouble down in Washington D.C. It is Hyon's desire to start a Legation at an enormous expense. It was opposed by Dolph (Counselor for the Commission), Chung and myself. In order to have money to carry out this scheme, he decided to discontinue our work in Philadelphia and Europe. I may tell you that the rent for the Legation is $300 per month, and the cost of maintenance and other expenses connected with it will perhaps be two or three times that much. In other words, his scheme will cost the Korean people a thousand dollars or more per month.

In order to be able to do this, he has cut out the other work. He has been intriguing the Shanghai Government by sending false reports that America is about to recognize Korea, and a Legation must be started at once. In his desperation to obtain funds, he took out $1,100 from the Commission last week by fraudulent methods. In this transaction, Chung was an unwitting accomplice.

I understand that Hyon asked for two signed checks from Chung for petty cash purposes. Chung unsuspectingly gave him the two checks with his signature on, and Hyon drew out $1,000 with one payable to himself and made out the other for $100 payable to J.H. Kim, his personal representative and adviser. He also went to the bank and told them that hereafter all the checks will be signed by himself without the counter signature of Chung, so that he will be in sole possession of all the money that belongs to the people.

Under the law we can prosecute him and have him put in jail tomorrow, but for the sake of Korea we want to remedy the evil by some quiet method. I have advised Chung and Dolph to notify the bank not to honor any checks signed by Hyon alone. Thus, we can conserve what little money they have down there until such time as when the matter can be straightened out.

The condition is so desperate that either the Government in Shanghai or the Korean people in this country will have to take drastic action to drive out this utterly dishonest person from the Commission. He is betraying his people, his country and his friends for the sake of having a luxurious home for himself and his comrade Kim. Incidentally, one American by the name of Stearn is instigating him to carry on this piracy so that Stearn himself will get some money out of the transaction. This is the report I have, and I have every reason to believe that it is true.

Chung has been working against me, but now he is in such a desperate position that he turned to me for help and advice. He has no sense, but at the same time he is not vicious or a thief like Hyon. In order to protect the money and property that belonged to the people, we will have to use Chung for the time being and let him obstruct Hyon's nefarious transactions.

Hyon has already signed the lease on the house. I do not know how he signed it, in whose name it was signed, but I hope the Korean people will not have to pay for it. We do not want to have this thing made public, but I think that people ought to know, so you may quietly tell the Koreans in Columbus the whole situation. Please do not let it get into the hands of Japanese agents or American newsmen.

I have advised Shanghai of the main facts of the case, but what they will do I do not know. If the Government will not do anything, then it will be desirable for the Koreans here and in Hawaii to take action immediately to avoid further damage to Korea.

Why the Reverend Hyon Soon, eloquent preacher of the gospel, stooped to such villainous conduct, and got himself tangled with the law is a mystery. Those who knew him characterized him variously as brilliant, ambitious, avaricious, and vainglorious. Perhaps he was something of all the above. The chairmanship of the Commission carried with it a great prestige and potentially fabulous wealth - the Independence Bonds - and his driving ambition for both led him to his undoing. On being told by Jaisohn in a direct confrontation that he had a choice of either quietly packing and leaving the Commission or facing prosecution and risk going to jail, the blustery acting Chairman of the Commission meekly resigned his position and left town. Curiously enough, although Rhee had nothing to do with Hyon's ouster, subsequently, the two became estranged and remained bitter enemies till the end.

Though Hyon's dismissal prevented further theft of the people's money deposited in the bank, the loss of the public's confidence in the Commission led to a drastic decrease in the sale of an Independence Bonds, and Jaisohn wondered how much longer he could carry on. In a desperate attempt to continue his work, he enlisted the services of three Koreans - Hong Un, Kim Won-jang and Kim Seung-je - who volunteered to raise funds among Chinese in Central and South America. They left on their mission in June but did not return until a year later. How successful they were is not known.

Four-Power Naval Disarmament Conference
(Washington Naval Conference)

In the mean-time, as if Jaisohn's worries were not taxing enough, there was another development in Washington, which he believed to be too much of a golden opportunity for furtherance of the cause of Korea to pass up. In July, 1921, President Harding announced that a 4-Power - the United States, Great Britain, Japan and France - Naval Disarmament Conference would be convened in Washington D.C. on November 12. Though there was practically no money in the Commission, and his own financial situation was no better, he decided that the Korean issue ought to receive attention by the powers and suggested to the Provisional Government that it appoint a delegation to the above-mentioned Conference.

The Shanghai Government promptly appointed a delegation which was as follows: Syngman Rhee, Chairman; Philip Jaisohn Vice

Chairman; Chung Han-kyong, Secretary; Fred A. Dolph, counselor; and Senator Charles Thomas, special counselor. Now Jaisohn's worry was money. The Provisional Government was, of course, in no position to be of assistance. Chairman Rhee had not yet returned to Washington D.C. Nevertheless, preparations for the Conference could not wait, and a budget of $20,000 was adopted. When consulting *KNA* leaders, they told Jaisohn that they would exert every effort to raise the amount. Gratified, he turned next to even more important matters, draft of a memorandum to be submitted to the Conference with supporting documents and a competent lawyer to act as the spokesman of the delegation. The Commission chose Senator Thomas to serve as a delegation special counsel. The remaining question was how to make Korea's case so convincing that the powers would find it impossible to ignore the Korean case.

In utmost secrecy, Jaisohn sent an urgent message to Lee Sang-jae in Seoul, a former colleague of his and most highly respected patriot, asking him to provide the delegation with a memorandum signed by representative leaders of Korea, along with an affidavit illustrating Japan's ruthless and intolerable rule over Korea. Jaisohn did everything he could. Now he could only wait. He was nervous. To a friend, he wrote:

> We have definitely engaged Senator Thomas to act as our special counsel. I think we have the right man. With him we can make a fight anyhow. The only thing that worries me is that we haven't any money. We have to pay the Senator the first installment of his fee on October 1st, and we haven't any to do it with.

To Jaisohn surprise and gratification, *KNA* leaders raised over $14,000. Also surprising was a donation of $7,000 from an anonymous source in Korea. Moreover, what he had requested of Lee Sang-jae - a memorandum signed by 342 representatives of the 13 provinces and 260 districts of Korea, consisting of *yangbans*, clergymen, teachers, merchants, farmers, factory workers and students, as well as an affidavit illustrating Japan's misrule, signed by over 25,000 persons in Korea - reached Jaisohn in the nick of time. With these impressive documents from the Koreans at home and Senator Thomas's legal brief, Jaisohn and his friends were sure of persuading the Washington conferees to take some positive action for Korea.

Jaisohn promptly paid Thomas's fee and hired a professional hostess who rented a house and took charge of the Korean delegation's social functions, entertaining diplomats and media representatives, etc. Chairman Rhee, who had returned to the capital tardily, kept himself in the background, and Jaisohn acted as head of the delegation.

As the Disarmament Conference got underway, Special Counsel Thomas submitted a powerful brief on behalf of Korea, together with copies of the memorandum and the affidavit smuggled out of Korea. The thrust of the Thomas brief was that since Korea was the focal point of international controversy in East Asia, no solution of the controversy was possible without resolving the Korean issue and that the resolution of the issue meant independence for Korea.

Jaisohn buttressed Thomas's argument with a personal call on Secretary of State Charles E. Hughes, Chairman of the Conference. Jaisohn had visited Mr. Harding at his home in Ohio following his election to the Presidency. At that time, the President-elect assured Jaisohn that he would instruct Mr. Hughes, his Secretary of State designate, to receive him and hear his views on Korea. Hughes was very polite. After listening to Jaisohn's presentation of the case of Korea and his urgent plea that it be included in the agenda of the Conference, Hughes assured Jaisohn of his personal sympathy for the plight of the Korean people. However, he informed Jaisohn that the U.S. delegation had decided not to raise the Korean question in public as it was believed more advantageous overall to induce Japan to make a concession on the larger issue, namely reduction of Japan's naval power in order to prevent her from disturbing the peace in the Pacific region. This, he said, would enable the United States to restrain Japan's conduct in Korea also. If, he continued, the United States insisted on airing Japan's harsh rule over Korea publicly and pressed her to reduce her naval strength as well, Japan might well walk out of the Conference, creating an international crisis. Hughes did promise to take up the Korean question in a private meeting with Prince Tokugawa, head of the Japanese Delegation, and request that Japan, in the interest of friendly relations between the U.S. and Japan, as well as for Korea's sake, institute humane administration in Korea.

Jaisohn appreciated the U.S. position. At the same time, he could not suppress his disappointment. He reminded Hughes of Theodore Roosevelt reneging on the U.S. treaty commitment to Korea and of Wilson's refusal to allow Korean delegates to attend the Peace Conference in Paris and told him that it was time for the United States to rectify the record. The Secretary of State reiterated his promise. He would make the strongest possible representation on behalf of Korea when met with Tokugawa, and added that, if the Japanese reacted negatively, the United States might reconsider its decision and take up the Korean issue publicly. Following the interview, Jaisohn wrote to a friend:

> The Japanese influence is very great. The American Government does not want to offend Japan unless she refuses to comply with America's request on the Far Eastern question as a whole. Till then, America wants to handle Japan in a most friendly manner and for that reason, the U.S. delegates are not pushing the Korean claim at this time.
>
> However, if Japan balks, ... America may change their attitude and bring up the Korean question before the Conference. That is the private information we have. As far as we are concerned, regardless of whether America or any other nation takes up the Korean question, it is our business to do all we can to call their attention to our case. We have no way of stopping them from ignoring us, but we must not leave any stone unturned in the way of attracting their attention. If we fail, there will be one satisfaction for us, and that is that we have done everything we can under the circumstances. Let us hope, however, that something will come out of it.

Hughes did hold a private session with Tokugawa. He told the Japanese that the United States was under no obligation to take up the Korean question in a formal meeting. However, the complaints by the Koreans in America were echoed by increasing number of American missionaries in Korea. If they succeed in raising their supporters at home who wield powerful influence, the Government of the United States would have to take the question officially. Something had to be done to appease the Korean people, and he was urging Japan to take corrective actions to that end before it developed into a major international issue between America and Japan. At first, Tokugawa sought to belittle the issue by saying that the Korean people were content to live under Japan and that the anti-Japanese agitation was the work of a few malcontents abroad who have lost touch with the realities in Korea. Hughes disagreed and emphasized the potential danger of sweeping the facts under the rug. By way of illustration, he produced his secret memorandum, and the support of affidavit spirited away from Korea. Tokugawa examined it and visibly shaken, he assured Hughes that 'within four months after his return to Japan, improvement in the administration of Korea would be affected.'

Was the much touted 'civil administration' of Japan's Governor General in Korea, Admiral Makoto Saito, the result of the warning by Secretary of State Hughes, using the documents submitted by Jaisohn as illustrations? Jaisohn thought so. Given America's desire for 'status quo' in the post-World War I era, the U.S. policy in the Pacific in general and toward Japan in particular, was one of not upsetting the apple cart. Simply put, it was a time of appeasement. Under the circumstances, the most Jaisohn and his colleagues could hope for was a behind-the-scenes verbal pressure by Hughes for Japan to be 'humane' toward the Korean people.

Photo: Syngman Rhee and Philip Jaisohn in Washington.

Photo: Members of the Korean Commission in America with Philip Jaisohn at the center of the front row (1921–1922).

Photo: Certificate of appointment issued by the Provisional Government of Korea in Shanghai for the Korean delegation to the Washington Conference. (November 1921).

The Four-Power Conference adjourned on February 6, 1922. On February 9, Jaisohn issued a brief report on the work of his delegation as follows:

> The International Conference, which began last November in order to deal with the questions concerning naval disarmament and the Far East, adjourned on February 6. I think Koreans at home and abroad are keenly disappointed by the failure of this

conference to take up the Korean question. I'm just as disappointed as our delegation did everything in its power to have it debated and acted on. However, does it mean that the conference has failed completely? What are the prospects for the future as far as the Korean people are concerned? Knowing that all of them are interested in answers to these questions, I wish to give my view briefly.

1. By means of the memorandum of our delegation, my speeches and press interviews and editorials and commentaries published in various newspapers, the American Government and delegates and participating powers were enabled to gain a better understanding of Korea and of the aspirations of the Korean people.

2. The justness of Korea's cause and the dignified and intelligent manner in which our delegates sought to enlighten the statesman of the world and the public in general, deeply and favorably impressed them, including the Japanese delegates.

3. Although there was no debate on Korea in the formal sessions of the Conference, there was discussion on the Korean situation in private meetings. Through these meetings, the delegates were made to realize that the independence movement in Korea is by no means the cry of a few malcontents instigated by us abroad, but that it is the grassroots movement of the Korean people. And Japan has pledged to institute reform in Korea. We will see whether Japan is sincere.

4. Finally, due to lack of funds, we regret to announce that the work of the Bureau of Information and of the League of Friends

of Korea must be terminated. However, should something extraordinary occur and my service is needed, I stand ready to do my part.

Still, reluctant to give up, he took the matter up with Rhee. In Jaisohn's presence he was all for continuing the activities of the Bureau as well as of the League and promised financial support. However, sometime after the Four-Power Conference, he slipped out of Washington D.C. without anyone knowing where he went. Letters by Jaisohn went unanswered, and Jaisohn surmised that he had gone to Hawaii. It was evident too, that he was not interested in what Jaisohn was trying to do. Hence, he told a friend of his: 'Dr. Rhee and his friends do not seem to think it is important, so under the circumstances I suppose I will have to get along without the help of the Koreans.'

For some months he carried on all by himself. However, with his own business getting steadily worse, Jaisohn became desperate. On September 21, 1922, he wrote to P. William Lee:

In regard to Korea Review, Dr. Rhee refuses to support it as he hasn't any money. Furthermore, he hasn't as much interest in it as he should. Under the circumstances, I do not care to incur any more debts. I published the review for the months of May, June and July at the firm's (his own) expense. But I cannot keep that up. Therefore, I suspended the August and September issues and do not know whether I can resume it or not. It all depends on what the Koreans are going to do about it. Judging from the looks of these things, no one is willing to support it, so I suppose it will die a natural death.

So ended the life of Korea Review, organ of the Provisional Government of the Republic of Korea, directed toward the English-speaking public after three fledgling years. For all practical purposes, Jaisohn, by then, was deserted by the Korean people, not because they had anything against him, but because they saw no ray of hope for Korea's independence, at least in the foreseeable future. Moreover, there were only about 7,000 Koreans in America and Hawaii, most of whom were struggling laborers, and a small percentage of them with extraordinary interest in Korea's freedom had about emptied their pockets for the independence movement up to that time. Jaisohn seems to have understood this. He was not bitter against them, but sad. In his letter to Lee, written on February 16, 1923, he wrote:

> There's nothing startling here except that I am trying to rehabilitate my business and to go out and speak for Korea whenever I get a chance. I spoke yesterday before the Philadelphia chapter of the Daughters of American Revolution. Next Sunday I will be speaking at the public forum of Cornell University, Ithaca, NY. This single-handed effort may not bring result for some time, but I will do my best. I will not lie down because others do. Rhee's gone to Hawaii. I do not know the object of his visit, nor do I know when he is expected back.

CHAPTER TWELVE

SECOND EXILE (II):

Down But Not Out

Driven to Bankruptcy

Jaisohn turned to his long-neglected business, which was in complete disarray. He put up a valiant fight to rehabilitate it. He began by dissolving the partnership in order to spare his partner from the effects of the business reverse. In order to hold down overhead expenses, he trimmed his firm's staff to the bone and moved to a new location and tried to stimulate sales. But it was at best a rear-guard operation against unavoidable failure.

The inevitable came to pass in 1924. That year, after three years of failure to attend to his firm's affairs while continuing to draw his living expenses from it, and of covering the costs of running the Bureau of Information at the expense of his company for more than half of the time, Philip Jaisohn and Co., Inc. was finally driven to bankruptcy. His shattered dream about a liberated Korea was a bitter pill to swallow. To see his business wiped out, and to find his sole remaining possession - his house - mortgaged to the hilt were doubly crushing blows to him.

Unable to either sleep or eat, he suffered a serious physical breakdown. His friends who saw him at the time were shocked. When one of his admirers expressed concern to Mrs. Jaisohn, she answered:

> "I am glad you saw the doctor, and I know you noticed an awful change in him."

A person who was very close to him described him as a 'nervous wreck, broken man,' and wondered if Koreans realized that it was because of them that the business failed. Jaisohn appreciated the love and concern of his family because a few years later, while holding a position in Washington D.C., he confided to a friend:

> "I miss my family, but some day we may join again here in Washington."

Nevertheless, there was still the spirit of an old warrior in him, and though he was down, he was not out. While he suffered deep in his heart, he held his chin up high and commenced a second try at business. With a group of Korean and American friends, he organized an import and export company. In the letter to a friend dated April 25, 1925, he described it in detail as follows:

> Yu Il-han (of Detroit, the 'Bean Sprout King') and a few other Koreans and Americans have organized a corporation for the purpose of doing import and export business in this country, in

China and in Korea, with me as its head, with offices in Philadelphia, Detroit and later other centers. The corporation is, for the time being, capitalized with $25,000. Already more than half of it has been subscribed. The purpose of the corporation is, of course, to make money, but it has another and more important object. We want to train Korean young men in the science of business and the secrets of cooperation through organizational activities. The only trouble has been that I did not have any capital to launch a corporation alone. I now find that Yu is able to join me with some money, experience and connections he has made. I think we can make a success of it and later it can be made the basis of starting a real corporation in Korea to develop the economic resources of the Korean people. If you have any money to invest, I will see that you receive some stock in this company. We have Chinese and American friends who want to join us, but we thought we ought to give Koreans the first chance.

Unfortunately, the corporation did not fare well. With China in the throes of civil strife and Korea closed to all Koreans whom the Japanese viewed as their enemies; it stood little chance of success. Jaisohn's connection with it was an asset in attracting investors in America, but in Korea he was a distinct liability. Outwardly, Jaisohn accepted his second abortive business venture with stoical calm, but it exacted a frightful toll physically and mentally.

Pan Pacific Conference

When his morale was at its lowest level, something happened to help lift it. The Institute of Pacific Relations scheduled to hold one of its periodic meetings, called the Pan Pacific Conference at Honolulu in July 1926, and Korean students in Chicago in cooperation with the Korean National Association in America invited Jaisohn to attend it as a representative of overseas Koreans as well as adviser to the entire Korean delegation. The Pan Pacific Conference was an unofficial gathering of prominent citizens of those nations bordering on the Pacific. Its purposes were to exchange information on economic, social and cultural affairs of those countries and help promote peace and progress in the region. Though it was an unofficial gathering, the governments of the nations concerned paid close attention to its proceedings, and many of the participants had close connections with their governments.

Jaisohn was glad to accept the invitation. It gave him a chance to put aside his business and financial worries for a while. More important, he learned that a delegation from Korea was expected, which would offer a golden opportunity for him to receive a first-hand report on conditions in the country. The Korean delegation from Seoul consisted of Shin Heung-wu (Dr. Hugh Shin), General Secretary of the Central Y.M.C.A. in Korea; Song Jin-wu, publisher of the *Dong-A Ilbo;* and Paek Kwan-sik, editor of the same newspaper. Dr. Shin had been a student of Jaisohn when he lectured at *Bae-Jae* Academy in the years 1896-98. When Jaisohn left for the Conference, his wife and daughters, glad that the Koreans had not forgotten him, entreated him to take advantage of the occasion and stay in Honolulu for a week or two following the adjournment of the Conference for rest and recuperation. They thought

317

that the Koreans who had invited him to represent Korea would provide him with an adequate expense allowance to enable him to do that.

Jaisohn found the Conference highly rewarding. The delegations participating in it included men and women of the highest caliber in intelligence and in concern for the peace and welfare of the people in the Pacific region. He was particularly impressed by the chief delegate from the United States, William A. White, who was the editor and publisher of the famed Emporia Gazette (Kansas). Elected chairman of the Conference, he presided over its sessions with strict impartiality. However, there was no doubt where his sympathy lay and when he felt compelled to speak out, he did so after requesting Dr. Jaisohn to take the chair in his place.

Jaisohn was also pleased to meet leading members of the Korean community in Honolulu and the Korean delegates to the Conference who had come from Seoul, especially talking with his ex-student Hugh Shin. He spent many hours with the latter, just listening to his reports on the conditions in Korea, as well as the news of Jaisohn's old comrades. Once the two men conferred far into the night, exchanging their views on the prospects of Korea's future.

Most rewarding of all to Jaisohn was the substance of the Conference itself. The initial plenary sessions were devoted to presentations of keynote addresses by representatives of various delegations. Each of the addresses was followed by a period of questions or comments from the audience. When Korea's turned arrived, the keynote address was delivered by Dr. Shin. It was a polite but forthright presentation of the truth of Japan's rule over Korea, the gist of which may be summed up as follows:

Since Japan's annexation of Korea, Japan has taken over more than 70% of the Korean farmland. At this rate, Japan may well occupy 100% of it before long. Therefore, countless Koreans immigrated to Manchuria and Siberia. Those who are left behind are no better off. We must pay serious attention to this.

When the address by Shin was finished, Jaisohn waited for a few moments to see if anyone cared to either question the speaker or comment on his speech. Seeing none, he got up and looking at the Japanese delegates said:

According to the Korean spokesman, Japan seems to have perpetrated very inhuman acts against the Korean people since her annexation of Korea 15 years ago. But before making up our own minds, we must hear both sides. I wish the Japanese delegates would respond.

The Japanese remained silent, so Jaisohn resumed:

Since there is no rebuttal from the Japanese delegates, it is evident that what the Korean spokesman said is true. That being so, we cannot close our eyes to the inhuman oppression of the Korean people by Japan.

At this point, the spokesman of the Japanese delegation, Mr. Kashiramoto, jumped up from his seat and declared:

Korea is a part of Japan. Therefore, the Korean question is an internal matter of Japan. This Conference has no right to interfere in the internal affairs of a nation. Moreover, the Korean delegate who has just spoken has been out of Korea for over a score of years and does not know the conditions in Korea. Since annexation, there has been unprecedented progress in Korea politically, economically and culturally. I move that this delegate be disqualified at this Conference.

Claiming his right to respond on a point of order, Jaisohn got up again and said:

The Philippines is a part of the United States, but the U.S. has allowed the Filipino delegates to participate in this Conference. Since this Conference is concerned with matters pertaining to all nations bordering on the Pacific, it has the duty to deal with the Korean issues. The Korean question is more than the concern of Japan alone. It is a concern of Asia, and indeed of the entire world.

An animated debate on the Japanese motion to disqualify Korean delegates followed. Canada's delegate, Mr. Nelson, warned that if the Korean delegation was disqualified, his would withdraw from the Conference as Canada was a part of Great Britain. He asserted that the Japanese demand was destructive. The Japanese motion was voted down and during the Conference Korea scored two additional victories. One was that Hugh Shin was elected against the Japanese objection to the Permanent Committee of the Pan Pacific Conference by a 5 to 1 vote.

The other was that Dr. Jaisohn was asked to serve as alternate chairman of the Conference, a subtle hint by Dr. White of how highly he regarded Jaisohn.

These pleased Jaisohn immensely because although they failed to drive Japan out of Korea, they showed that Korea and the Korean people received their due recognition at the international gathering. There was another cause for him to exult. During the hassle over Shin's remarks, the Japanese delegates sought to portray the U.S. as 'no better than' Japan by pointing out that it had annexed the Philippines, to which Jaisohn replied: "The date of the Philippine independence has been set." The sheepish Japanese sat down without a word.

Unfortunately, the Jaisohn travel was not adequately financed. This was not due to any lack of good intention on the part of his sponsors. They had done their best to raise a sufficient amount to adequately cover his expenses, but without success. They were furthermore unaware of how straightened he was financially. They had understood that he was a successful businessman in comfortable circumstances. Actually, he had borrowed money to attend the Conference. On the way to Honolulu, he stopped over in Chicago and Los Angeles to see his sponsoring organizations. However, when he saw that the amount of money they offered him fell short of what he needed, he decided to return home as soon as the Conference ended. When his family received his telegram to that effect, they were deeply disappointed, as they had hoped he would spend some time resting on the island. His wife confided in a friend:

"Don't you see that fighting for Korea is meat and drink for your great leader? It makes me actually weep when I think of his coming back and struggling, struggling to keep the wolf from

321

the door at times, looking so worn and haggard when he ought to be at the head of that nation of sorrowing souls, lifting them out of their prison, unfettering their lives and setting them free! God knows I would not put a stone in his way if he could return (to that role) and I would willingly go with him."

Jaisohn returned home physically fatigued, but much lifted in morale. He was glad to have helped enhance the image of Korea before the gathering of representatives of the Pacific nations. He was proud of the delegation from Seoul, for its members were superior to those of many other delegations. Evidently, he himself had commanded the respect of the participants in the Conference. At the conclusion of the Conference, the chief delegate from Japan came up to ask him if he would meet with him in private and discuss the Korean question, to which Jaisohn replied: "No, this is the matter which must be discussed in public."

Photo: Philip Jaisohn with Korean students attending the Pacific regional conference in Hawaii (June 1925)

But alas, what he had done was so meager compared to what was needed. He was glad to be home again with his family, which was a source of pride as well as comfort to him. His wife pinched pennies to make dollars last longer and kept reassuring him: "These days of hardship will not last long, my dear. I know, know, KNOW, it is only temporary and that the future will be better."

Photo: The Honolulu Bulletin reported Jaisohn's arrival (June 1925).

P. Jaisohn, Kim Hwal-lan, Shin Heung-woo

Photo: Jaisohn with the Korean delegation in Hawaii. (June 1925).

Return to Medicine

Jaisohn abandoned the idea of third business venture. Instead, he decided to return to pathology and took a position in Washington D.C. He liked the work and the people he was associated with there. However, the position did not offer him the security he needed. While he earned a decent salary, the expenses of maintaining a home in Media, PA and living in Washington D.C., as well as repaying his debts, kept him in constant penury. He confided this in a letter to a friend, dated December 1, 1927:

> I have been trying to send you some money ever since October but could not do so. I have to keep home going in Media and I have to pay for my living expenses here. Besides, the taxes, interest on the mortgage, coal, etc. keep me broke most of the time. I enclose herewith a check for $25 and will try to send you more from time to time. I must repay a part of it at least.

Additionally, he was unhappy because he did not wish to be separated from his family. So, he decided to start a medical practice in Media, PA. However, since he had been long out of touch with medicine, he felt the need to take a refresher course. With full support and encouragement from Mrs. Jaisohn, he borrowed $2,000 through negotiation of a second mortgage on their house and entered the Graduate School of Medicine at the University of Pennsylvania. His return to school at the age of over 60 was big news, and the *Dong-A Ilbo* fittingly treated it as such in a feature article. Later recalling this period, he said: "It was a rough going, but my wife was happy that I was returning to my medicine, and we were full of faith and hope."

324

After completing his study, Jaisohn found it necessary to take a position as a pathologist for a while in order to build up cash to start his practice with. In the years, 1930-34, he was associated with several hospitals as acting or visiting pathologist. He was happy because, in addition to his regular duties, he was able to pick up outside orders for special diagnostic research on the side, which were not only adding to his income but also very interesting. For example, on one occasion during this period he diagnosed the cause of an epidemic of unknown origin, which claimed many lives - it was trichinosis. At this time, too, he became a member of the American Association of Neoplastic Diseases and attended lectures at Johns Hopkins while conducting cancer research in which he was deeply interested.

Thus, he was well on the way to realizing his overriding ambition, which was to open his own practice. Suddenly, however, the stock market crash of 1929 wiped out his savings, and the Great Depression which followed brought virtually everyone an unprecedented hard time. Undaunted, Jaisohn looked everywhere for a way to realize his plan and found a way, or he thought he did. Early in 1932, on the suggestion of a friend, he wrote to Kim Sung-soo in Korea, founder of the famed newspaper *Dong-A Ilbo* and new proprietor of *Posong* College (now Korea University) for a loan of $5,000. Kim turned him down with apologies. The financial strain on Kim caused by his acquisition of the college was just too severe to enable him to advance the loan.

Disappointed though Jaisohn was, that was only half of his trouble. In 1934, while he was working strenuously to build up cash in order to start a practice, he became a victim of tuberculosis. Apparently, an old lesion in his lung flared up. Perhaps it was a result of over-work on his part. Perhaps it was a delayed reaction of the traumatic effects of the previous years. At any rate, on his doctor's advice, he entered the Pinecrest Sanitarium in West Virginia. How shocked he was, yet how heroically he conquered the TB was poignantly described in his article entitled 'A Daydream at Pinecrest.'

At the sanitarium, he made rapid progress after initial few weeks of absolute rest, which he found most difficult to endure, and occupied his time doing research on projects for the American Association of Neoplastic Diseases and treating patients there. One of them had a very unresponsive lung condition. Jaisohn put him through certain X-rays, and the patient was found to have had for years a nail lodged in his lung. In a little over half a year Jaisohn was well again and returned home.

Photo: Philip Jaisohn during his time immersed in medical research.

CARCINOMA OF THE EPIDIDYMIS

PHILIP JAISOHN, M.D.

AND

E. V. JORDAN, M.D.

CHARLESTON, W. VA.

The infrequent occurrence of malignant tumors in the epididymis, particularly carcinoma, can be judged by the paucity of literature on the subject. Recently we found a case of primary cancer of the epididymis in the course of our routine work. We looked up the literature on the subject, as we had never seen a case before. To our surprise we found only twenty-one cases of primary malignant tumors of the epididymis reported, of which fifteen are sarcomas or teratomas of various sorts and six carcinomas. Three of the six are of doubtful histologic descriptions for carcinoma, which leaves only three authentic primary cancers in this organ as far as we could find. Undoubtedly more cases had occurred than those found reported, but such a small number in the world's literature indicates the rarity of the occurrence.

Photo: Research paper by Philip Jaisohn published in Journal of the American Medical Association. (JAMA 1933, 100: 1021-1022)

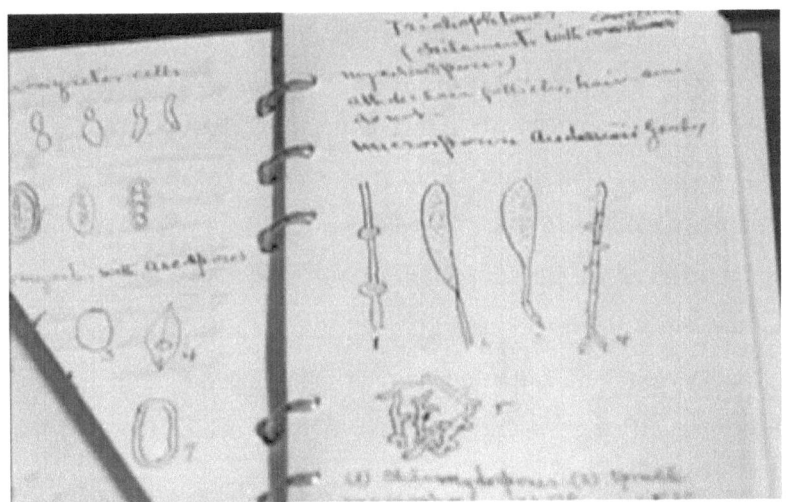

Photo: Philip Jaisohn 's handwritten medical research notes.

PHILIP JAISOHN, OF WASHINGTON, DISTRICT OF COLUMBIA, ASSIGNOR TO ALFRED A. SMITH, OF SAME PLACE.

THERMOMETER-CASE.

SPECIFICATION forming part of Letters Patent No. 545,366, dated August 27, 1895.

Application filed April 23, 1895. Serial No. 546,942. (No model.)

Photo: Philip Jaisohn 's U.S. patent.

Opening a Medical Practice

Now Jaisohn decided more than ever firmly that the time he should begin his practice had come. So, with 'faith, hope and conviction' that this was the right thing to do, and with the full support of his family, he opened his office in Media, PA, complete with laboratory.

At first, there were not many patients, as it is usually with most new practitioners. Moreover, as the nation was still in the throes of depression, many who needed physicians' care could not afford it. But those who came found him a competent and dedicated physician. They were greatly helped. Gradually, as the word spread that he was not only knowledgeable but also deeply interested in his patients as individuals, and as the depression receded, the number of his patients steadily increased. He was never interested in money. He never bothered to send out bills for collection. Some of his patients could not pay or paid only a small amount of the fee. As F.D. Roosevelt's New Deal began to take effect and the gathering cloud of war in Europe and Asia forced the United States to rearm, hastening the return of prosperity, more patients flocked to his office, while old ones paid up their unpaid bills.

In five years, he had a thriving practice, keeping him busy from morning till well into the evening. In addition, he was the doctor for several school districts, for the State Reformatory, for a private school: he was visiting pathologist to what is now Crozier Chester Medical Center, PA and conducted a clinic specializing in diseases of the skin. When the Second World War broke out, he volunteered his services as examining physician to the Draft Board, and by the end of the war he had examined more than 2,000 inductees. For the service he received a medal from Congress and a citation from President Truman.

As is true with most successful persons, behind Jaisohn's success as a physician and statesman was Muriel Armstrong Jaisohn, his devoted wife. She stood by him when the going was the roughest and encouraged him. Each morning, she would pack a delicious lunch for him. She played a tremendous part in the saga of his life, always smiling, never cross, full of hope, kind and selfless. She lived to see him as a successful doctor, happy in his work. She passed away in July 1941, thoroughly happy in her accomplishment. At this time, Philip Jaisohn was 77 years old.

The Future of Korea

In spite of his busy life as a successful physician, Jaisohn's interest in the events abroad, especially in Korea, remained undiminished. As the ultimate defeat of Japan became more and more certain, Koreans in America, who were anxious for the liberation of their country, called on him to discuss the future of Korea with him and to seek his advice with increasing frequency. He was never too busy to see them, to listen to them and to give his views until, and unless, he found them to be rank self-serving opportunists trying to exploit him. He never turned down requests for help from the Korean organizations of proven reliability.

Whenever he was free between visits with his patients, he would sit at his desk with a writing pad in his hand and write in long hand an article or address requested by Koreans. Naturally, he was most frequently sought after as speaker by Korean organizations. His articles were also eagerly solicited, and he wrote frequently for The New Korea, the oldest and for many years the only Korean newspaper published in the United States, and the Korean Student Bulletin, a quarterly published by the Korean Student Federation in America in cooperation with the Committee on Friendly Relations among Foreign Students in America (a sub-division of the International Council of Y.M.C.A.).

Notable among the articles were the series under the titles 'My Days in Korea' and 'Random Thoughts' published in The New Korea. While his articles were on subjects of a wide variety, on the whole they were around three main themes:

- patriotism,
- mutual cooperation, and
- practical knowledge.

As an author, his style was lucid. As the speaker, he was captivating with humor and eloquence. The following article was originally delivered before a Korean student gathering. It was later written up and published in the Korean Student Bulletin. Because it represents his deeply held thoughts and typifies him as a writer, it deserves quoting in full:

On What Korea Expects of Its Youth

Do you know what Korea expects of you? No doubt all of you have heard of the historic message Admiral Nelson sent to his command at the Trafalgar's Bay on October 21st, 1805, just before engaging the combined fleets of France and Spain. All he said to his men was 'England expects everyone to do his duty.' This laconic yet inspiring seven-word message brought to England the momentous victory that has made her the undisputed mistress of the sea ever since.

I have no official authority to speak for Korea, but I happen to know what she expects of you, and I'm going to tell you about it. Korea expects you to lead her out of the shame and misery in which she is now submerged. She has no one else to look to for rescue, and she certainly has the right to expect it of you. She possesses not only hope, but places implicit faith in you, that you will be bound by the mystic chord of patriotism and the love of liberty and come forward as champions of Korea. As to the success of such a movement, she has no doubt because history tells her that Korea has always managed to emerge from terrible situations without sacrificing her rights as a self-governing nation. She quelled the Mongolian and Chinese invasions and frustrated the ambitious designs of Hideyoshi of Japan. That indomitable and resourceful blood is still in the veins of Koreans and will show it sooner or later.

The present weakness that retards the more rapid progress of the national movement is due to lack of experience in harnessing and organizing for common purpose. The inherent power that is in her teamwork or the spirit of cooperation among her own people is not yet fully developed, and constant clash of individual opinions and personal jealousies throws a dampening effect on the whole movement. However, this is not an insurmountable obstacle because in time the best element will become the controlling factor, and its influence will harmonize all discords that irritate our ears.

Korea expects you to be the nucleus of the element that makes you love Korea more than wealth, individual honor, and life itself. No one doubts the sincerity or universality of patriotism of the Koreans. But there are many who doubt the intensity of it. In other words, are they ready to pay the price of political and economic freedom? Korea expects you to pay that price, even in blood if necessary. Can you refuse her?

I believe your main object in life is to do your duty to your country, and for that reason you are all studying and preparing yourselves for that great task. Of course, knowledge is indispensable for intelligent leadership, so you must acquire it as extensively as you can. But besides the cultivation of intellect, you must develop your moral and spiritual forces. Absolute honesty of the heart and deeds is essential in leadership. Honesty alone nurtures a sense of justice. Therefore, an honest person is generally just. I know of nothing that begets the confidence of others like honesty and justice. Your country demands that you be honest and just. Can you refuse her?

Leadership in any enterprise must be the source of the dynamic force that irresistibly carries everybody with it. The motive power must be generated by leadership, and the one who leads must work harder and longer than anyone else. Inaction and easygoing spell failure in any enterprise. Korea expects you to be the source of that force which will lift her out of that quagmire and place her on the highway of freedom and prosperity. Can you refuse her?

Last but not the least is to learn how to work in unison with others. Korea is not interested in any excuse for failure but expects you to accomplish that which she desires. Do not play or work alone, but, whenever possible, with others. You will do better and accomplish more if you get others to share your labor. And let them participate in formulating the plans. Even if they do not furnish better ideas, they will check up your own, which is valuable in itself. Korea expects you to be broad-minded and tolerant. Can you refuse her?

So, you can understand that your country expects a great deal from you. But I have faith in you. Like the men under Nelson at Trafalgar, you will not disappoint Korea.

Loyalty to the United States

Jaisohn's fidelity to the United States was as steadfast as was his love for Korea. Though he deeply regretted the failure of U.S. representatives in Korea to cooperate with his endeavor for reform in the late 1890's, he concluded that they did not exemplify the principle espoused by the United States and volunteered his service in the Spanish-American War on his return to the United States. Though he was deeply hurt by Theodore Roosevelt's violation of the U.S.-Korea Treaty, he chose to believe that it was an aberration on his part and supported America's war effort by becoming a member of the National

Security League during World War I. He was bitter when the United States pursued an appeasement policy toward Japan in the inter-war period. However, when his adopted country was threatened by Japan and Nazi Germany, the countries it had sought to appease, he volunteered his services as a medical examiner for inductees, continuing until the end of the war. Though he was profoundly disappointed in Franklin Roosevelt's equivocal stance regarding Korea in the Cairo Declaration in 1943 and was severely critical of Truman's cavalier decision to partition Korea on the eve of Japan's surrender in 1945, he told a visitor following V-J Day (Victory over Japan Day) that he stood ready to serve the United States and Korea in any capacity, if requested.

Liberation

V-J Day was followed by the division of Korea into two parts at the 38th parallel and by the Soviets occupying the northern zone, while the U.S. occupied the southern half. U.S. occupation forces under the command of Lieutenant General John R. Hodge arrived in Korea on September 8. In the ensuing months, many of Korea's emigrated patriots, leaders of the Provisional Government in China and the head of the Korean Commission in Washington D.C., returned to Seoul as 'private individuals.' Others, such as Kim Il-sung and Kim Du-bong, returned to *Pyongyang*. But in the face of lively speculation among observers when or whether he was returning to Korea, Jaisohn calmly continued his medical practice in the suburb of Philadelphia for a year. He was almost a forgotten man, while Syngman Rhee, Kim Koo, Kim Kiu-sik, Yoh Wun-hyong, etc. filled the headlines of the South Korean newspapers.

To occasional visitors who ruefully observed that U.S. occupation authorities in South Korea appeared to be stuck in the quagmire of free-for-all squabbles among Korean politicians, Jaisohn said:

> "Let us hope that the Koreans, as well as Americans who hold the destiny of Korea in their hands, will prove their statesmanship by helping the Korean people enjoy freedom and better livelihood."

He hoped, too, that the United States would prove worthy of its reputation as the leader of the free world by rectifying its past mistakes and helping establish 'a reunified democratic and independent Korea.' Asked whether he would like to return to Korea once again and offer his service, Jaisohn replied:

> My heart is there, but as a plain citizen, it is not up to me to make the decision. To go there without an invitation is being an intruder. Besides, Korea seems to be suffering from an overdose of 'leaders' at the moment.

The choice of General John R. Hodge as the commander of the U.S. Army of Occupation in South Korea was an unfortunate accident for the United States, as it was for Korea. It illustrates how inefficient the United States was and still is, in discharging its role as a superpower. Until Japan sent out in early August 1945 an SOS confessing that she had had all the punishments she could take, Washington had acted almost as if Korea did not exist. Its attitude seemed to be that Korea was an insignificant piece of real estate at its disposal, either to be used as a bargaining chip, should the United States be forced to conclude a negotiated peace with Japan, or to be thrown to the Russians as a sop for the latter's cooperation in the final defeat of fanatical Japan, or even placed under international trusteeship in which it would play a dominant role.

Meanwhile, the U.S. was too busy dealing with what it regarded as major issues such as the post-war Taiwan with 10 million people and Okinawa with less than 1 million inhabitants to bother with such trifling country as Korea, though she was a land of 30 million souls. It was only when Japan went to her knees that Washington suddenly realized the existence of Korea. By the time it dawned on the U.S. that Korea was too important a country to lose by default, there was no time to deal with it properly. Soviet troops were already pouring into northern Korea. However, since the American forces nearest Korea were on Okinawa, three days' journey away, there was no way in which they could preempt Korea ahead of the Soviets.

Hence, all that Washington could do, short of declaring war on the U.S.S.R., was a proposal to divide Korea and occupy her jointly, the northern zone by Soviet troops and the southern zone by American, and to receive the surrender of the Japanese forces in their respective zones. When the Kremlin consented to it, Washington was relieved, but it had to move in its troops without delay or it would face dire consequences. All possible speed being of the essence, Washington had no alternative but to rush into South Korea the 24th Army Corps which at the time was mopping up the remnant of the Japanese forces on Okinawa.

Lieutenant General Hodge

Thus, it was that Lieutenant General John R. Hodge, commander of the 24th Corps, was sent to Korea. To say that his selection was unwise is not to cast reflection on him as a person, for he was a man of competence, integrity and dedication. As such, he was the most surprised man on receiving the assignment. A professional soldier, he disdained politics. Yet as commander of the U.S. Army of Occupation, he ran straight into the vortex of Korean, and U.S.-Soviet, politics. Until he received his orders, he was abysmally ignorant about Korea.

Born in a rural downstate Illinois town, he studied engineering. During World War I he enlisted in the Army and served in Europe. After the war he remained in the Army and during the Second World War he won fame as a tank commander in the Pacific theatre. A blunt man by nature, he would never have volunteered for the job in Korea. However, as a soldier, he was not a man to disobey his Commander in Chief. He made a valiant attempt to discharge his duties well, and in view of the enormity and complexities of them, it may be said that few others could have done better.

Photo: John R. Hodge (1946).

However, his initiation to his job was a disaster. On arriving in Korea, he proceeded to deal with the Koreans as he had done with the Okinawans. To him, the Koreans were the 'same breed as Japs.' The Koreans were appalled. While most Okinawans were emigrant Japanese, Koreans were of an entirely different ethnic origin and were proud of their heritage. Consequently, his attitude did little to endear the occupying authorities to the local population. It was a rude awakening.

If Hodge was surprised to realize how ill-equipped, he was to deal with the Koreans, he was shocked by the degree of unpreparedness of his government to deal with Korea. In the wake of Japan's surrender, Korea was in a shambles. With the bulk of its managerial personnel driven into hiding by the irate populace who vowed to 'get rid of the pro-Jap collaborators,' the nation's governmental, industrial and financial machinery ground to a halt. Due to a reckless printing and distribution of paper currency by Japanese officials in a frantic effort to buy the good-will of the Korean people, a runaway inflation threatened everybody. A growing food shortage was made worse by the influx of emigre Koreans from Japan, China and the North. The country was on the brink of chaos; yet he had under his command merely two Army divisions.

Washington sent him no detailed directives and no trained personnel to serve as administrators. Out of his entire group, only one person - a minor Navy officer who had been born in Korea of missionary parents - had even a smattering of Korean. And this was more an embarrassment than some help, for he had picked it up from domestic servants. Desperately short of manpower, Hodge tried to let the Japanese government apparatus continue to function under his direction. But this stirred such vehement opposition among the Koreans that President Truman ordered him to ship the Japanese back to Japan forthwith.

The alternative was to deal with the Korean People's Committee for National Reconstruction, a nation-wide organization with as effective control on all levels as any of its kind could have. Initially, it consisted of virtually all groups and points of view, leftist, rightist, moderate, agricultural, workers, and intellectual. One group the committee pointedly excluded was that of 'collaborators with the Japanese.' Its leader, though personally of progressive leaning, declared that in the interest of national unity he would be willing to yield his position to such leaders as Syngman Rhee and Kim Koo. But General Hodge's orders were to recognize no Korean regime and to set up a military government in the southern zone, pending agreement with the U.S.S.R. concerning future disposition of Korea.

Accordingly, he divided his command into two groups, the United States Army Military Government in Korea (USAMGIK) and the 24th Corps. Retaining the overall command of both himself, he appointed a Major General to the post of Military Governor to take direct charge of USAMGIK, and another officer of the same rank to the post of Chief of Staff under him. The Military Government established its headquarters in the Central Administration Building, formerly the Government General Building under the Japanese, while the headquarters of the 24th Corps was in the *Bando* Hotel.

In establishing the Military Government, the problems facing Hodge and his Military Governor were legion. To cite some of them, they were: cultural and language barriers, food shortages, budgetary constraints, shortage of trained manpower, restiveness of Korean politicians and the north-south relations. It was earlier pointed out that Washington had failed to train occupation personnel for Korea and that there was but one person under Hodges command who could speak some Korean.

Hence, the first problem was to find enough Koreans to act as interpreters for the American officers manning various administrative positions. While some Koreans were competent enough as interpreters, the rest were miserably inadequate, and the Military Government reminded one of the House of Babel. Equally vexatious was a cultural conflict between Korea and America. Aware of the sensibilities of the Korean people about dealing with anyone who had worked under the Japanese masters, Hodge gave strict orders not to hire those with any such record. But no sooner had a Korean been hired than cries of protests were raised in the press. When it was pointed out that none of those who were hired had any pro-Japanese record, the rejoinder was that they were either the brothers or cousins of the beneficiaries of Japanese imperialism and hence were as 'dirty' as their relatives.

At the outset of the U.S. occupation, General Hodge envisaged it to last a year or two at most and was not disturbed by Washington's directive or lack of it, which in effect told him to maintain law and order and preserve status quo. It quickly became plain, however, that the occupation could not be terminated any time soon. The Joint Commission of the American and Soviet Commands, established in accordance with the decision of the Foreign Ministers' Conference at Moscow in December, 1945 bogged down in dispute over procedural matter. The Foreign Ministers' Conference instructed the Joint Commission to 'consult with the Korean democratic parties and social organizations' on the formation of the Provisional Government for a reunified Korea and to coordinate the administrative and economic affairs of both zones. Also agreed to at the Foreign Ministers'

Conference was establishment of a Four-Power Trusteeship for Korea for a period of up to five years.

At the initial session of the Joint Commission, the Soviet delegate served notice that only those parties and organizations which supported the Moscow decision should be consulted. Since all parties and organizations in South Korea except *Namno-dang* (Communist Party) had openly opposed the Four-Power Five-year Trusteeship, the American delegation interpreted it as signifying that the Soviets were intent on setting up a communist Government of Korea. Rightist politicians in South Korea, led by Syngman Rhee, thought it a waste of time to continue meeting with the Soviets and pressed for a separate government in South Korea.

But on Washington's instruction, Hodge refused to break off the talks entirely. At the same time, he proceeded to 'Koreanize' the USAMGIK by replacing American officials with Koreans, but keeping the Americans attached to their old positions as advisers, and to create an interim legislature composed of members, one half of whom were elected and the rest appointed. This was intended as an assurance to the Soviets that the United States was keeping its door open for the establishment of an all-Korean democratic Provisional Government, and to the Koreans that it was moving toward their self-government.

The net result was negative. On the one hand, the Kremlin charged that Washington was violating the Moscow agreement while, on the other, Rhee and his colleagues attacked it as appeasement 'to the Communists.' There was, also, criticism among Koreans that the 'Koreanization' of the Military Government was a farce because the American 'advisers' still exercised their old authority; that, in the face of pressing problems crying for solutions, all that the 'advisers' government' did was to function as a care-taker regime; and that no one knew how long that would last.

As it became patently clear that the occupation of South Korea would last longer than anticipated, General Hodge found himself facing two serious problems. One was 'economic.' With her fledgling industry at a stand-still and her farmland virtually barren through lack of care, South Korea was sinking. To maintain status quo under the circumstances was to court disaster. Yet Washington did not seem to care, although it professed to be seriously concerned about the menace of the communist bloc. Hodge feared that if something drastic to revive the economy of South Korea was not done immediately, South Korea would be lost by default.

The other problem was one of 'too many cooks.' Hodge had not wanted his job but, having been assigned to it, he wanted to succeed for the sake of Korea as well as the United States. Realizing the enormity of it, he was anxious to have around him a group of advisers who were well informed about Korea and Koreans and were also above partisanship. Thus, it was not long after he arrived in Seoul that he was quite intrigued when an application for return to Seoul by Syngman Rhee reached his desk. He had never heard of him before. On inquiring about him, Hodge found out that while sources close to the State Department expressed opposition, fearing that he might be a divisive influence, some of his military officers who knew Rhee were decisively in favor of permitting his return, pointing out his strong anti-communist stance. In the end, Hodge decided to approve Rhee's return. His reasons were

- first, a memorandum from General Douglas MacArthur's headquarters together with Rhee's application made it clear that he would support the U.S. command in Korea,

- and secondly, the information obtained from local Koreans, which was highly favorable; to them Rhee was 'the father of the Korean Republic.'

In mid-October 1945 Rhee was the first and best-known Korean exile to return as a 'private citizen.' His return proved to be the most popular decision Hodge had made-up to that time, and the American commander made the most of it. He personally introduced a septuagenarian ex-President of the Korean Government-in-exile to the Koreans in a huge reception in Rhee's honor in these words: "I present to you your leader, Dr. Syngman Rhee." The entire people of South Korea followed it in the press and through the radio, while the crowd at the reception in Seoul went wild. Shortly thereafter, Hodge appointed him chairman of his Advisory Council and happily looked forward to a fruitful association.

The Hodge-Rhee 'entente cordiale' did not last long. The purpose of Rhee's return ahead of his potential rivals was not to serve Hodge, but to build up his political base. Hodge's flattering introduction of Rhee to the Korean people was intended as an attempt to enhance his own position by the recruitment of so popular a Korean leader as Rhee. But it only served to boost Rhee's ego, causing the Koreans to believe that the United States was grooming him for the Presidency of Korea. Although Hodge found him courteous and pleasant, whenever they met

('He was all smiles'), away from him, Rhee conducted himself as if he were the President of South Korea.

Everyone with ulterior motives of their own flocked to Rhee: 'pro-Japs' with money, landlords who were anxious to retain their holdings, opportunistic politicians and high-level Korean officials in the American Military Government who wish to secure appointment in the anticipated Rhee regime. Though no one knew how long the Military Government would last, everyone knew that it was only a temporary one. Hence, many of the latter group were 'Hodge's employees during the daytime and Rhee's servants in the evening,' as many observers quipped. Hodge was concerned lest the Korean official's efficiency declined, but he felt that so long as they performed their duties as expected, what they did on their own time was their business. He did consider Rhee's lifestyle unseemly, to say the least. Rhee, who had reportedly solicited money among Korean vegetable growers in Montana, Oregon and California for travel expenses to Korea, moved into a sumptuous mansion shortly after his return to Seoul and lived the life of luxury surrounded by a large retinue of attendants.

What led finally to a bitter split between Hodge and Rhee was Rhee's persistent, vociferous attacks on the United States policy in Korea. While professing to be grateful to the U.S. for the liberation of Korea and to favor the unity of all Koreans for the establishment of a democratic and unified Korea, he was in effect fomenting disunity with his hysterical anti-communist outcries and coddling of collaborators with the Japanese. After fruitlessly appealing to him to tone down his rhetoric, Hodge warned Rhee that he was jeopardizing the accomplishment of the very objective he claimed to support. Rhee retorted that Hodge was appeasing the Communists. When Hodge reminded him that what he was doing was in pursuance of the policy adopted by the United States, Rhee's rejoinder was: the Democratic administration in Washington was soft on communism - a faint McCarthyist threat.

The pipe-smoking, muscular Hodge not only looked like Popeye the Sailor, but also was as tough as he. In a stormy but brief session, he told Rhee that he had no intention of listening to anyone insulting his own Government. Asserting that as a soldier who had sworn to defend the U.S., it was his duty to obey his government, be it Democratic or Republican, so long as it was legally in power. He reminded Rhee of his pledge to honor the authority of the United States Military Occupation Command in Korea.

During the ensuing months, members of the Korean government-in-exile in China, headed by Kim Koo, Kim Kiu-sik and scores of lesser luminaries, returned home. They returned as private citizens to *'assist'* the American occupation authorities in establishing a reunified, democratic Provisional Government of Korea. Their return, however, produced confusion rather than cohesion among Korean politicians. Although they had cooperated with one another for the duration of World War II, their difference had never been healed. Soon after their return, their differences resurfaced and multiplied. Their original and running difference was ideological, conservatism versus liberalism. Kim Koo, a conservative, joined Rhee who was a rock-ribbed conservative. Kim Kyu-sik and his followers formed a middle-of-the-road coalition in conjunction with like-minded leaders inside Korea.

Difference of opinion developed also on the issue of collaboration with the Japanese. On this issue, the members of the exile government were united in refusing to have anything to do with the 'pro-Japs,' but since Rhee had already embraced the 'pro-Japs' and received financial support from them it was very awkward, to say the least, for Kim Koo to collaborate with Rhee. The political climate for South Korea became more tense each day with charges and countercharges.

It was during this period that some Koreans, as well as Americans, suggested to Hodge that in order to help calm the tumult, he might consider inviting to Korea a man who could help him accomplish his goals better than anyone alive. The man was a Korean American named Philip Jaisohn, who lived in a suburb of Philadelphia, PA, they said. The General's initial reaction was: "Add another one to the already too many cooks?" Having been repeatedly disappointed with repatriate leaders, he was getting weary of them. They understood his position. Moreover, unsure of whether the Korean American was able or willing to accept the invitation (he was an octogenarian), they did not press the matter.

But Hodge could not forget their suggestion. The more he pondered it, the more it occurred to him that the elderly patriot might be the person whose advice he should seek. He was, in Hodge's view, too old a man to entertain political ambitions of his own. Since, too, he was a naturalized citizen of the United States, it might deter his ambition even if he were ambitious for political office. Above all, all who knew him assured Hodge that Jaisohn was a man of sterling integrity. He decided to sound out discreetly his availability.

Early in 1947 an officer on General Hodge's staff was given a leave in the United States. The officer (Major Clarence N. Weems Jr.) was told to call on Jaisohn, explained the situation in Korea and inquire about Jaisohn's availability. This the officer did. He informed Jaisohn that if he was able and willing to return to Korea, Hodge would like him to assist in the capacity of Chief Adviser on Korean Affairs to the

Commanding General of the U.S. Army Forces in Korea (Hodge). Jaisohn answered that he would be pleased to accept the offer as he believed it to be his last chance to serve the United States as well as Korea both of which were very close to his heart.

Photo: Major Clarence N. Weems, Jr. — at the request of Lt. Gen. Hodge — visits Philip Jaisohn in Media, PA. Soh shows him a copy of *The Independent*, the newspaper he once published. (1947)

(**Editor's Note:** Major Clarence N. Weems Jr.'s father, Clarence N. Weems, came to Korea in 1909 as a Southern Methodist missionary with his wife and two sons (David and Clarence Jr.). He served for 23 years in *Kaesong*, ministering and working as the principal of *Songdo High School* and as the district superintendent of the Methodist Church in the *Kaesong* area. The second son, Clarence N. Weems Jr., attended a foreign school in Korea and was fluent in Korean. After serving as a U.S. Army officer during World War II, he returned to Korea as an adviser to the U.S. Military Government. He made significant contributions to the study of Korean history, particularly by editing two books on Korean history originally published in 1905 by missionary Homer Hulbert. Hulbert's History of Korea. Edited by Clarence Norwood Weems. New York: Hillary House, 1962. 2 vols.)

CHAPTER THIRTEEN

SECOND RETURN (I):

The Dead Come Alive

Following the visit by General Hodge's emissary, Dr. Jaisohn sent me(Dr. Liem) a note suggesting that I come to see him at my convenience. He gave no reason for the request, but since it was unusual for him to do that, I telephoned him and said I was coming the next afternoon. When I arrived in his office as promised, he was seeing his last patient. After that we went to his residence and had dinner. Following the dinner, Dr. Jaisohn and I went to his room and there he confided his reason for wishing to see me. He wanted me to go with him to Korea as his aide. For several reasons, including his difficulty in conversing in Korean, he said he needed someone to assist him. Then he related the visit he had with an army officer who was sent by General Hodge in Seoul.

I was so excited and thrilled by the sudden prospect of returning to Korea - a dream for 18 years - and by the trust Dr. Jaisohn placed in me that I sat speechless for a long time. When I was able to speak, I acted like a spoiled youngster. Forgetting to thank him, I asked: "Can I bring my family with me?" He hoped so, but we had to wait and see, he answered.

Another month's wait and early in March 1947, while Hodge was back in Washington D.C. for consultations, he invited Jaisohn to the nation's capital for a personal meeting. During a long conversation, the General described his relations with Korean leaders and his Russian counterpart in *Pyongyang*. He spoke of his hopes and frustrations, and of how Jaisohn could be of help in carrying out his mission. In brief, he needed someone of influence and knowledge with whom he could freely consult and whose advice would be without bias and ulterior motive. Judging from all that he had heard, he said, Jaisohn was the man. He expressed the hope that, barring Jaisohn's health, the latter would accept his offer.

Jaisohn thanked Hodge for his kind words and for briefing him on the situation in Korea. As for his own health, he said 'he felt as fit as any man his age (he was now 83 years old), perhaps better, and he would be glad to do anything to help the General discharge his historic duties for Korea as well as the United States.' Jaisohn made one request that he be allowed to be accompanied by an assistant, Channing Liem. Hodge promised to arrange for that.

However, Hodge's request to the War Department for Jaisohn was caught in a sticky web of bureaucratic and political intrigues in both Seoul and Washington. In Korea and Washington Rhee partisans, on learning of it, mounted behind-the-scenes campaign against bringing out Jaisohn. Though their real motive was to deprive Hodge of the prestige Jaisohn's presence in Korea would accord him, their ostensible argument was that he was too old. "Korea has enough fossils without him," they said. This was a persuasive argument to the bureaucrats in Washington, who were uninformed about the facts in the case.

Moreover, ripples of Korean politics had already reached Foggy Bottom and the Pentagon, causing many middle-level officials to lean toward or against Rhee. Major General Archibald Arnold, first Military Governor in Korea now reassigned in Washington, was one inclined toward Rhee. Noting that Jaisohn's health record revealed that he had had TB, Rheeites argued against 'risk-taking.' After prolonged silence, the War Department sent Jaisohn a form letter, notifying him of its rejection of 'your application for the reason of poor health.' The news was flashed across to Seoul where Rhee partisans saw to it that it received headline treatment. Hodge and admirers of Jaisohn were very disappointed, and the press learned of it. An AP correspondent called on Jaisohn at his office and asked about the state of his health. Jaisohn's answer was as follows:

> "I am at my office every day of the week except Sundays. My office hours are from 9 a.m. until often 10 p.m. My health is excellent."

Asked by the reporter if Jaisohn thought that there were those who opposed his going to Korea and were using their influence to prevent it, Jaisohn replied: 'No comment.' The AP article was published both in Korea and the United States and helped undoubtedly to counteract the earlier publicity about Jaisohn's health. However, what clinched the matter in favor of his going to Korea was a campaign in its favor by his supporters in America, especially Congressman Wallace Chadwick. They pointed out that Jaisohn had not initiated his application, but that the Commanding General of the American Forces in Korea, wishing for his service, had persuaded Jaisohn to come to Korea as his adviser. General Hodge was well aware of Jaisohn's advanced age, they said. Chadwick, influential member of the House of Representatives from Jaisohn's district and a friend of his, was furious. He wrote a stern letter to Secretary of War Patterson, chiding the Department's insult to so great a man and accusing it of non-cooperation with its Field Commander. Since Chadwick was head of the House Appropriations Committee, Patterson evidently chose not to cross swords with him. After looking into the matter personally, he answered the Congressman that if Dr. Jaisohn would waive all claims against the United States arising out of his possible illness while serving abroad, he would order the immediate confirmation of his appointment. This was done, and the War Department hastened with Jaisohn's appointment after three months' procrastination.

However, it was not possible for me(Dr. Liem) to accompany him. When Hodge learned that his requisition for Jaisohn was running into a snag, he concentrated his efforts on getting Jaisohn's clearance and tabled, for the time being, requisition for me. Clearance for Jaisohn did not automatically enable me to go with him; it was necessary for Hodge to request my appointment separately. In the meantime, noting the uncertainty of Dr. Jaisohn's return to Korea, I had already accepted reappointment as an instructor at Princeton for the year 1947 - 48, and I felt it my duty to at least complete my first semester's teaching. My request for release from my contract at the end of the first semester was granted, and I joined Dr. Jaisohn in February 1948.

Return to Korea

Dr. Jaisohn, accompanied only by his daughter, left for Korea in June 1947. His family and I saw them off at the 30th Street Pennsylvania Railroad Station of Philadelphia, PA, in the clear, warm evening of June 10, 1947. Dr. Jaisohn looked much younger than his age and very happy.

At the time of Korea's liberation from Japan, most Koreans assume that Jaisohn had passed away and had become a part of history. On learning that he was still alive and active in the United States, and that the United States Military Government was reportedly planning to invite him back to Korea, virtually the whole nation was excited. The press, sensing the mood of the people, vied with one another to print the latest news about him. No sooner had one reported the Military Government's confirmation than another came out with the claim that he might be returning 'around the middle of March (1947).' Still another claimed a scoop by asserting that it would be toward the 'end of March,' while the fourth editorial called on the entire population to turn out to welcome home 'the old independence warrior' whenever he arrived, and a fifth carried a paid advertisement for a 'Dr. Jaisohn Reception' with the notice that admission would be limited to ticket holders, with tickets costing 3,000 *won* each. In U.S. currency, the charge would have been $30 at the black-market rate and $200 at the official exchange rate. However, at the time, it was not at all certain whether he would return. That Koreans made so much ado about it under those circumstances was proof of how highly Jaisohn was regarded. It showed, too, that not all who waited for him so anxiously did so out of unselfish and patriotic motives.

Their wait was not in vain. After months of silence, the Military Government spokesman announced that Jaisohn was expected in Korea in early July. The announcement in the papers and on the radio electrified the nation. While on the one hand, the Government rushed into elaborate preparations for his welcome from his landing in *Incheon* to his arrival at the *Chosun* Hotel, on the other civic organizations - from surviving members of the old *Independence Club* to the Soh Clan Association - sought to outdo one another in honoring the 'Father of Korea's Independence Movement.'

The day of Jaisohn's return, July 6, 1947, came at last. On that day he set foot on the soil of his native land from which he had been ejected forty-nine years previously. How different this homecoming was compared with his first in 1896! Then he slipped in secretly for fear of a possibly hostile reception by the people. Now he was returning to the hero's welcome. On hand to greet him at the pier in *Inchon* were fifty of the highest Korean and American dignitaries, including Syngman Rhee and the Military Governor Lerch. After cordial handshakes with the V.I.P.'s and the presentation of bouquets by two colorfully dressed little girls, an official, chairman of the Dr. Jaisohn Welcoming Committee, escorted Jaisohn and his daughter to the head of a long caravan of cars waiting several hundred yards away.

On both sides of the passage-way stood thousands of welcomers - mighty and humble, Korean and foreign - who waved to him and shouted: "Soh Jae Pil *Paksa Mansei*!". As the limousine, its banner reading, "Welcome, Dr. Jaisohn" slowly led the caravan through the port of *Inchon*, with honor guard officers on horseback accompanying, the streets were filled with people greeting him with shouts of "*Mansei!*" Virtually all the way from *Inchon* to Seoul, passers-by stopped either to wave or to bow to him, and on arrival in Seoul, he was greeted by welcomers, estimated to be in the hundreds of thousands. They lined the streets and repeatedly raised shouts of welcome to the sound of a siren signaling his approach. The tumult lasted until he reached his hotel.

Photo: Philip Jaisohn and Miss Muriel being welcomed upon their arrival in *Incheon*, with Kim Kyu-sik greeting them on the right. (July 1947)

Photo: Prominent figures awaiting Philip Jaisohn 's arrival (July 1947)

So delighted were the people by the return of Dr. Jaisohn that in the weeks which followed he would have been overwhelmed by an endless stream of welcoming ceremonies, had he not sternly forbidden it. He consented to just one reception by the South Korean Interim National Assembly. It was held at the Seoul Stadium on July 12 with some fifty thousand people in attendance. Many of them came from all parts of South Korea to have a glimpse of the legendary hero and to hear from his own lips that the independence of Korea with the elimination of the division at the 38th parallel was at hand.

Photo: In the car en route from *Incheon* to Seoul — seated on either side of Dr. Soh are Kim Kyu-sik and Yoh Woon-hyeong. (July 1947)

The crowd gathered at the stadium was thrilled when Jaisohn emerged from a throng of escorts and walked up to the platform, escorted by Kim Kiu-sik, President of the South Korean Interim Legislative Assembly and chairman of the meeting welcoming Dr. Jaisohn. Tall and erect, though grey-haired, he seemed defiant of the march of time. It was as though the clock had stopped ticking and eight decades of tumultuous developments, of which he was a leading figure, had come alive in him. One in the gathering was heard to exclaim in jubilation: "What a miracle - a living corpse reminding us that the spirit of Korean independence is not dead!" Another chimed in: "Yes, he has come back from the nether world to complete the work he left unfinished."

Photo: Philip Jaisohn (November 1947).

From Enthusiastic Joy to Disappointment

However, as Jaisohn rose to speak, following remarks of welcome by several dignitaries, including Kim Kiu-sik, the enthusiasm of the crowd was dampened. What he said was drowned out, as it were, by how he said it. He spoke in English, and an interpreter translated it into Korean. Though the interpreter was an admirer of his and performed his duty ably, Jaisohn seemed so distant, so foreign to his listeners. Not realizing that languages, including one's mother tongue, are an acquired skill which can be lost through disuse, they were incredulous. They muttered: "How can he who loves Korea so much forget his native language? Can he not say in a few simple Korean words that he is delighted to be back in his ancestral country with us?"

Jaisohn had not forgotten Korean. He was out of practice. His Korean was old-fashioned, and he found it very difficult to express himself in Korean when addressing large audiences.

Disappointing to his listeners, too, was his pointed reminder to them that he returned as an American. With all due respect for his loyalty to the country of his adoption, they could not help but wish he would choose to be a part of them and spend the rest of his life as a Korean. They said to themselves: "Since he has been an American for over half a century, is it not fair for him now to become a Korean again and lead us?" Given emotional predilection, their reaction was understandable. Jaisohn appreciated their feeling.

Anticipating it, he had tried, before returning to Korea to brush up on his Korean. One of his reasons for wishing me to accompany him was that I might help him with his Korean while on route. Since he was expected to travel by train and ship, which was the normal mode of travel at the time, he had nearly a month's time for it. Hence, he regretted that circumstances beyond our control rendered that impossible. It was our intention that he should not only give his Korean a brush up but also work up a few short speeches and rehearse them to enable him to speak in Korean before public gatherings. In fact, he commenced his Korean lessons as soon as he returned from his first meeting with General Hodge in Washington D.C. early in 1947, thinking that we might be leaving for Korea within months. The lessons were interrupted when his proposed return to Korea hit a snag. As noted earlier, after a prolonged delay, clearance for his return came through suddenly and in all haste to prepare for the return, he was unable to overcome his linguistic handicap. On arriving in Seoul, he was able to converse in Korean in private meetings with Korean friends. However, feeling incompetent to address public gatherings, he secured the services of an American-educated physician as interpreter.

Jaisohn's American citizenship was another obstacle to affinity of the grassroots toward him. On his part, rightly or not, it was his conviction that one can serve two masters - Korea and the United States - and proceeded to practice it. A man of principle, he never doubted that he loved Korea as much as ever when he became an American citizen. By the same logic, he believed just as firmly that whether he retained his American citizenship, his love for America would remain unaffected. Why, then, did he choose to retain it notwithstanding the wishes of the Koreans to the contrary?

He did this at his first public appearance in order to serve notice to the entire Korean people that he returned to Korea not to seek any political office, but to help them become truly self-supporting and self-respecting people, which alone would lead create independence. As soon as his return was announced, the news was received with conflicting interpretations. In spite of Hodge's explicit statement that he was coming as an American to be his chief adviser, some chose to view it as the American occupation commander's subtle move to groom Jaisohn as Korea's President and were wary.

On the other hand, many rejoiced, looking upon him as the alternative to Syngman Rhee. Jaisohn was aware of this and, believing that unless these views were scotched at the outset, his usefulness in Korea would be seriously impaired, he repeated what Hodge had said;

> he was and would remain an American, signifying that as a U.S. citizen he could not, even had he wished, to qualify for Korea's Presidency.

Most of the audience did not comprehend it and were disappointed. On the other hand, those who perceived his inner thought admired him more. How well they remembered his often-expressed disclaimer for political ambition: "I am not interested in any political office, not even Emperorship of Korea."

Before many days had elapsed, Jaisohn realized what his role in the American occupation of Korea should be. Many of the ways of the Korean people remained unchanged. They had to be changed. One of them, for example, was the clan system, which he believed to be inimical to the unity of the Korean people and to the growth of Korea as a viable nation. One day, a group of white robed men called at his office. Bowing before him with regal dignity, their spokesman informed Jaisohn that as representatives of his clan, they came to extend to him an invitation to a reception to be tendered in his honor by his clansmen. He inquired:

How large is the Soh clan?
It consists of approximately three hundred thousand people, sir.

How many people are expected to attend the reception?
We expect about fifty thousand to be there, sir.

I hope you will have a good time there without me. I am sorry I cannot come to your party. Good day, gentlemen.

He fully anticipated a slander campaign against him by his irate clansmen. From the traditional Korean point of view, it was a serious social crime, but he felt that Korea must choose between the unity of the people, leading to Korea's true independence and fragmentation which could not help but result in her weakness and downfall and that she had to choose the former. When, sometime later, the same delegation wished to see him, he was sure they came to inform him of the indignant decision of the Soh clan to write his name off the clan's list. It was a surprise to him, therefore, to learn the purpose of its call. The delegates came to apologize for having offended him. Their spokesman told him: we had no right to claim you merely as a member of our clan. You belong to all Koreans.

Another habit of the Korean people, which Jaisohn believed detrimental to them was their propensity for idleness. A stock answer of many Koreans, when asked what they did for living was: "I don't do anything," implying they were well to do. But they were not. One day, he ordered one of his close relatives out of his office. The relative showed up almost every day. One day, when he asked his relative what his purpose of the calls was and told that he came to be close to him, Jaisohn told him: "You can be very close to my heart by spending your time gainfully."

On returning to Korea, Jaisohn found the popularity of the American Military Government (AMG) at a very low ebb. After nearly two years' control of the country south of the 38th parallel, it had been unable to make any headway towards solving her economic or political problems. Unemployment was rampant, 20,000 families were sleeping in the streets, and South Korea's industrial machinery was operating at 20% of its capacity. The *samnam* (North and South *Kyongsang, Cholla and Chungchong*) provinces, the traditional rice bowl of Korea, were producing barely enough to feed their own inhabitants. South Korea was dependent on U.S. grain imports to feed its burgeoning population. Complaints such as 'Things cannot go on as they are much longer' were voiced by increasing number of people. Kim Sung-soo, founder of the

Dong-A Ilbo (East Asian Daily) as well as of Korea University and a man highly respected by General Hodge, told a fact-finding mission headed by Paul G Hoffman: "The military government must be replaced by a Korean Government soon or South Korea will go down the drain."

On the political front, too, the AMG came increasingly under criticism. Leaders of the defunct People's Committee for National Reconstruction, which had briefly functioned as the de facto government of South Korea before the arrival of the U.S. forces, charged it as repressive as the Japanese Government General through which Japan had exercised absolute control over Korea. The rank and file accused it of having packed the police force with the hated ex-policemen who had worked for the Japanese. Politicians assailed it as a regime of alien incompetents who were intent on prolonging it indefinitely.

By the time Jaisohn returned to Korea, Rhee and Kim Koo had been feuding with Hodge for a year, now as allies and now at cross-purposes. In order to see how beleaguered the American commander was, it may be well to review briefly the controversy over the Moscow Agreement. Following the division of Korea into two and the occupation of the northern and southern zones by the Soviet forces and U.S. troops respectively in 1945, the Foreign Ministers of the United States, Russia and Britain met in Moscow and decided to place Korea under a Four-Power Trusteeship (consisting of the above plus China) for up to five years. They also instructed the two occupying commanders to establish a Joint Commission which would 'consult' with democratic parties and organizations for the purpose of organizing a Provisional Government of Korea.

It was an unrealistic order and personally Hodge opposed it, but as a soldier, he felt that it was his duty to follow orders and do his best to implement it. The Joint Commission was set up. However, as was previously described, no sooner had the Moscow Agreement concerning the 5-year trusteeship been made public than a storm of protests against it flared up in South Korea, in which an overwhelming majority of the people participated. The Soviet side of the Commission served notice at the beginning of its meeting that only those parties and organizations supporting the Moscow Agreement would be consulted. Since only the Communist Party (South Korean Labor Party) had not opposed the Moscow Agreement, an acquiescence in the Soviet demand appeared tantamount to turning over the entire peninsular Korea to the communist rule, and the American side refused.

Yet the United States decided against being the party to break up the Joint Commission, and a deadlock resulted. During the ensuing year, Hodge and his allies searched hard for a formula which would hopefully satisfy all parties concerned. Finally, the formula they came up with was that all consultants would sign a document agreeing to the validity of the Moscow Agreement but stating that they were not bound by it. The Russians gave their tacit consent to the formula. Most of South Korea's leaders, including Kim Koo's and Rhee's lieutenants, were in favor. Still, the two rightists themselves refused adamantly.

While sympathizing with the recalcitrant rightists, Hodge regretted their action, feeling that it may lead to their exclusion from a future Korean government which might consequently be dominated by leftist groups. Had the two leaders let it go at that, their relations with him might have remained cool but cordial. But they decided to go further. They started what appeared to be a campaign to undermine the U.S. Military Government. This was intolerable and Hodge called them in separately. He began in a conciliatory manner by appealing to them for support of the formula. He said he himself did not consider it an ideal one but contended that it was acceptable to most of the parties concerned and that if accepted by the two leaders also, it would lead to the formation of a broad-based Provisional Government of Korea. They disagreed that the formula was either acceptable to the Korean people or that it would lead to the establishment of a broad-based Provisional Government. They asserted, on the contrary, that it would result in the domination of the Provisional Government by the Communists. To prove his contention, Hodge produced a list of organizations supporting the formula. Kim and Rhee refused to be impressed and insisting that the organizations received little support from the people, they claimed that only their organization, the National Committee for a Rapid Realization of Independence, was truly representative of the people.

Hodge challenged them by asking: "Do you mean that the Korean people want to take a course which will lead to war?" And he added that their totally inflexible position would only result in war. Instead of answering his question, they observed that 'the people' would not remain docile in the face of his dictation. Plainly angered, Hodge asked them in measured words 'whether they were threatening the U.S. occupation command.' They denied it, but ignoring their denial, he told them that 'lately there were reports about a movement to stage a general strike against the Military Government and reminded them that in the light of the reports, what they said sounded like an orchestrated threat.' Rhee took pains to reassure Hodge that 'he' had intended no such thing, while Kim Koo remained silent. Hodge discerned a hint of their concealed dissension.

Actually, under the surface of cordiality, Rhee and Kim Koo were at odds. The idea of a general strike was Kim's. A paralyzing general strike against the Military Government was thought very likely to lead to a take-over of power by the former exile regime. Rhee, on the other hand, was for a 'separate election' in South Korea and replacement of the U.S. Military Government by the elected one, which he calculated he himself would lead. Yet both gave polite support to each other. To Rhee the talk of a strike itself served as a show of force for his proposal, and to Kim, the idea of a separate election was repugnant, but he went along with Rhee, thinking that he stood no chance of success. (Kim was uninformed about America and about the mood of its people.)

The two rightists went away sulking. Kim Koo thought Hodge looked like Popeye the Sailor but acted like Bruto - an app characterization of the United States. "All that you Americans know is how to bully others," he said to himself, "and it would inevitably drive the Korean people into the communist lap." Rhee called his close aides together for a secret conclave. He was shaking with anger, frothing at the mouth and convulsively gesticulating. He told them of the 'stormy' session he had with the 'crude and insolent' American General. In an emotional tirade, he denounced at length Franklin D. Roosevelt for having started 'all this mess,' and castigated Harry Truman for trying to complete the job of handing Korea over to the Communists. Then he announced his secret plan:

> I have decided to go to the United States. I will appeal to the American people over the head of the Truman administration for Hodge's recall. The U.S. Congress is with me, and if the American people know that Hodge is about to turn Korea over to the Communists, they will raise such hell that Truman will have to get Hodge out of here. Now here's what I want you to

do. Raise 30,000,000 won - one won from each of our 30 million people - as the Salvation of Korea Fund. With it I will bring home our national independence.

There was no audible dissent among those who were present, though some were dubious. Kim Sung-soo, perhaps the wealthiest among them, later expressed his regret for having supported Rhee. When asked why he had contributed so much (1,000,000 *won),* he replied that he had been requested to give many times more than the amount. Besides, he said, the contribution was from his brother. Others in the group divided themselves as captains of committees, which would assume the responsibility of raising the fund among various groups. Some would shake down 'pro-Japanese collaborators.' Some would contact Korean officials in the American Military Government with demands for maximum contributions, thinly hinting that they would land them jobs in the proposed Korean Government, and some would canvas farmers and store owners throughout the country, demanding that they either make fat cash contributions or purchase Rhee's photographs. Within a few months, their goal had been more than reached.

Rhee converted $10,000 worth of it at the official exchange rate (15 *won* to $1) but changed the remainder into U.S. currency illegally. In a secret deal with Helen Kim, President of *Ewha* University, he gave her 30 million won in exchange for her authorization to the *Ewha* Foundation in the United States to turn over to him $300,000 at the rate of 100 *won* to $1. This black-market deal was forbidden by the U.S. Military Government in Korea, but the *Ewha* Foundation might have been unaware of it.

With this war chest in his possession, Rhee went to see Hodge. Wearing a disarming smile, he asked Hodge for permission to visit the United States to attend to his personal business, including the disposal of his house in Washington D.C. Hodge gave his approval, quite unaware of his real purpose and of his illegal financial transaction. Hodge was soon to regret his approval. No sooner had Rhee arrived in Tokyo on his way to America than he held a press conference in which he called for the removal of U.S. troops from Korea and for the holding of elections in South Korea. It was a bid to American isolationists, who at the time were powerful among the Republicans. Then, arriving in Washington D.C., he installed himself in the fashionable Carlton Hotel and, with the help of several high-priced American advisers, drew up a six point 'Solution to the Korean Problem' which he sent to the State Department. His six points were:

1. An interim government should be elected for southern Korea to serve until the two halves of the country could be reunited and a general election held immediately thereafter.

2. Without disturbing direct Russian-American consultations on Korea, this interim government should be allowed to negotiate directly with Russia and the United States concerning the occupation of Korea and on other questions.

3. Korean claims for reparations from Japan should be given early consideration to aid in the rehabilitation of Korean economy.

4. Full commercial rights should be granted to Korea on the basis of equality with other nations and with no favoritism extended to any nation.

5. Korean currency should be stabilized and established on the international exchange.

6. United States troops should remain in Korea until the two foreign armies of occupation withdraw simultaneously.

Quite apart from ambiguities and inconsistencies apparent in the proposals, the 'Solution' was so radically at variance with the Moscow Agreement that the State Department ignored it. Some minor officials, however, thought it worth consideration, if only as a gesture toward Rhee as a political leader in South Korea and as a cold war strategy against the Russians. John H. Hildring, Assistant Secretary of State for Occupied Territories, was a member of this group. Even Hildring emphasized that his interest in Rhee's 6-point Proposals was a personal one and not the State Department's. When Rhee released the proposals to the press, styling it as an 'understanding between him and the State Department,' the Department released a statement of its own, pointing out that no new policy for Korea had been adopted. Rhee returned to Korea without having had access to any officials of the State Department higher than Hildring, who was closer to the Pentagon, as he was a Major General. On his return to Seoul, however, Rhee's followers hailed him as a 'magic diplomat.'

Of course, he was unsuccessful in forcing the recall of General Hodge, who was coincidentally back in Washington D.C. on official business at that time. Nor was he successful in his behind-the-scenes efforts to block the return to Korea of Dr. Jaisohn. Jaisohn and Rhee met briefly in Washington D.C., while Jaisohn was visiting in the capital at Hodge's invitation. He found Dr. Rhee a paranoid. His dislike of Hodge, according to Jaisohn, was visceral. Virtually the whole time they were together, Rhee poured out his anger at the General. His only comment, on being told that Jaisohn was planning to go out to Korea was that he had heard of it and that "your friends would be glad to see you."

Then quickly returning to the subject of Hodge, Rhee declared that for the good of Korea, Hodge should be removed as the commander of U.S. forces in Korea, and that there was a growing question about his fitness among high officials in Washington. Jaisohn conceded that there had been an occasion when Americans raised the question of his fitness for the role as the Commander of U.S. forces in Korea, but he said that it was at the beginning of his arrival in Korea and in relation to a different issue. The issue was resolved, he told Rhee. Jaisohn went on to remind his one-time protege that though Americans were more interested in what went on in South Korea, they were not aware of any cause for which they wanted their commander there relieved of his duty. Jaisohn suggested to Rhee that he was wasting his time. Jaisohn was right. Hodge was not only sent back to Korea, but President Truman also underscored his confidence in him by receiving him at the White House and publicly complimenting him for his performance.

When Jaisohn arrived in *Inchon*, Rhee was among the dignitaries to welcome him there. After Jaisohn settled down in his suite at the *Chosun* Hotel, Rhee and his wife paid him a visit. Jaisohn had hoped to take the opportunity to discuss the situation in Korea with him and tried to steer the conversation toward it, but Rhee politely refused and excused himself and Mrs. Rhee soon thereafter.

However, Kim Koo called on Jaisohn for a lengthy conversation, during which he made it clear that he did not think much of Rhee. Kim Koo visited for the second time not long after the first one, accompanied by Kim Kiu-sik. They were deeply disturbed by Rhee's campaign for a separate government in South Korea, as this would make it much more difficult to achieve the reunification of Korea. Jaisohn expressed the hope that this would not happen. He also hoped that the Russians would show more flexibility. If they did, he said, it would be easier to force Rhee to abandon his effort. He added that, for their own information, there was a definite swing to the right on practically all issues among the American people, and that Rhee was likely to sense it and feel that the tide was with him.

On July 17, 1947, Jaisohn sent out a form letter to the representatives of various organizations, which was as follows:

Dear Friends:

As you know, I have returned to Korea for the sole purpose of serving the Korean people in an advisory capacity;. therefore, it is my duty to learn all I can about the views and objectives of the leaders and active participants of the different political, social, economic and cultural organizations. If I know these facts, then it will be possible for me to formulate some plan by which I may be of some assistance to these organizations.

In order to avoid unnecessarily lengthy writing, I wish you would briefly state in writing the primary objectives of the organization which you represent. Also, please answer the following questions for my information:

1. Do you and your organization advocate the unification of North and South Korea under one independent democratic Korean Government?

    a. If your answer is yes, what is the best plan the Korean people should adopt in order to bring about the unification without losing much time and causing confusion?

   b. If your answer is no, give your reason for not wanting it.

2. Do you and your organization advocate a pure democracy, that is, let the majority of voters decide every national question by referendum, or representative democracy such as that in the U.S. by having three branches of government?

3. What do you and your organization advocate on economic policy of Korea? Do you desire free enterprise with profit motive by private citizens or the socialistic theory of public control and government direction for all business and industry?

4. What would you do with the property formerly owned or controlled by the Japanese government or Japanese nationals?

5. Do you believe in the inviolability of the rights of the minority in a democratic country?

6. What is your definition of personal liberty?

Your early reply will be highly appreciated.

Yours truly,

(Signed) Philip Jaisohn

Special Counselor

CHAPTER FOURTEEN

SECOND RETURN (II):

Serving Two Masters

Jaisohn was lodged in the old *Chosun* Hotel suite No.1. Elegantly fitted out with antique French furniture, it consisted of four rooms: a large reception room, 2 bedrooms and a bathroom. One of the bedrooms was occupied by his daughter, Muriel, who attended to him day and night. He was also provided with a commodious office (Room 206) in the Capitol Building with an adequate staff. A chauffeur-driven automobile was assigned to him to transport him to and from the office each day and to be used whenever he needed it.

His title was Chief Adviser on Korean Affairs to the Commanding General of the U.S. Army Forces in Korea. As such, his duties were to act as confidential adviser to Hodge on such matters as the Commanding General chose to consult with him, to give counsel to Korean political, social, economic and cultural organizations or their representatives, to serve as a member of the American-Russian Joint Military Commission and to help promote the knowledge of the Korean people by means of the government-owned radio.

However, since the Joint Military Commission was all but moribund owing to the interminable wrangling described earlier, and since Hodge and his staff agreed that Jaisohn's role as counselor to the above-described Korean organizations would occupy a major share of his time, he was given the office in the Capitol Building, Room 206. Although the sign posted on his office door read 'Dr. Philip Jaisohn, Special Counselor,' it was inaccurate. It should have read 'Dr. Philip Jaisohn, Chief Adviser to the Commanding General of the U.S. Army Forces in Korea and Special Counselor on Korean Affairs.' Later, the office was occupied by the Chairman of the National Assembly. The World News (*Seke Shinbo*) published by the Office of Civil Information, USAFIK Issue No.11 reported on 'A Day with Dr. Jaisohn' as follows:

> In Room 206 of the Capitol Building, behind a huge desk, sits Dr. Philip Jaisohn of Media, PA. Dr. Jaisohn hasn't always been in Pennsylvania. Of Korean parentage, many of his earlier years were spent in Korea.
>
> After studying at various institutions in the United States, he returned to Korea in 1896. He was responsible for such acts as starting the first newspaper in the Korean language, sponsoring a public discussion club at Independence Hall, and having Independence Gate built as a symbol of freedom from foreign domination.
>
> He went back to the United States several years later to study and practice medicine. Returned to Korea again on behalf of the Independence Movement.

Today he has two jobs - chief adviser to Lieutenant General John R. Hodge, Commander of U.S. Army Forces in Korea, and that of special counselor to the Military Government, Major General Aecher L. Lerch. Coming from the Chosun Hotel where he lives with his daughter who acts as his personal secretary, Dr. Jaisohn is in his office from ten to twelve each morning. He also spends three hours there each afternoon.

At the Chosun Hotel, he receives many people, some on business, others who want to know and talk with him. Recently, he attended a reception which the Korean Medical Society gave in his honor.

To the farmers of Korea, Dr. Jaisohn says; Your first duty is to produce as much as possible, more than you need, if conditions permit. Then you can use the surplus profit to buy improvements for your home, new farming equipment and to educate your children.

The only way for you to live comfortably is to produce a surplus. If not, you will be poor. These things are the duty of a good citizen and are the foundation for building the country. You don't have to be a politician to help your country. Strive for betterment and improvement within your home, raise your standard of living and you will have helped your country.

At first, in order to reduce the pressure on his time, as well as to better acquaint himself with the objectives of the organization seeking his counsel, he had sent out a brief questionnaire. However, the recipients were more desirous of seeing him and hearing his views from his own lips. He soon realized, too, that restricting his callers to those with 'legitimate businesses' deprived him of the opportunity to meet 'average, forgotten citizens.' He ordered the screening of his visitors kept to a minimum, and in this way he did more good for Koreans than he had foreseen.

People of all walks of life, all ranks and from all parts of the country came, some to discuss momentous issues with him, mainly just to look at him fondly and to make such remarks as: "Just think how lucky I am to meet this grand old patriot" or "The poor old soul, how old he looks" and so on, thinking that he did not understand Korean. Of course, Jaisohn knew what they were saying and hated it at heart but knowing well that that was their way of complimenting him, he sat through it all, keeping mum. Of course, he was aware that to them age is revered and that their remarks were supposed to be compliments.

Jaisohn's appointment book reveals that during his first month, beginning from July 8, he received about 100 visitors - more than half of them prominent in their fields of endeavor and 20 of them nationally known personages. Among the twenty were such political leaders as Syngman Rhee, Yoh Woon-hyong, Ahn Jae-hong, Kim Kiu-sik, Kim Won-bong, Hoh Hon, and Kim Pyong-no; such educational leaders as Helen Kim, Paul Choe (President of Severance Medical College), Yu Ok-kyom, Alice Appenzeller, Chang Lee-wuk and Lee Kap-soo (President of Women's Medical College); such civic leaders as Kim Sung-soo, Paek Sang-kyu, Kim Yo-su and Shin Heung-wu; such religious leaders as former Bishop Yang Ju-sam of the Korean Methodist College; and such journalists as Pang Eng-mo, Sol Eui-sik and Kim Yong-jeung. To each and every one of these visitors Dr. Jaisohn gave his unstinted time and counseling – never seeming to care how long it took.

In spite of Jaisohn's crowded schedule, which necessitated careful screening of those wishing to see him, he made every effort to receive men and women of all strata and every walk of life, including some who wished to have a glimpse of him whom they fondly called 'a living corpse.' However, he gave orders to his aides to keep out those without justifiable business or those go-getters who sought his help in receiving appointments to important positions in the government on the ground that they had either been members of the *Independence Club* founded by Jaisohn or 'suffered persecution' under Japanese rule. Once one of such braggarts whom he had ordered kept out of his office came to his hotel suite carrying a box of gifts. How he had passed guards at the gate was a mystery. Anyway, Jaisohn lost his patience and led him downstairs into the entrance, dragging him by the collar where a guard escorted the uninvited caller out.

One of Jaisohn's unpublicized activities as Chief Adviser to the Commanding General, John R. Hodge, had to do with the preparation of 'A General Plan for Supervision of Possible South Korean Elections,' which he personally hoped would never come to pass. Originally, it was the intention of the occupation authorities to prepare a draft plan for supervision of the Unified Korean Government Elections. However, as the realization of such elections appeared impossible, they revised their plan.

Upon arrival in Korea, Jaisohn was appointed as a member of the American delegation to the American-Russian Joint Military Commission by Hodge, and he attended few meetings with the Joint Commission which had been resumed after many months' lapse. But those brief sessions with the Russians, as well as his talks with Korean political leaders, convinced him and his colleagues in the American delegation that it was doubtful whether the Joint Commission would succeed. If not, they agreed that a move towards self-government, even in the southern half, had to be made as the people were increasingly restive.

Meanwhile, the South Korean Interim Assembly was also of the same view and following due deliberations, passed the 'Law for the Election of Members of the Korean Interim Legislative Assembly' and was promulgated on September 3, 1947. The existing Assembly which passed this law consisted of members, one-half of whom were elected and the other half appointed by the Commanding General (Hodge). Hodge instructed Major General Albert E. Brown, Chief of U.S. delegates to the U.S.-U.S.S.R. Joint Commission, to examine the law and to recommend the methods and procedures of its implementation, should it become imperative. General Brown and his fellow delegates to the Joint Commission held a series of meetings during September and early October, and on October 17 he submitted his delegation's 'Recommendations for Possible South Korea Elections.' With certain modifications, they served as the guide to the UN-observed elections in South Korea in May 1948.

Weekly Radio Talks

Jaisohn's most publicized activity was giving weekly radio talks. Though the people wished he could deliver them in Korean, they tuned in on him every Friday evening at 7:15 p.m.; the talks were on timely and down-to-earth subjects and delivered in a simple and forthright manner. Anxious to communicate in Korean, he promised his audience at the outset that as soon as he could, he would broadcast in his mother tongue. The subject of his first talk was 'The Privileges and

Responsibilities of Citizenship.' Since it set the tone of his subsequent talks, it seems worth quoting it in full:

> The day is not far off when Korea will have its own government, elected by a democratic method according to the wishes of the majority of all Koreans. It is therefore fitting that we who desire to hasten the day when Korea is independent, unified and democratic, prepare ourselves now by asking ourselves: "What are the principles of democracy and how do they affect us in our daily life?" Through today's talk and through similar talks each week, we can become better informed on these matters, thus becoming worthier citizens of our democratic state.
>
> First, we must realize that the privileges of individual citizens in any democratic society are great. They represent freedom, security and improved personal welfare, none of which are common to undemocratic nations. We have only to reflect upon life in Korea in the forty years before the recent liberation to realize how true that is.
>
> But with democratic privileges come responsibilities that are equally important. These do not restrain our privileges. Instead, they guarantee those privileges. Responsibilities amount to respecting the rightful desires of our neighbors, our friends, and other citizens. When they observe their responsibilities, they are respecting our privileges.
>
> For example, in a democratic society, you have the privilege of religious freedoms. Your neighbor may wish to worship in another way, but he does not interfere with your way of worship,

just as you do not interfere with his. This mutual respect for the privileges of others is typical of democratic living and ensures greater happiness for everyone.

Generally, then, what makes one a good and useful citizen in a democratic state?

First, a good citizen must be honest and sincere so that he can command the respect and confidence of his fellow citizens.

Secondly, a good citizen must earn his daily bread by honest labor.

Thirdly, a good citizen must obey the law of the land whether he likes it or not. If the law is unjust or works hardship on a large portion of the people, it could be changed by a lawful method.

Fourthly, a good citizen must be loyal to his country at all times, whether in peace or in war.

Fifthly, a good citizen must be willing to make personal sacrifices for the cause of his country and the welfare of his fellow men.

Sixthly, a good citizen must learn to cooperate with others if he really desires to accomplish any worthy objective of public interest.

Seventhly, a good citizen must be well informed by reading and listening to what others say. A conclusion arrived at by a well-informed person is more likely to be correct than the one reached blindly.

Eighthly, a good citizen must vote for those who have the best record in public office, rather than for their party's record in the past.

Ninthly, a good citizen must not accuse others of any wrong-doing without convincing proof.

Tenthly, a good citizen must always remember that all virtues or vices are not the exclusive property of any individual or party. Therefore, it is wise to listen to those who do not agree with him as well as who do.

There are many other qualifications for a good citizen in a democratic state, but I do not want to say too many things at one time. So, I will close tonight's broadcast with the suggestion that you make a note of the gist of what I have said for further reference and consideration during your leisure time. Later, I may be able to talk to you in Korean and dispensing with the service of an interpreter, which takes time.

On August 27, *Jayu Shinmun* (The Free News) published an editorial entitled 'The Last One of the Familiar Broadcast,' in which it commented in part as follows:

Tonight, the elderly reform leader, Dr. Jaisohn, who will be soon leaving his native land, will deliver his last radio talk. On June 30 last year, the octogenarian statesman returned to Korea after an absence of 48 years. . . . Since then, he has tirelessly endeavored for the cause of Korean reunification and independence. Among his many activities was his weekly addresses, which he made over the Seoul radio, some forty times beginning last September 12.

In these talks, he exhorted his listeners to strive diligently for the building up of industry and achievement of a unified and independent Korea. The people will miss him but will thank him for what he has done. Keeping the voice of his wisdom alive and putting his advice into practice will be our thanks to him.

Photo: Philip Jaisohn and Muriel (1947).

Photo: Philip Jaisohn in the New Year's event of the Interim Legislative Assembly. Philip Jaisohn is fourth from the left in the front row (1947).

Photo: Philip Jaisohn with students, (1948).

Photo: Philip Jaisohn speaking during a radio broadcast (1948).

Photo: Philip Jaisohn and Muriel at the *Independence Gate* (1948).

Jaisohn returned to Korea fully intending to stay clear of Korean politics. Upon arriving in Seoul, he made this explicit in both action and words. But in spite of his intention, he was drawn into it step by step, and within eight months he found himself in the whirlpool of Korean politics. There were several causative factors.

One was the United States decision to toss the Korean issue onto the lap of the United Nations in November 1947. It roused a storm of controversy throughout South Korea, many of its leaders denouncing it as the first step toward a permanent division of their country, and some hailing it as inevitable and necessary in view of the Russian intransigence. Rhee immediately claimed credit for it, asserting that the 'long overdue action' was the result of his persuasion. Rhee's political stock soared. Hodge, expressing support for his Government's action, nevertheless insisted that Washington made the decision entirely on its own initiative. Though most Koreans believed Rhee's contention more convincing, the facts tended to support Hodge.

The Truman administration, smarting under the attack of its critics as being soft on Communism, yet anxious to avoid a military confrontation with the U.S.S.R., took the above-mentioned step in order to circumvent Soviet obstructionism and to get the Korean issue off dead center. At that point, it was not concerned whether the beneficiary of the probable outcome - a separate government in South Korea - was a rightist such as Rhee, or a moderate such as Kim Kiu-sik. The proof of this was the Truman administration's backing of its verbal denial of Rhee's claim with the sending back of Hodge to Seoul.

During consultations in Washington D.C., Hodge made clear his opinion that the election of Rhee to the Presidency of South Korea would most likely be a prelude to a war in the Korean Peninsula. In support of this, he cited Rhee's fiery calls for '*bukjin*' (northward invasion) and his claim that since the United States had split Korea into two parts, it was its duty to help him reunify her. Hodge reported that the majority of the Korean people were for peaceful unification of the country and that, should an agreement with the Russians on the establishment of a unified democratic Government of Korea proved absolutely impossible, they would settle for a broad-based government in the South led by moderates, which would push ahead for a peaceful unification with the North.

Drawn into the Political Maelstrom

Regardless of what prompted the United States to turn the Korean question over to the United Nations, there was no denial that it gave apparent evidence to Rhee's claim, for the U.S. action followed by only several months his lobbying activities for a separate government in South Korea. His followers asserted that he held the U.S. State Department 'by the throat.' Hence, unless the moderates could quickly put up a viable candidate of their own, they could very well lose the Presidency by default. Prospects for them were not bright. Hodge, being a professional soldier, was resigned to eat crow and support Rhee's candidacy, but the moderates were not willing to 'throw in the sponge' so easily.

A few of them called on Jaisohn and inquired about the facts of the Rhee-Hodge controversy. As a man who was never afraid of speaking the truth, Jaisohn told them what he knew to be the facts. The facts were:

- that during the entire period of Rhee's visit in Washington, his visits were mainly with Republican politicians - Senators and

Congressmen - whom he had known, journalists of conservative persuasion, and those members of the Korean-American Council, an organization he had established during World War II, who were particularly close to him, such as John W. Staggers and J. J. Williams;

- that, his boasts notwithstanding, the highest official in the State Department whom he saw was John H. Hildring, Assistant Secretary of State for Occupied Areas, and
- that the State Department spokesman specifically denied that there was any 'understanding' between the Department and Rhee.

The news about this interview soon reached to the Rhee camp, and naturally, it did not endear Jaisohn to Rhee and his aides. They spread the gossip that Hodge brought out Jaisohn in order to help boost Kim Kiu-sik's candidacy as a moderate.

Another factor sucking Jaisohn into Korean politics was the erosion of the moderate forces. In December 1946 Hodge set up the South Korean Interim Legislative Assembly with 50% of its members elected by the Koreans and the rest appointed by the American Military Governor. Kim Kiu-sik was elected to its speakership. As a political leader, he was less known than Rhee and Kim Koo, but to the intelligentsia of Korea, he ranked first among the 'Big Three.' From the first day of his return to Korea, he became known as the leader of the moderates, and it is true that Hodge had a high regard for him.

(**Editor's Note:** Kim Kyu-sik earned a Master's degree in English Literature from Princeton University in 1903. He returned to Korea in

1904 and worked for missionary Horace Underwood until 1913, after which he went into exile in Shanghai.)

Unfortunately, however, as a result of his entanglement in two incidents, he announced 'his retirement from politics,' meaning that he was resigning not only as the Speaker, but also from the Interim Assembly. One of the incidents was, in reality, a series of incidents provoked by a bloc of the Assembly members who belonged to the *Hanmin Dang* (Korean Democratic Party). As representatives of conservative landowners, they were against the U.S. Military Government for its 'land reform policy.' As the principal backers of Syngman Rhee (later they split from him), they had a very low opinion about the United Nations, mainly because Rhee felt that way and whenever they had nothing else to vent their frustration, they waged an anti-Communist 'crusade' by criticizing the UN as the 'hot bed' of Communism. As Speaker of the Assembly, Kim Kiu-sik was increasingly irritated by their mindless behavior.

(**Editor's Note:** The land reform policy implemented after Syngman Rhee became President—planned under the U.S. Military Government—allowed tenant farmers to purchase the farmland they cultivated from the Oriental Development Company. They were required to pay 20% of their annual income to the newly established '*Shinhan Gongsa*' over a period of 15 years. In the case of farmland owned by landlords, the Government issued 'land price bonds' (*jiga jeungwon*, 地價證券) in compensation, which could be used to purchase former Japanese-owned enterprises ('enemy property') left behind after the colonial period. This reform made a decisive contribution to preventing Communism from taking root in South Korea by enabling tenant farmers to become landowners. On the other hand, the landowner class used the bonds to establish or acquire companies that became the foundations of major conglomerates such as the SK Group, OB Beer and *Doosan* Group, *Hanwha* Group, and *Dongkuk* Steel, which would later grow into the driving forces behind the so-called 'Miracle on the *Han* River.')

However, when the United States turned the Korean question over to the UN in November, these same Assemblymen who had been as critical of the U.S. as they had of the UN, suddenly turned pro-U.S. and pro-UN and moved to adopt a resolution of commendation. Speaker Kim felt compelled to oppose it on the ground that it was sheer opportunism. The Assembly voted to reject the motion. Thereupon, the *Hanmin Dang* bloc decided to send a 'minority resolution' to the UN's Little Assembly. Speaker Kim denounced it as an 'unruly, unprincipled and unpatriotic act.' The *Hanmin Dangites* countered, calling him, in effect, a pro-Communist.

The other incident was called the '7,000,000 *won* incident.' It occurred during a heated debate in the Assembly over a bill proposing the banning of 'public prostitution.' An envelope containing a certain sum of cash was sent to the Speaker's residence by an anonymous sender, and his family, quite unaware of the nature of it, left it on the Speaker's desk. Before he had had an opportunity to notice it, the newspapers carried the reports of the '7,000,000 *won* bribe.' Kim turned the envelope with the cash over to the police, but by then enough damage had been done to his political reputation as to influence him in his decision to resign.

Jaisohn was so infuriated on learning about it that he felt it his moral duty to condemn the political climate which produced such character assassinations. To a reporter of *Chosun Chung-ang Ilbo* (Korea Central Daily), dated March 17, 1948, he said:

Partisanship is quite familiar with seekers of power and position. Recently, Dr. Kim Kiu-sik has fallen into a trap. It is well known that baser politicians use slander, intrigue and other schemes as their political weapons. Politicians who lack scientific knowledge are especially inclined to use such weapons. As a whole, Korean political leaders are ignorant of science.

Jaisohn was even more saddened by the other cause of Kim Kiu-sik's resignation from the Interim Assembly, namely the *Hanmin Dangites'* rank opportunism. In the course of the same interview referred to above, he said:

> I wonder how many Korean politicians make efforts for industrial construction and to solve the economic problems. Do these politicians know that there is no independence without autonomous economy? We cannot call Korea independent even if she has a President and a few ministers while 30 millions of her compatriots are beggars. I shout at the top of my voice that every member of the nation should become the master of the country.
>
> Patriotism is not to love such individuals as Dr. Rhee Syngman or Mr. Kim Koo, but to love one's compatriots and territory. Every man and woman except the sick, children and the old, should work. We should not be like the lice or bedbugs that live by sucking human blood. We should be like a wise man who earns his living by the sweat of his brow. If we would do this, our country will become rich and strong. This is being really patriotic.

Korean people should learn to respect honesty and honor. It is a shame that those among us who strut about as leaders or patriots frequently resort to lies, plot against others, and rejoice in the downfall of their adversaries. Hearing the details of Dr. Kim's resignation as Chairman of the Legislative Assembly, I was deeply saddened by the stories that he resigned his position because members of the Assembly from the *Hankuk* (Korean) Democratic Party wanted to send a letter to the Little (UN) Assembly urging an election in South Korea. This is contrary to their earlier position. The *Hankuk* Democratic Party formally shouted for an autonomous election, saying that they could not trust the UN. But when the UN Commission came to Korea, they shifted their position and argued in favor of UN conducted elections. Their purpose in sending a letter was to show that their position coincided with that of the UN. Such an action would only reveal their opportunism.

Hodge received the news of Kim Kiu-sik's 'elimination of himself from politics with mixed feelings. He regretted it because he was now left without any viable middle-of-the-road candidate to oppose rightist Rhee. But he was also relieved because he had been irritated by Kim's open opposition to the UN-observed elections. To see a man who was widely known to be his choice for the leadership of the anticipated separate South Korean government openly oppose him was embarrassing, to say the least. Before long, Hodge came to hate Kim Kiu-sik only slightly less than Rhee. To his surprise, Kim had not retired from politics. The house of the ex-Speaker of the Interim Assembly became the headquarters of politicians of moderate inclination. He learned that Kim Koo had broken off from Rhee on the UN-supervised election issue and joined hands with Kim Kiu-sik. Hodge ordered Kim's telephone disconnected, provoking the latter to comment: 'How petty he can get.'

The growing estrangement between Hodge and Kim Kiu-sik in no way drew Hodge and Rhee closer to each other. Rhee was still a 'bastard' to Hodge and to Rhee Hodge was a 'dumbhead.' All the same, Hodge rendered a yeoman's service to Rhee until he turned the reign of government over to him, now the President of South Korea, on August 15, 1948. One day in March 1948, the news of Kim Koo's open defection to Kim Kiu-sik's camp so infuriated Rhee that he kept blowing at his raised hands impulsively for nearly thirty seconds and then broke into a long tirade against his former colleague, against Kim Kiu-sik, Hodge and Jaisohn for 'ganging up' on him.

But there was no need for him to do that. Hodge delivered a crushing blow at Kim Koo, eliminating him as a presidential contender against Rhee. A month earlier (July 19), Chang Dok-soo, the leader of the conservative Korean Democratic Party, was shot to death by youths, allegedly on orders of the Communists. Prior to this assassination, On June 28, 1947, General Hodge sent a letter to Syngman Rhee stating, "I hope the accusation that you and Kim Koo are planning acts of terrorism is not true," and urged him to "cancel any assassination plans against anyone."

(**Editor's Note:** Source – Weekly Intelligence Summary Report No. 3 of the G-2, U.S. Army Command in Korea: February–August 1947)

In response, Syngman Rhee publicly refuted the letter through the *Chosun Ilbo* on July 2, stating, "Your letter dated June 28, in which you suspect Mr. Kim Koo and myself of involvement in terrorism and assassination, has once again confirmed our belief that you do not understand the Korean people and their leaders."

However, just 17 days later, on July 19, 1947, Yeo Un-hyeong was assassinated. Then, five months later December 2, Chang Dok-soo was assassinated. The assassins were apprehended. During their interrogation, however, they squealed on their immediate superiors, who in turn, on being grilled, squealed on their immediate superiors, who also squealed on their superiors, and so on up. When the trail got hotter and hotter, leading not to the Communists, but to Kim Koo and Syngman Rhee, the astonished prosecutors stopped and reported their finding to their supervisors.

The Chief Prosecutor and his American Adviser faced a dilemma in view of the fact that the final authority on the prosecution under the Military Government rested with General Hodge. Should the prosecution call Rhee and Kim before the court as alleged instigators of the murder of Chang Dok-soo, they might well accuse Hodge of political persecution. On the other hand, not to do so when the accused had implicated them would constitute a violation of due process of justice. In the end, the matter was laid before Hodge, who after mulling over it, ordered: "Leave damn Rhee alone. I don't want to thwart his political ambition and be accused of being vindictive."

Kim Koo alone was put on the witness stand. The assassins, perhaps thinking that being called as a witness was an honor, were heard to mutter: "Why not call Dr. Rhee, too? They both called Chang a traitor." The prosecutor, flushed, went through the motions of questioning Kim

Koo and excused him. Though he was exonerated, the fact that he was brought to the court as an alleged instigator of a murder dealt him a deadly political blow.

North-South Negotiations

Thus, politically, the two Kims were down but not out, not yet. In fact, they were convinced that the United States would pay dearly for the misguided course it was taking in Korea, and that Rhee and his partisans could not escape condemnation before the bar of history. Though they were powerless to persuade them to see their way, they believed they had a weapon - the weapon of public opinion - and decided to use it accordingly. They wrote to Kim Il-sung and Kim Du-bong, leaders of North Korea at the time, proposing the convening of the leaders of both sides who were opposed to the separate elections. The northern leaders accepted the proposal.

On learning that the United States had decided to establish a separate government in South Korea, Jaisohn's feelings were mixed. On the one hand, given the Soviet non-cooperation, Washington's impatience was understandable. Ideally too, if the emerging government was wise and responsible, it could better cope with South Korea's pressing economic ills and more speedily effect Korea's unification than the U.S. Military Government could. On the other hand, prospects for the future of the Korean people were far from bright. It appeared certain that Rhee would be elected to the Presidency, and Jaisohn had no confidence in him. In his view, Rhee as President would most probably turn his government into an inept dictatorial regime and polarize the North and South.

But the die was cast, and the only thing he could do was to help enlighten the people in the hope they might be able to safeguard their rights and assist the government in the building up of their nation. Accordingly, while directing his weekly radio broadcast to that end, he began weekly evening meetings devoted mainly to the discussion on parliamentary rules and procedures. At first, they were intended for newly elected assembly members. Later he opened them to anyone who was interested.

Unfortunately, the country was in no condition to warrant such a hope as he entertained. The United States decision split the Korean people into two opposing camps. Heading the one in favor of separate elections was Syngman Rhee, with Kim Sung-soo, Lee Si-yong, Lee Pom-sok, Cho Pyong-ok, etc. supporting him in varying degrees and for conflicting reasons.

Opposing separate elections were Kim Koo (rightist), Kim Kiu-sik (moderate), Ahn Jae-hong (former Civil Administrator in the U.S. Military Government), Cho So-ang (ex-Foreign Minister in the Korean Provisional Government in exile), etc. with such moderates as Shin Ik-hi and such ex-Communists as Cho Pong-am and others opposing separate elections in principles but supporting it in order to 'control Rhee from within.' Undoubtedly, Rhee enjoyed by far the greatest popularity. However, this also posed his worst threat, for his backers were either uninformed peasants who were led to believe that Rhee was a magic man and would satisfy all their wants, or such unconscionable opportunists as predatory landowners and former pro-Japanese collaborators.

In contrast, the leaders of the opposition camp, Kim Koo and Kim Kiu-sik, had far less following than Rhee, but their supporters were intellectuals and nationalists to whom separate elections meant a permanent bisection and doom of Korea. Kim Koo, Kim Kiu-sik and their allies were so profoundly of the view that they insisted that at the least, the proposal should be aired in front of the whole people before being implemented. Hence, as pointed out earlier, they wrote to the North Korean leaders on February 16, 1948, proposing that a North-South Joint Conference of all concerned leaders be held prior to separate elections. Their proposal included five principles on which the conference would be based. These were:

- democracy and opposition to dictatorship,
- opposition to monopolistic capitalism but recognition of the right to private property,
- unification of the North and South under one government after national elections,
- opposition to the establishment of military bases in Korea by any foreign power, and
- withdrawal of U.S. and Russian troops by a date to be set by the two powers themselves and to be publicly announced.

On March 10, 1948, the North Korean leaders accepted these principles. The North-South Joint Conference with 695 participants - 395 from the South and 300 from the North - met in *Pyongyang* from April 20 to 28, 1948, and resolutions embodying the principles were adopted and sent to Generals Hodge and Stikov, commanders of U.S. and Soviet occupation forces, respectively.

On May 5, the day the two Kims and their chief aides returned to Seoul, Hodge made clear America's rejection of the Joint Conference's resolution in a statement released to the press. To this, Hodge added a comment of his own to the effect that the two Kims were playing into the hands of the Communists. This was the same language with which

Rhee had castigated the Kims, saying "Now, at last, the "dumbhead" was awakened." There was a sardonic smile on Rhee's twitching face.

Jaisohn, on being told that the two Kims were preparing to leave for *Pyongyang*, joined Hodge in warning them, but for different reasons. He knew them too well to think that they would act in any way that would be in detriment to Korea. However, he was against their northern pilgrimage for two reasons.

- Firstly, since the Soviets held real power in their hands, their conference with the Korean leaders in *Pyongyang* would only be an exercise in futility unless the Soviets chose to support them, which was not likely.

- Secondly, he felt that they should accept the dictates of the circumstances and actively enter the separate election contest with a powerful coalition slate of candidates.

If their platform clearly stated that they would vigorously push for peaceful unification of the North and South, Jaisohn believed that they stood a good chance of gaining control of the National Assembly, or at least of preventing Rhee from dominating the legislature. He believed that this offered a better chance of reuniting Korea.

Alas! The Kims and their allies knew well that Jaisohn in his idealism was blind to the reality: given the abnormal conditions created by the escalating East-West cold war, fair and honest elections in the South could not be expected. That Rhee backers, by fair means or foul, would win by landslide margins was a foregone conclusion under the circumstances. To participate in the elections was to help divide and destroy Korea. This they would not do.

Supporters of Rhee were soon to prove what the Kims and their backers said would happen. Following the *Pyongyang* Conference, the two Kims announced their intention to boycott the separate elections scheduled for May 10, 1948. Kim Koo retired into a monastery, while Kim Kiu-sik secluded himself in his house. Thus, with Rhee's two main rivals out of the way, there was no cause for concern about his victory. Nevertheless, his lieutenants knew him too well. He did not just wish to be elected. He wished to be elected in a spectacular way, and they decided to confer on him the distinction of being the 'unanimous choice' of his election district. Through a media blitz and door-to-door canvassing, they made it clear that Rhee was to be the sole candidate in his election district 'in accordance with the will of the people.'

Such arbitrary tactics could not help but stir resentment among the people. One of them, a colorful, energetic man who was in the prime of his life, offered to challenge Rhee. His name was Choe Neung-jin, but he was popularly known to Americans as Danny Choe. Though an unknown figure compared with Rhee, the graduate of Springfield, MA, Y.M.C.A. College and a former college instructor in physical education attracted wide following among younger people. But no sooner had he announced his candidacy than he was forced to go into hiding because threats against his life by Rhee backers became too menacing. Against staggering odds, Choe succeeded, with the determined aid of his supporters, in securing the required number of signatures on the petition for his candidacy. A half hour before closing time on the last day to file the petition, Choe, with his aides protecting him, approached the Election Commission Office carrying a briefcase containing his petition. Suddenly they were ambushed by a large group of ruffians and within minutes the attackers made off with the briefcase. With the petition stolen and the filing date deadline passed, his protest at the Election Commission proved in vain.

Since Rhee's sole opponent was thus 'disqualified,' there was no need to hold an election in his district, and Rhee was declared 'unanimously elected.' None dared to protest the blatant illegality. Rhee went on to win the Speakership of the National Assembly shortly thereafter and to capture the Presidency of South Korea.

Danny Choe's effrontery still rankled him, and the same year he had Choe arrested on a trumped-up charge of subversion and locked him up in Westgate Prison. When the Korean War broke out in 1950, the Rhee regime, before fleeing from Seoul, brought him out of his cell and shot him to death.

Such was precisely what Kim Koo and Kim Kiu-sik had foreseen. Such was what many others had feared. The uneasiness of Koreans of a wide political spectrum about the prospect of life under the Rhee regime was so great that thousands in desperation appealed to Jaisohn to allow his name to be put up as a candidate for the Presidency. They were confident that if Jaisohn agreed to give up his U.S. citizenship, announced his candidacy and was backed by General Hodge, he would easily capture the majority support in the National Assembly, which had the responsibility of electing the President. How pathetic the political conditions in South Korea were may be gleaned by my letter to my wife dated April 26, 1948. It said in part:

> On arriving in Seoul (early March), I found the relations between the U.S. high command and the two Kims terribly strained. They have improved somewhat since then, but not much. They are also 'tainted' with scandals in the eyes of the

public, although those in the know consider them innocent. Kim Kiu-sik is said to have been involved in the so-called 7-million-won scandal, while Kim Koo's name was drawn into the Chang Dok-soo assassination. Hence, the prevailing view here is that, however closely the two Kims stick together, their combined forces cannot match those of Rhee.

In surveying the political climate here during the first several weeks, I have found South Korea Syngman Rhee's *chonha* (world). It is also evident that unless the Russians show quickly willingness for give-and-take, Washington will go ahead with separate elections. Should the condition be allowed to remain unchanged, South Korea would be holding elections with only one candidate. Had I told you this the first time I realized this, you would have clamored for my immediate return. Having mulled over the gloomy prospect for some time, I talked over it with Dr. Jaisohn. He agreed with my assessment, but didn't see what could be done about it. I told him that unless a way was found to offer the people a chance to make a choice, I would rather return immediately to my family in America and came away.

The next day I had an unusually large number of visitors in my office, among whom were one each from *Kaesong*, *Kyongsangdo* and Seoul. I asked them, as well as others, what they thought the attitude of the people was toward Dr. Jaisohn. Their answer was that generally the people supported Rhee only because there was none better. They thought that should Dr. Jaisohn announce his availability as a candidate, people would be decisively for him. I also talked with a man who was close to the two Kims. He said since they definitely ruled themselves out of the running, he believed that they would welcome Dr. Jaisohn's candidacy.

I reported the discussions to Dr. Jaisohn and said that there should be at least one other candidate. Since there seemed to be no one else, and since he was so highly thought of, would he consider being a candidate if General Hodge, Kim Song-soo and the Kims offered their support, I asked. He said that he had never intended to and was very reluctant to descend to the world of Korean politics. However, he let it be known that should he be solely needed, he could not shirk his duty. At the same time, he would do no more than authorize me to test the water without in any way hinting at his willingness.

The following morning, I called on Hodge. I told him how unhappy I was about the political state of affairs, adding that the holding of elections with only one candidate made it no different from those of the Nazi Germany and Soviet Russia. He agreed and told me that in order to prevent it from happening, he had tried his best, in the face of charges that he was a Communist, to help form a coalition slate of moderates, but Kim Kiu-sik refused to cooperate. I asked him: "But should not an attempt be made to avoid the tragedy while there is still a chance?" He agreed. I then told him that on the basis of my inquiries, Dr. Jaisohn was the only viable alternative and asked what he thought of urging him to run. He said: "Will he run?" I answered: "If you, Kim, Song-soo and the two Kims are for him, he will be persuaded. The two Kims are, I am told, for him." He thought that was an interesting idea and promised to think about it.

About 10 days later, I called on him again. He said he had made some inquiries but found it unfeasible. He implied that Kim Song-soo thought it was too late to stop Rhee, although he much preferred Jaisohn to Rhee. However, he was willing to let me continue contacting influential leaders, adding that I should make it clear to them that I was doing it strictly on my own.

Unfortunately (or should I say, fortunately), just at the time Hodge was inquiring through indirect means about Kim Sung-soo's view concerning Dr. Jaisohn's candidacy, Dr. Jaisohn's remarks about Korean politicians in general, which he had made to a publisher thinking that he was off the record, was published in a newspaper. Since it could be construed as an attack against Rhee, he and his aides were naturally enraged. The *Dong-A Ilbo* came out with a stinging denunciation of Dr. Jaisohn. I am told that some people contend that I've come out to direct Dr. Jaisohn's presidential campaign, while others claimed that Hodge is waging a vendetta against Rhee. In view of the furor the Jaisohn interview has created, I thought it best to lie low for a few weeks. Now the storm seems to have calmed down.

I wanted to call on the two Kims first, but since I learned that they were definitely in favor of Dr. Jaisohn, I decided to visit Kim Sung-soo before seeing them. I had a three-hour visit with Kim Sung-soo. My impression about his thinking is similar to Hodge's. Although he is definitely dissatisfied with Rhee and holds Jaisohn in high esteem, he is unwilling to make an open break with Rhee for fear that it will split his party and cause many of its members to lose election to the National Assembly. Therefore, he plans to let Rhee win the Presidency but restrain him by having the National Assembly adopted a cabinet system constitution. I said: "If you cannot restrain him now when he is a plain citizen, how can you restrain him when as President he commands the military, economic and police power? No constitution, whatever its nature, can restrain him." He couldn't answer.

W. Bullit   P. Jaisohn   Muriel   Rhee

Photo: Ambassador W. Bullitt visiting Korea as President Truman's special envoy (1948).

Photo: Philip Jaisohn and General Hodge — their final meeting before Dr. Soh's return to the United States (1948)

The Movement to Nominate Philip Jaisohn

Now that the worst fears of the people were borne out, their appeals to Jaisohn became more urgent. In the weeks following the elections, appeals to him came from newly elected National Assembly members as well. In my letter to my wife, dated July 11, 1948, I wrote:

> First, let me report on the meeting of last Friday evening. As I told you before, this was the latest of the weekly sessions which Dr. Jaisohn conducts on parliamentary rules and procedures. Last Friday there were more Assemblymen at the meeting. As usual, he talked for about an hour and offered to answer any questions the audience wished to ask, and several questions were put to him. He gave his answers in fluent Korean, and I was pleased. Then someone, I think he was an Assemblyman, suggested that he renounce his U.S. citizenship and 'lead' the Korean people. Dr. Jaisohn answered that he was a Korean at

heart and that he prayed for Korea. Then he broke down and cried.

Such appeals to him were made not by politicians alone. Prominent personages such as ex-Bishop Yang Ju-sam of the Methodist Church, Kim Byong-no, Justice of the Supreme Court, General Lee Chong-chon, Army Chief of Staff of the Korean Provisional Government in Exile, Shin Heung-woo, ex-General Secretary of the National Y.M.C.A. of Korea, many influential members of *Heungsa Dan* (Young Korean Academy), whose founder was Ahn Chang-ho, and many others were secret backers of Jaisohn. Dr. Lee Yong-sul, ex-President of *Heungsa Dan* sighed: "If only he had returned to Korea a year earlier." Kim Koo and Kim Kiu-sik quietly encouraged their followers to support Jaisohn actively. Pang Eung-mo, publisher of the *Chosun Ilbo* and Ahn Jae-hong, former Civil Administrator of the U.S. Military Government, were open supporters of his. Surviving members of the old *Independence Club* founded by him offered to revive it and work for his election, but Jaisohn discouraged them, saying: "It was never mine; it belonged to all Koreans."

That Jaisohn stood head and shoulders above Rhee in the esteem held by the people was shown on May 31, 1948, the day of the opening of the National Assembly. Almost at the last minute before the opening ceremony, Rhee asked Jaisohn to say a few words of well-wishes. Jaisohn accepted the invitation. When Rhee got up to deliver his opening address as the Assembly's temporary chairman, he was greeted with silence, but when Jaisohn rose, he was greeted with thunderous applause.

One day about 10 youths came to my office. Announcing that they were representatives of the *Daehan* Youth Corps, they told me that a simple statement from Dr. Jaisohn promising to serve if elected to the Presidency would be sufficient to put him in the Presidential chair. Jaisohn, of course, declined. Whether their assertion was factual or fanciful could not be ascertained. What was factual was that within a few weeks, without receiving any encouragement from Jaisohn, they collected more than 50,000 signatures for a petition appealing for his candidacy. Jaisohn was deeply touched, but his mind had been made-up over a month earlier. When I told him what Hodge and I had found out about Kim Sung-soo's position as the leader of the *Hanmin Dang*, he was relieved. Hodge regretted that Jaisohn was not 20 years younger, for he honestly believed Jaisohn to be a truly great statesman. When we lunched together two days before Dr. Jaisohn and his daughter Muriel left for America, Kim Sung-soo regretted that he had not mustered the courage to throw his support openly for Jaisohn.

Photo: A petition urging Philip Jaisohn to run for the presidential office, (1948).

Jaisohn was relieved when Kim Sung-soo found it impossible to support him, which in turn led Hodge to conclude that, under the circumstances, he could not urge the 'Doctor' to run. Jaisohn had devoutly hoped that he would not have to change his mind about not being involved in Korean politics. He was aware, too, of his limitations. Guiding the truncated and poverty-stricken Korea through its trying days to reunification and economic recovery was obviously 'too onerous a burden for a man of his age.'

Nevertheless, despite his repeated statements disavowing interest in any political office, tens of thousands of his admirers persisted in urging him to run for the Presidency. Hundreds of organizations, political, civic and religious, petitioned to him, assuring him that one short sentence, "I will accept the position if offered," would result in his election by a landslide. Reinforcing the urging were, as shown earlier, the confidential appeal by the majority of the newly elected members of the National Assembly, that of two-thirds of senior officials of the South Korean Interim Government, the Korean counterpart of the USAMG, as well as that of many newspaper publishers.

Jaisohn, though deeply moved, firmly declined while thanking them for their support, he urged them to throw their support behind another candidate of their choice, and once a man was elected to the Presidency, they should support him as their leader.

On July 19, 1948, Syngman Rhee, whose unanimous election to the National Assembly had touched off widespread cries of corruption, was elected President of South Korea. He received 180 votes to 16 for Kim Koo, who had declared that he would not accept any office, and one for Jaisohn. On being told that he had received one vote, Jaisohn laughed and said: "Whoever cast that vote must be shot." There were acrimonious charges of ballot rigging, while members of the UN Observer team expressed unhappiness in private. But one of them, Paul

Boncour of France, commented: "All elections are corruption prone. The Korean elections were no exception. But what's the alternative?"

Photo: Members of the Interim Legislative Assembly casting their votes in the presidential election in Korea (July 1948).

Jaisohn was one of the earliest to send congratulatory messages to the new President. This done, he told me of his intention to return to the United States, adding that he would like me to go with him unless I strongly wished to remain in Korea. Of course, I would do as he did, I assured him, for I fully understood the reasons. Rhee had never been comfortable anywhere with Jaisohn around. He had been against Hodge's invitation to Jaisohn to return to Korea. As President, he would have more reason to be uneasy about Jaisohn's presence in Korea. He might well become the rallying point for opposition. Jaisohn had no such intention, and this was one reason for his decision to leave. Besides, he felt that Rhee, like all newly elected chief executives, deserved a 'honeymoon,' and if he could help provide it, he would do so by all means. It was his opinion that in view of my intimate relationship with

405

him, my staying in Korea could be interpreted as an indirect means of spying on the Rhee administration.

Returning to the U.S.

As soon as the presidential election was over, there arose widespread speculations in the press and among ordinary people as to what Jaisohn would do. Would he remain in Korea, or would he return to the United States? He announced that he had decided to return to America, although he would consider serving as an adviser to the Government at some future date, if invited. The people took this to mean that he would stay now, if asked, and called on the Government to offer him the invitation now so he might 'bury his bones' in his native land. Many newspapers echoed this editorially, pointing out that this would help forging unity in the nation. The National Assembly passed a resolution urging Jaisohn to reconsider his decision. Day after day, streams of visitors poured into his office, asking him not to 'desert' Korea.

All those demonstrations of affection for, and confidence in, him were gratifying to him. At the same time, they placed such physical and mental strain on him that toward the end he secluded himself in his hotel suite, leaving me to act as his surrogate. Prominent physicians offered to build a hospital to be headed by him. If he would stay, some civic leaders invited him to serve as the publisher of a new newspaper, which they would establish. Some educational leaders volunteered to found a university bearing his name and to be headed by him.

Numerous cultural and youth organizations adopted resolutions urging him to remain in Korea, which were in many cases brought to him in person by their representatives. One such appeal submitted by

'Concerned Youths of Masan' reminded him of the inseparability of Korea and Jaisohn and said: "If you still insist on leaving, please take all of us with you." One evening a group of youths went to see him at the Chosun Hotel and warned him that unless he changed his plan, some of their friends might commit suicide in front of the hotel. Jaisohn was scared and advised them in the most fatherly way "to go to see my assistant Channing Liem, who will explain my entire situation'. Kim Sung-soo, head of the conservative *Hanmin Dang* (Korean Democratic Party) and one time supporter of Rhee, and Cho Bong-am, ex-Communist who had just been appointed Secretary of Agriculture by Rhee, were two of the secret callers who attempted to talk Jaisohn out of leaving Korea. Conspicuously missing from the list of all the personages and organizations trying to dissuade Jaisohn was President Syngman Rhee, who alone could have swayed Jaisohn's decision. Through silence Rhee made it clear he wanted Jaisohn out of Korea.

Deep in his heart, Jaisohn wanted to remain in Korea. He felt he could be a 'missionary' for democracy and peaceful unification of Korea without touching on the sensitivity of the Rhee administration. But he was against accepting any of the offers of financial support from the organizations mentioned above. Grateful though he was for their offer, he thought it was more of a charity on their part - this he would never accept. He had mixed feelings about accepting an invitation from the Korean Government. Part of him said it was all right to accept it, should it be offered, because the Government was the representative of all the people. But part of Jaisohn opposed it as Rhee would most likely consider the Government as 'his' and regard the invitation as his personal favor to Jaisohn. In a vague sort of way, he fancied the United

States keeping him in Korea as adviser on Korean-American relations. I agreed that there was a need for a 'watchdog.'

However, I questioned whether he could fill the role without raising the doubt as to his impartiality in the minds of the Korean people while he was under the payroll of the United States. He agreed. Furthermore, such an offer was never made to him. There was no doubt that millions of Koreans wished him to remain in Korea. I agreed with them too, if a way could be found which would enable him to do so without being beholden to anyone, for his mere presence might well serve as a restraining influence on the Rhee government. Undoubtedly, too, should he decide to remain, he would receive numerous job offers befitting his status. However, in view of the generally low salary scale in Korea, I believe that he should not depend entirely on his position for his living expenses. So, I asked him about his financial situation. He said, "I have only a house in Media and about $3,000 in the bank." That ruled out any feasibility of his staying in Korea. I then asked him how he planned to support himself in America. "By returning to my practice. That's the only way I know," he answered.

The last and most prominent leaders to try to dissuade him were Kim Koo, Kim Kiu-sik and Ahn Jae-hong. They wished to confer with him in privacy in an undisclosed location, but it was virtually impossible for the four of them to meet without the knowledge of the press. Therefore, it was decided that I should host a farewell dinner for them at Dr. Jaisohn's hotel suite. The press was informed about it but were not allowed into the *Chosun* Hotel. The reasons for which the three men sought to persuade Jaisohn to stay in Korea were:

Firstly, their fear that unless Rhee was restrained by the presence of leaders of such moderating influence as Jaisohn, he might provoke a war as a means of reunifying the nation; and secondly, that on the basis of conversations the two Kims had had with Kim Il-sung and Kim Du-bong at Pyongyang, they believed that Jaisohn enjoyed the respect of the people of the North also. Hence, they believed that his presence in Korea would greatly increase the possibility of reunifying the North and South peacefully.

They assured him that if he wished to stay, there would be no problem with finding the means for his support.

Dr. Jaisohn answered by thanking them and the millions of the Koreans who expressed their wish for him to stay. He also shared the uneasy feeling the three leaders had about Rhee's weaknesses and possible dangers of his policies. Nevertheless, his decision to leave Korea, at least for a while, remained unaltered. He assured them that he believed his decision to be in the best interest of Korea. He said:

> If the people respect me, it must be because I try to live according to the principles I cherish. Whether I am in Korea or in America physically should not make much difference. Wherever I may be, my concern for Korea will be not a whit less. On the other hand, there are two reasons why I think it is wise for me to return to the United States.
>
> First, since wisely or not, the people have elected Rhee, he deserves a 'honeymoon.' I for one want to let him have one unless he commits serious mistakes.

Secondly, Rhee feels uneasy about my being around. Although I have made it clear that I am not his rival for office and my comments are for the benefit of Korea, he seems to feel that I am his habitual critic.

He is wrong in so thinking, but so long as he does, I intend to obviate any excuse for him to entertain such a feeling, at least for a year or so, God willing. I hope you gentlemen will do likewise.

Though the three leaders still regretted his leaving, they were impressed by the reasons he gave them. They were also encouraged by his use of the phrase 'for a year or so,' which seemed to indicate that he was thinking of returning to Korea. Kim Koo agreed, but added, "But I have a premonition that the future for Korea is bleak." Within six months, Kim Koo was gunned down by an assassin. The assassin, Ahn Doo-hee, was arrested, tried and sentenced to death, but the sentence was never carried out. Instead, he was quietly released and allowed to live under an assumed name.

Jaisohn's final weeks in Korea were a painful period for him. In addition to the pain caused by his new ill-fitting denture, he was deluged with last minute pleas for reconsideration of his plan to return to the United States. Those urging him to stay were not his long-standing admirers alone; many who had praised Rhee as the 'savior of Korea' till a few months before flocked to him with the request that he not 'desert Korea.' Some offered to found a university bearing his name and to have him head it if he would settle down in Korea. Some would establish a hospital to be named after him and to be headed by him should he decide to spend the rest of his life in the land of his birth. Some of his more youthful admirers went so far as to threaten physical violence on themselves unless he consented to remain. In my letter to my wife, dated August 22, I wrote.

> At 2:00 p.m. today (Sunday), I went to see Dr. J. at his hotel. He was sitting up in his bed alone. He said he felt better, though not a whole lot. His denture still gave him pain. What bothered him more, he said, was that some of his followers might go berserk. He told me that yesterday a young man came to see him after reading the reports of his plan to return to America and tried to talk Dr. J. out of it, with tears in his eyes. Finally, the youth warned the Dr. J.: "If you persist in abandoning us, some of us may try to stop you by committing suicide." Dr. J. told me that he had advised the youth to come to see me and talk over the matter with me as I could explain to him and his friends why his returning to America is a good for all concerned, etc.

Numerous invitations to farewell functions in Jaisohn's honor kept pouring in. Although he declined most of them, a few which he accepted proved taxing on his energy. One day during our hectic week, Lee Ki-poong, Rhee's secretary, walked in bearing an invitation to dinner for Dr. Jaisohn, Muriel and me from President and Mrs. Rhee. I reported it to Jaisohn. His previous engagements made it impossible for him to accept the invitation and he declined it with thanks.

It has been contended by some writers that following Rhee's election to the Presidency, Jaisohn called on him to offer congratulations on the latter's election. That is incorrect. Jaisohn did not congratulate Rhee in person but sent him a note of congratulations to which he replied:

Dear Dr. Jaisohn: Thank you for your congratulatory message. It reminds me of the days when you served at my request as adviser to the Korean Commission, hoping to get some sort of recognition for our government in exile.

Photo: Farewell gathering in Seoul before Philip Jaisohn 's return to the United States (1948).

The author recounts: On the eve of Dr. Soh's third and final departure from his homeland, I went to the lobby of the *Chosun Hotel* hoping to see him. As I entered, I saw National Assembly Speaker Shin Ik-hee leaving. When I went upstairs, I found Dr. Soh lying face down on the bed, weeping. He murmured to himself, "I am a lonely man. My home life was like that, and very little in my public life went as I had hoped." I waited for him to calm down before starting a conversation.

From what I could gather, what weighed on Dr. Soh's heart was the emotional distance he had felt throughout more than 40 years of living with his foreign wife, unable to truly share the depth of his thoughts with her. And despite all his efforts for Korea's full independence and democratization since the *Kapsin* Revolution, the results remained unclear and unfulfilled. Quietly in his heart, he had hoped that the National Assembly might name at least one main street in Seoul after him—'*Jaepil-ro*' (Jaisohn Street). But at that time, the Assembly had no capacity or will to consider such ideas. When I said,

> Considering your seniority and the situation, it should have been President Syngman Rhee who visited you to offer his farewell. Instead, you went all the way to the *Gyeongmudae* (Presidential Office) to bid him goodbye, but you couldn't even meet him and had to return to the hotel. Then later, the President came to the hotel and spoke with you for only three minutes before leaving. I find this deeply regrettable.

Dr. Soh replied,

> I didn't go there to meet Syngman Rhee as a person. I went to pay my respects to the President of the Republic of Korea.

CHAPTER FIFTEEN:
LAST EXILE

September 11, 1948. Jaisohn was up before 6:00 a.m. It was a bright, crisp morning. By 6:30, he was ready to receive Kim Koo, former head of Korea's Exile Government.

Promptly at that moment, the veteran nationalist leader arrived. For a half hour the two men met alone. He sought the early appointment because though he wished to see Jaisohn off at *Incheon*, he did not feel it safe to venture out that far. Besides, he wished to unburden the worries that plagued him to the man he deeply admired and whom he might not see again.

Their mutual admiration had blossomed only recently. They had not met until they both returned to Korea following Japan's defeat. They met on several occasions since then. However, in Kim's estimation Jaisohn was above all a 'foreigner,' probably as a result of Rhee's influence. To the latter, Kim was a 'war lord,' a characterization of him current among the U.S. authorities in Korea who had never understood him. Following Kim Koo's break with Rhee on the issue of separate elections, however, he came to grasp the true dimensions of Jaisohn through his association with Kim Kiu-sik and other moderates. Jaisohn's view of Kim Koo also underwent change. Though he differed with Kim on the separate elections issue, Jaisohn admired Kim Koo's courage to stick to a principle he believed to be right. During the summer their mutual admiration deepened, and Kim wanted to assure Jaisohn of this.

Having done so, he recounted how Rhee had consistently and successfully tried to alienate the U.S. Military high command from him, while using him whenever it was to his advantage. He went on to report that Rhee's drop in popularity since his election was so alarming that he ordered his secret police apparatus beefed up and that 'anyone suspected of being his potential rival was put on its purge list.' Then, almost in a whisper, he said that he had an eerie feeling that 'something unusual was going to happen before long.' As described earlier, he was assassinated in the summer of 1949.

At 7:00 a.m. Jaisohn had breakfast with his daughter and Channing Liem, his secretary, and when they emerged from the *Chosun* Hotel, the courtyard was nearly filled with people who turned out to say goodbye to Jaisohn and his party. Some managed to utter a few parting words, but most were too overcome with emotion to say anything. Danny Choe, who had dared to challenge Rhee in the Assembly election, stepped forward, made a bow before Jaisohn, and turning to me, shook my hand and said in a somber tone: "See you in the nether world." He was imprisoned within a year and at the start of the Korean War, he was executed.

It was past 7:30 a.m. - time to leave. Dr. Jaisohn and I climbed into a waiting limousine, and his daughter and representatives of the U.S. Army in another car. Nodding fondly to the weeping, waving crowd, the

Jaisohn party headed for *Inchon*. For a long time, he was silent with his eyes closed. I broke the silence and asked: "How is your toothache?" "It hurts," he said, "but what hurts even more is the report about ominous happenings in the making, which Kim Koo gave me. I'll tell you more about it later." More silence. I wondered what the report might have been about. I had an idea. Well, no matter.

When we arrived at *Incheon* at about 8:40 a.m., a crowd appearing to be more than a hundred had gathered near the pier. Among them were Dr. and Mrs. Kim Kiu-sik, Shin Heung-wu, Paek Sang-kyu, Kim Dong-won, Vice Chairman of the National Assembly, Kim Hyung-min, Mayor of Seoul, and Jaisohn's relatives. Kim Kiu-sik, who had been the first to shake his hand, waited till the handshaking was over and said:

> Friends, this is no time for weeping. For, in truth, Dr. Jaisohn is not leaving us for good. Twice in the last 60 years he was thought to have gone for good, but twice he returned. He will be back again. He is leaving behind his love for Korea. Where his heart is, he is bound to be. So let us be cheerful!

And he led the cheering crowd with three shouts of "Philip Jaisohn *Paksa Mansei!*"

Obviously moved by the show of affection, Jaisohn stood speechless for a minute. Then in a halting voice, he said:

> Thank you very much. I've already spoken enough about how much I care for Korea and the Korean people, so I will not repeat it. God bless you all.

With these words, he turned toward the waiting U.S. Army Transport General Hodges and walked slowly but steadily, flanked on both sides by his daughter, Muriel, and Channing Liem, his secretary. When the three of us and two army officers boarded a small ferry boat which took the party to the transport, Dr. Jaisohn looked at his friends on the pier and waved his final goodbye.

On the transport, General Hodges, Jaisohn, Muriel and I were assigned adjoining first class cabins. They were airy, immaculate and comfortable. After unpacking, we went up on deck and settled down in wicker chairs to sun ourselves, take in the refreshing sea air and relax. No sooner had we sat down than our attention was attracted to a mild commotion below. Among hundreds of G.I.'s (U.S. soldiers) on the port side who were being ferried to the transport General Hodges saw a touching scene involving some home-bound servicemen and their pet dog, which they were not allowed to bring. They held and petted the animal until the last moment and when they left it on the small ferry boat and climbed aboard the ship, the dog jumped into the water in a desperate attempt to follow the boys. The dog was picked up and put back on the ferry boat, but oh, what a parting sorrow it was!

Photo: *Chosun Ilbo* reported the departure of Philip Jaisohn to the U.S.

Photo: Army transport ship General Hodges (1948).

Final Pacific Crossing

The General Hodges left *Incheon* at 12:30 p.m. Saturday. It was a delightful day and the sea was calm. It continued to be so the next day and the day after. But Jaisohn was not well. He complained of body aches all over, of loss of appetite and of inability to sleep at night. Initially, Muriel and I thought that he was suffering from the physical overexertion in the weeks prior to our departure and that he would recover after a few days of rest. When this did not happen, we were fearful of something terrible happening on the high seas. He himself seemed to suspect that he might be terminally ill, for he insisted on dictating to me a memo to John Muccio, U.S. Ambassador designate to Korea, to whom he had promised to write upon arrival in America. It read:

> This is the memorandum which I promised to send you as soon as I reached California. It is not necessary for me to write at length on the situation in Korea, as I think you have already learned it a great deal.
>
> What I wish to tell you is something about a few key men in the present Korean government. While I do not know many

of them personally, I am familiar with some of them. I have known Dr. Syngman Rhee for many years. In fact, I know him better than any other persons in his government. I also know some members of the National Assembly and have found them to be willing to do what is right for their country. But all of them, including Dr. Rhee, have had no practical experience in government or business and have little education, except perhaps Dr. Rhee, who has had an American college education.

Dr. Rhee is a man of some ability and of patriotism for his country, but his views are narrow and some of his ideas are impractical. This is due to a lack of experience. His cabinet is composed of men and women who do not seem to enjoy the confidence of the majority of the Korean people. However, I rather think the present sentiment against the Rhee cabinet is unjust because it has not had time to demonstrate whether it is or is not capable of serving Korea as it should.

Before I left Seoul, I advised the Korean people to give the Rhee government a chance to show what they can do. I think a year's trial will definitely tell whether it can or cannot do the job expected of it. I am in hopes that the people will give Rhee and his cabinet that chance, and I sincerely hope that they will make good for their own sake as well as that of Korea. I think with your advice and Washington's friendly direction; they will be kept in the right path. However, you will have to watch their actions closely and if you find that they do anything to deviate from the right path, you will need to give them your friendly advice. At times you may even have to be firm. This is a confidential communication, and I hope that you will treat it as such.

On the fourth day out of *Inchon*, Jaisohn went to the ship's dentist office for a check up on his denture. The dentist, a very competent looking Army captain, asked him how he felt. 'Rotten,' Jaisohn answered. The dentist examined his denture carefully. Then, holding it firmly between his thumb and forefinger, he deftly pulled it off. The resultant pain nearly knocked Jaisohn off the chair, but in minutes he got up feeling much better. He had been unwell due to an ill-fitting denture whose rough edges had been pressing against his oral nerve. The dentist corrected it.

From then on, Jaisohn enjoyed every minute of the voyage. He slept soundly at night, his appetite returned to normal, enabling him to enjoy his meals, especially his breakfast with soft-boiled eggs with toast and tea. He spent hours on deck every day, sunning himself and chatting with fellow passengers; and he relished recalling some of his pleasant as well as not-so-pleasant experiences he had had during the fifteen months he spent in Korea.

He told me of the unusually early morning visit by Kim Koo. Kim had requested a confidential meeting. Since the only time Jaisohn had was before breakfast, he had told Kim's messenger that he would see Kim at 6:30 a.m. in the morning of September 11. What Kim Koo told him were:

- firstly, that much as he hated to see Jaisohn leave, he thought it was wise for Jaisohn's personal safety,

- secondly, Rhee's fast-melting support in the country, especially in the National Assembly, so alarmed him that, according to a reliable source of information, Rhee had decided to shore up his position with strong-arm tactics, and

- thirdly, he had given orders to his secret police to watch his potential rivals and to liquidate them, if necessary. Kim Koo felt himself to be in danger. Well, he might as he was Rhee's chief rival.

On another occasion, Jaisohn told me that he had just talked with few Army officers who were on board, homebound as we were. They had served as advisers to the Korean prosecutor-general and were present when pre-trial hearings of the assassins of Chang Dok-soo were held, which were, of course, closed to the public. They told of 'how frightened the interrogators were when the confessed murderers mentioned Kim Koo and Syngman Rhee as individuals who declared that Chang was a traitor and should be put away.' The Koreans told one another that it would be suicidal for them to allow the name of 'the future president of Korea' to be dragged into the open court and that they were against it. I asked Jaisohn: "Is it not probable, then, that Rhee would not have been called as a witness even though Hodge had not intervened?" "Probably," was Jaisohn's reply.

Jaisohn also met with the Korean students who were going to the United States on the same ship. They consisted of twenty male and eleven female students who had been accepted by American and Canadian colleges and universities. Desirous of securing as much information as possible on the 'dos and don'ts' while pursuing education in America, they request meeting with Dr. Jaisohn and myself. Through the kindness of the captain of the General Hodges, I secured for them a room where they met for that purpose. During his informal meetings with them, they would discuss a wide variety of subjects, from their studies to health care to politics, and Jaisohn would answer their questions, treating them as mature and conscientious persons. When a young man remarked, somewhat facetiously, that what he dreaded most was the prospect of having to live on Occidental food and that he did not think he'd ever get used to it, Jaisohn said: "Better give it a chance. 200 million Americans find it appetizing as well as healthful. "

As the U.S.A.T. General Hodges approached the International Date Line, most of the Korean students were too seasick to venture out of their cabins. Muriel was out on the deck painting. That left Dr. Jaisohn and me to stay on deck, conversing or reading and being on the alert for the arrival of the dateline. Finally, it did, and at that point it was either September 19th or 20th, depending on which side one chose to be. A moment before, it was September 20th. Now it is September 19th.

On September 25, the final day of our voyage, as the ship docked at San Francisco, I was surprised to see scores of photographers and reporters waiting at the pier. Thinking for a moment that they might be for Jaisohn, I turned to him and whispered that the moment of the due recognition of him appeared to have arrived at last. However, no sooner had I said it than a loud voice from behind ordered us to step aside and clear the way. I had overestimated the sense of importance of the American press.

The noisy reception was not for the man who had turned down the Presidency of Korea to remain a plain citizen of the United States, but for a young *Nisei*, nick-named Tokyo Rose, an alleged war criminal, who was being brought back from Japan for trial. I had seen her on deck, sitting apart from the other passengers and playing cards with a couple of young woman guards who, I thought at first, were her friends. Only days later did I learn that they were her guards. Before long, everyone on board knew who she was. But throughout the entire crossing of the Pacific, her fellow passengers neither showed curiosity for nor animosity toward her. This was fitting and proper. On arrival in the United States, however, she was given what looked like a V.I.P. treatment. If she was a war criminal, American perception of an important person is warped, I thought. If the fuss was not a V.I.P. treatment but a public humiliation, should she not be accorded a presumption of innocence until or unless she was proven guilty in a court of law?

Back in His Adopted Homeland

As for Jaisohn, a surprise was indeed in store. Shunted aside though he was by an army of eager press reporters and photographers who were flocking around the frail, nervous Japanese-American woman, on his landing a sizable crowd of his friends and relatives gave him a hearty reception. His elder daughter, Mrs. Stephanie J. Boyd, came out all the way from Media, PA. Several missionary friends who had returned to America a few weeks earlier stayed on in San Francisco in order to welcome him back. A large number of Koreans in the Bay Area, including a few of his distant cousins, were on hand. That evening, Dr. Jaisohn, his two daughters and I were guests at a dinner given by local Koreans, during which Jaisohn made a brief speech of thanks and advice. After recounting the event in Korea leading to the election of the Rhee Government, he said:

"The people made their choice. Now it is up to the Government to live up to their expectations. It is the duty of all Koreans at home and of American friends of Korea to help the Government deliver its promises."

Photo: Liem, Philip Jaisohn , and Muriel on the deck of the ship (1948).

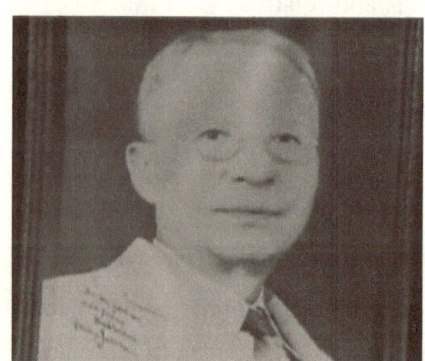

Photo: Philip Jaisohn

424

Photo: Philip Jaisohn and Muriel arriving at Los Angeles, being received by the president of the *Korean National Association* and Philip Ahn (son of Ahn Chang-ho) (1948).

The following day (September 26, 1948), I said goodbye to Jaisohn, Muriel and Stephanie. They were planning to spend several days in San Francisco. After that, they were booked to go to Los Angeles for a week's visit with friends there before returning to their home in Media, PA. That night, I boarded a train bound for Princeton, NJ – and for a reunion with my family.

Following a few days' rest at the Mark Hopkins Hotel in San Francisco, Jaisohn and his daughters went on to Los Angeles. There they were met by movie actor Philip Ahn, Jaisohn's namesake and son of the late nationalist leader Ahn Chang-ho, and leaders of the *Korean National Association* in America. After nearly a week of busy rounds of public and private receptions tendered them by the LA Koreans, Jaisohn's heart was thoroughly warmed but physically, he was exhausted. Though his daughters urged him to stay a week or two more and rest in a quiet place in the sunny Southern California, his purse told him otherwise, and he returned home without tarrying. In his first letter to me after returning home, dated October 10, 1948, he wrote:

> I reached home Friday afternoon and I'm very tired and exhausted. Will consult the dentist and throat specialist tomorrow or the day after. The Koreans in LA treated us most cordially, regardless of their factional affiliations. The Korean National Association people were particularly kind to us. I want to know how you are faring, so if you can please come and see me. P.J.

I telephoned him right away and tried to encourage him and cheer him up. As soon as I had settled down in our new house, into which my family had just moved, I promised, I would come to Media for a reunion. A few weeks later, I fulfilled my promise. As I approached his house, I became nervous, wondering how to cheer up a man who I knew was exhausted mentally as well as physically. Upon arriving in his house, I was met by Muriel, who took me to her sister's house, where her father was watching a televised ball game while waiting for me.

There was no need for me to cheer him up. He was in fine spirits and cheered me up with a warm embrace. When I remarked that 'you did not at all look or act like an exile driven from the land of your birth by your own ex-student and that you looked 20 years younger. ', he answered that

> in every situation there are two sides, the bright and gloomy sides, and that I chose to see the bright one.

That did not mean, he added, that 'he was not aware of the ominous future facing the Korean people and the regime.' However, reminding me that we had promised to give Rhee a 'honeymoon,' he proposed to 'refrain from criticizing him for a period, perhaps a year.' He thought it best for us to turn our attention to our mundane affairs. Saying he planned to resume medical practice; he expressed the hope that 'you might find a teaching position real soon.'

I answered that 'barring an unexpected break, I was not likely to land one before the next academic year. But that for the current year I planned to accept an itinerary lectureship offered by two professional Lecture Bureaus in New York. While it entailed travelling a great deal which I did not cherish', I pointed out that 'it would offer my living expenses as well as give me an opportunity to reach wider audiences.' I assured him that I was confident about securing a teaching position in the course of the year. He was relieved but his concern for me did not abate. His second letter dated December 31, 1948, was as follows:

Many thanks to you and your wife for the Christmas remembrance. I hope you all had a pleasant Christmas. We stayed home all day, and in the evening, we went to Stephanie's house for dinner. It was a very nice dinner. I have not done anything else. I still feel very tired and weak, although I am better than when I left Korea.

There are many changes going on in Korea. And it seems that Washington is going to help the Rhee Government for a while until it stands on its own feet. I hope that Rhee and the

National Assembly will do their part. I do not think they are anti-American any longer.

I hope you will find something good soon. Please keep me posted as to how you are making out. If I can be of any help, just let me know.

Wishing you and your family a Happy New Year. PJ.

With the arrival of the year 1949, his health showed a marked improvement. His letter of February 21, 1949, told of his plan to visit friends in Washington D.C. and ended by saying that he was thinking of getting an office for medical practice the following month. In his March 5th letter, Jaisohn reported on his trip to Washington D.C. as follows:

We spent two days in Washington D.C. and came home Wednesday afternoon. We went to the reception given by Mr. Chang Myun in Wardman Park Hotel and met several American people whom we knew in Korea and some Koreans, including Helen Kim. I did not know she was still here. I also met Mr. Muccio, who was here for a short time on some business. He will return to Korea in a few days and will present his credentials as U.S. Ambassador as soon as his nomination is acted on by the Senate. Mr. Chang will do the same simultaneously in Washington. Chang seemed a very presentable person. He will get a new house for the Korean Embassy, and it will likely be financed by the Economic Cooperation Administration.

By June, he was definitely ready to resume his medical practice. He opened a new office at 330 West State Street, Media, PA and announced his resumption of practice in local newspapers. His office is mentioned in Media's brochure of famous places.

His office hours were 2:00 to 5:00 p.m., Monday through Friday. He felt fine and found it a pleasure to be 'in harness again.' However, that was nullified by reports about the assassination of Kim Koo and the conflict between the northern and southern armies in Korea. They caused them great anguish. In his letter of June 28, he wrote:

> I am very sorry to hear the news about the assassination of Mr. Kim Koo. I did not know the reason for the crime, but it hurts the reputation of Korea in the eyes of the world. I hope the culprit will be punished.
>
> Today I heard over the radio that a dispatch from the UN Commission in Korea reported a fight or battle between the northern and southern Korean armies. I don't have details, but I'm much concerned about the report.

In May, I accepted a position at Chatham College in Pittsburgh, PA. Jaisohn was much relieved and promised to come to Princeton for a visit with me and my family before we moved to the Steel City in September. In July, he and Muriel drove to Princeton for a very pleasant visit.

C. Liem (Author)　P. Jaisohn

Photo: Philip Jaisohn visiting the author and the author's wife, Bobae, dressed in traditional Korean *hanbok*, in Princeton, NJ (1949).

He looked well. I promised to visit him in his new office during August, but due to heavy pressure of chores relative to moving and preparing for my teaching, I was unable to keep the promise but kept in touch with him through telephonic conversations. They revealed that his health was not as good as he wished and consequently, his financial condition gave him concern. As always, however, Koreans generally could not believe that he was in severely straitened financial circumstances. 'Dr. Jaisohn must be well off' was their consensus.

Photo: Philip Jaisohn in his later years, resting at his home in Media, PA.

Photo: Philip Jaisohn with his beloved dog at his home in Media, PA.

Jaisohn's letter dated September 21, 1949, shows his uneasiness about the Rhee regime:

I hope that by this time you are well settled and that you are getting along OK. There's nothing new with us here. I received the enclosed letter from Mr. Ahn Jae-hong. It was written in Korean. Please give me the gist of what he says. I cannot make out some parts of his letter.

I got another letter from Bishop J.S. Yang today in which he says the Government arrested 17 members of the National Assembly on the charge of conspiracy against his Government. Rhee is ruling with an iron hand.

His letter of January 27, 1950, shows that despite his painful, debilitating illness, he was following developments in Korea with the same alertness. It said:

I have received yours of the 12th. I am feeling better but not as strong as I would like to be. I have a letter from Kim Kiu-sik. He wants to be remembered to you. He says he wrote you not too long ago. It is a pity that a man of his caliber is not active in the work of national reconstruction at this time.

I understand that the Korean aid bill will be considered again by the Congress and will pass the next time. Some $60 million for industrial rehabilitation and a few more millions for military equipment.

His letter of April 12 reveals his deepening fears of Rhee's authoritarianism.

Your note of April 10 is received and I'm glad to hear from you. I'm getting along fairly well, but not entirely well. I am eating better and feeling stronger. I have gained some weight.

I read in the paper that Mister Shin Ik-hee, Chairman of the National Assembly, and three other Assembly members were visiting Washington D.C. So, I wrote to Shin that he might come and see me on his way to New York. I got a letter from him written in Los Angeles to the effect that he was hurriedly and unexpectedly called back to Korea so he could not come and see me. I think the State Department told them to go back and carry out the National Assembly election in accordance with the Constitution, which mandated that the election take place in May this year. I understand that Mister Muccio is on his way to Washington D.C. for further consultation. It will be wise for Dr. Rhee to watch his step.

I had a letter from Hugh Shin (Shin Heung-wu) who was sent to Japan as Korean Ambassador in January, but he has already resigned his job and is going back to Korea. What is the meaning of all these lightning changes? Whatever is the cause, it clearly indicates instability and unreliability of the Rhee leadership. Rhee and his Ministers have no experience in selecting leaders and they do not recognize the proper ones who can help them. The situation is really very difficult.

I'm sorry you could not come during Easter. Hope to see you in June.

Jaisohn was right in thinking that the United States brought pressure on President Rhee to hold the National Assembly election in May as ordered by the Korean Constitution. Not only was Shin told to hurry home and urge it on a reluctant Rhee, but in addition, Dean Acheson, Secretary of State, publicly warned Rhee that 'U.S. aid was predicated upon the assumption that it was in the interest of both countries that the Rhee Government promote democracy by living up to its constitutional obligation.'

Rhee had tried to do away with the election or to postpone it indefinitely, for he feared that his popularity at that time was dangerously low. One had only to take a quick glance at his record to see how true that was. At the outset, Rhee packed his administration with people who were loyal to him. Such criteria as qualifications and reputation hardly mattered. For the ministership of commerce and industry, he chose a woman whose only qualification, in the opinion of observers, was that she had been one of his staunchest followers for over two decades. Yun Chi-yong, whom Rhee had picked to head the Ministry of Interior, had been one of his close aides since the 1920s. He had had no training or experience for the post, and he had reportedly asked for the Foreign Ministership. Chang Taek-sang, who as police chief of Seoul, had proven his loyalty to Rhee by offering him physical protection, was given the portfolio of Foreign Minister despite his preference for the Interior Ministership. The choice of Lee Pom-sok for the post of Premier was another case in point. Raised in China and a career soldier in the Chinese Nationalist Army, he was considered the least qualified for the post because, as the President's deputy, he was expected to maintain close working relationship among the diverse and contentious members of the cabinet. The only qualification he could offer Rhee was that he was the founder and leader of the most powerful and militantly anti-Communist Youth Corps.

The United Nations Temporary Commission on Korea, noting that disquieting development, reported that 'there was widespread criticism of the personnel appointed to the Cabinet, and the feeling was expressed that the President had failed to utilize fully the best talent available.' Not only did Rhee fail to tap the best talent available, but he was also preoccupied in detecting any tendency on the part of his appointees to initiate constructive policies. Evidently, this was to prevent his ministers from developing independent following of their own. Under the circumstances, the Rhee administration was utterly incapable of solving the nation's pressing economic and social problems.

The outbreak of mutiny in the fledgling R.O.K. Army, known as the *Yosu and Soonchon* incident, was a reflection of this. Yet the Government, instead of instituting long overdue reform while seeking to restore order and discipline in the Army, reacted with vengeance. Determined to stamp out the 'Communist menace,' it indulged in wholesale, indiscriminate executions of men and women on mere suspicion. Under the reign of terror, not only the peasants in *Yosu and Soonchon* regions, but the peasants in rural areas throughout the South fled to the hills or cities, leaving the farms in waste. This resulted in shortage of grains and spiraling inflation which had already reached a dangerous stage due to lack of consumer goods. By early 1950, South Korea was in grave peril, and the dissatisfaction of the people was evident everywhere.

Still, the Rhee administration was smugly going about politics as usual, with Rhee keeping a suspicious eye on his ministers, his wife diligently interfering with his affairs, and his ministers vying with one another fawning over Rhee. The letter by Shin Heung-wu, referred to above by Jaisohn, dated April 17, 1950, offers a glimpse of the Rhee administration:

Please allow me to express to you my very sincere thanks for your kind remembrances and also to ask your pardon for my dilatoriness in acknowledging them. In Seoul, I did not feel free to answer your letters as I would have liked to because I knew my letters were going through the hands of censors. So before going back home, I wish to write you and unbosom my thought to a certain measure because I'm going back home in a few days.

Towards the end of last year, Dr. Rhee asked me whether I would be willing to come to Tokyo and replace Mr. Chung Han-pum, with whom he expressed himself as dissatisfied, and I said that I would try my best in whatever position he saw fit to place me. So, on January 19th I came here. Since my arrival, from General MacArthur down all the persons in the SCAP (Supreme Command of Allied Powers) have shown me every consideration and courtesy, and even the Japanese officials, including Mr. Yoshida and Mr. Shidehara, veteran statesman and diplomats, showed a good deal of courtesy and goodwill. The Korean residents began to show signs of putting things in order, and I also began to think things along constructive lines.

But something I had not foreseen intervened. Mrs. Rhee, who from the beginning did not favor my appointment, started intrigues, machination and work of alienation of relations between Dr. Rhee and me. I have had to go through all sorts of annoyances that I finally came to the conclusion that my position was untenable no matter how much I tried, and I wrote to him that I was going to quit. He seemingly was hoping and expecting my resignation and accepted it with alacrity. So, I with my family, I'm leaving on Tuesday the 11th not to return.

Parenthetically, Mrs. Rhee's avarice, meddling and underhanded interference in governmental matters, together with Rhee's blindness and hair-trigger impulsiveness are doing untold damage to our nation just now. I am infinitely sorry to note that informed opinion in America is getting to be more and more unfavorable to Korea. Unless something is done in Korea, and that very quickly, I fear that our future will become more and more precarious, that something will have to be along constructive lines that will help the common people. Otherwise, everything will be a loss. I very sincerely and ardently hope that there will be a day soon when you will come again and lend your leadership.

The summer of 1950 was one of worsening physical pain compounded with mental anguish for Jaisohn. Adding to his illness, which was later diagnosed as cancer of the bladder, was the news of the Korean War. When following a year-long border clash between northern and southern forces, the war broke out in earnest in the early hours of June 25, Korean time, the U.S. reaction was that it was an 'unprovoked aggression' perpetrated by the Kremlin in a bid to conquer the entire Korean Peninsula. Accordingly, the Truman administration decided to let the Russians know that 'they could not get away with it.' Jaisohn accepted the United States version and was grievously pained by the thought that the Koreans in the North were sacrificial lambs of the Soviet aggressors.

In a letter he had dictated and sent to me through his eldest daughter, Mrs. Stephanie Boyd, Dr. Soh expressed his feelings as follows:

> I hope to see the war come to a swift end, and at the same time, I hope that our compatriots will not serve as the paw of the cat that pulls chestnuts out of the fire for some cunning foreign government. The Soviets have already made fools of the Korean people. Koreans have gained nothing and lost everything.
>
> I hope that both the people of the South and the North will come to realize their mistakes and strive together to build a unified, independent, and democratic nation for all.
>
> Soh Jai-pil

Actually, the cause and nature of the Korean War were far more complex. Some partisan critics in the United States blamed Dean Acheson, Secretary of State, for the war. According to them, his speech before the National Press Club in Washington D.C. on January 12 excluding Korea from America's defense perimeter in the Pacific was tantamount to an invitation for the Communists to 'come and take' South Korea. To be sure, the speech was a wrong one at the wrong time, but hardly a causative factor. There is no evidence that the Russians began to prepare for the war because of the Acheson speech.   Furthermore, they would have been foolish to take it so seriously. Unreliability of American politicians' words were all too well known. Had not Theodore Roosevelt reneged on America's treaty pledged to defend Korea's independence? Did not Woodrow Wilson win reelection in 1916 on the slogan, 'He kept America out of the European war,' but lead the country into the war? Had not Franklin Roosevelt told the American people, "I tell you again and again and again that your boys will not be sent to war," yet did exactly the opposite, following his election to a third term in 1940?

Again, some argued that U.S. concessions made at Yalta in 1945 led the Russian Bear to the back door of Korea, which foredoomed her. That, too, is untrue. On the contrary, at Yalta President Roosevelt obtained a promise from Stalin, which was that in three months, after Hitler's defeat, the U.S.S.R. would join the U.S. in bringing Japan to her knees. Naturally, the Soviet ruler demanded a price in return. It was that the U.S. concur in Russia's repossession of its territories lost to the Japanese in the Russo-Japanese War of 1904-1905. Roosevelt, confident that it was a small price to pay for the defeat of Japan, agreed. The deal turned out to be a boon to Russia and bane for the United States for three months after Germany's defeat, Japan had had enough punishment and 'sued for peace.' With an atomic explosion over Hiroshima thoroughly unnerving the Japanese, Russian entry into the war was no longer needed. By then, however, Russia was ready to jump on Japan and declare war on her. Within weeks, Red Army forces in pursuit of fleeing Japanese troops crossed into the northern border of Korea.

How did the supposedly winning bargain at Yalta turns so troublesome for the U.S.? America's miscalculations were responsible for it. Its assessment of Japan was consistently faulty. Before Pearl Harbor, it had dangerously underestimated the might of Japan. After that, the United States policymakers were slaves of their overestimation of Japan. It was such miscalculation which led them into believing that the war against Japan would last till 1947 and produce the loss of American lives running into the millions.

Similarly, miscalculations characterized U.S. policies with respect to Korea. The cavalier manner in which the United States split the ancient, homogeneous and compact nation into two is a classic example of it. Having secured Soviet sanction to divide the country and to jointly occupy - the U.S. south of the 38th parallel and the U.S.S.R. north of it - to receive the surrender of the Japanese troops there, they were surprised to find the Koreans warmly friendly one day and icily hostile the next. Remembering the Cairo Declaration, which stated that Korea in due course would become free and independent, the Korean people expected that 'the United States would quickly reunify their country and help establish its independence.' However, when the Americans refused to say when Korea would be reunified and become independent, but proceeded to set up military rule over them, they felt betrayed. Failing to realize the depth of the Koreans' yearning for their country's reunification and freedom, the United States and the U.S.S.R. converted it into a cold war battlefield.

Thus, it was that the Korean War of 1950 was a combination of a duel between the two superpowers and the inept but fiercely anti-Communist Rhee government and the Communist government of Kim Il-sung. The war ended in a draw, and an uneasy truce has remained in effect since 1953. However, in view of the implacable will of the Korean people for their country's reunification, the superpowers must either honor the will of the Koreans or face another Korean War, which may well spark a nuclear World War.

To return to the Jaisohn story, during the 1950 Christmas holidays I paid him what turned out to be my last visit. He was bedridden at home and was being attended by his daughters. Muriel, who lived with him, was his nurse on 24-hour duty. Sensing that I was struggling to hide my alarm at his physical decline, the old warrior for Korea's independence and human rights lightened the moment, saying, "I am ready."

Then, as if it made no difference to him whether he was physically alive or not, he insisted on talking about the subjects closest to his heart - the welfare of the Korean people as well as of the American people, and the necessity of their cooperation in building a better future for both and for all humans. In spite of his physical discomfort, mentally he was as alert as ever and wished to continue our conversation. I briefed him on the latest development of the war in Korea - the entrance of China in the conflict and the dramatic reverses suffered by the South Korean and UN forces. Realizing that in all probability this might be our last personal visit, I stayed with him till almost mid-night when the last train out of Media was scheduled to leave. Though I tried to persuade him to lie down quietly and conserve his energy, he preferred to discuss the subject which was of interest to both of us. That was the Korean War. The substance of what he said may be summed up as follows:

> This war was begun out of foolishness. At this point in history, anyone who thinks he can capitalize out of war is a fool. In an atomic age, to resort to war as an instrument of national policy will be forever condemned by posterity. It is justified only when the survival of a nation is clearly at stake. The Korean War has now turned into a World War, fought in a tiny, densely populated country with weapons hitherto unprecedented in destructive power. Koreans are caught helplessly in the savage crossfire. Hundreds of thousands have already been killed and maimed. Millions more will be killed unless the war is quickly brought to an end. How I wish I could do something to help stop

the madness! Yes, where possible, I would go anywhere, to Pyongyang, Seoul, Washington, Moscow and Peking to plead with the leaders for an end to this tragedy.

I have faith in humanity. The human beings are of good and bad faculties. They, as rational beings, somehow manage to restrain the bad and utilize the good in them. History bears witness to this. Likewise, I have faith in the Korean people that ultimately, they will learn to live together and work for the common good. Therein lies the road to a unified, independent and democratic Korea.

With great reluctance, I bade him goodbye. After a 30-minute ride on the Media-Philadelphia local train, I boarded a Pittsburgh-bound express. As I closed my eyes, the sage of the man I had known for twenty years and deeply admired unfolded before me. A man of extraordinary intelligence, of robust physique, and of insatiable curiosity about things new and better, Philip Jaisohn was unique among all the persons I had known, unsullied by his aristocratic environment, hungry for knowledge, ever ready to take part in patriotic and humanitarian endeavors, yet modest about his many accomplishments and philosophical in adversity. He had many firsts to his credit:

- member of the first Korean student group to be sent abroad,
- the first Korean college graduate in America,
- the first Korean to obtain an M.D. degree in America,
- founder of the first Korean newspaper and
- the leader of the first reformist uprising in Korean history, etc.

But he never bragged about these. To him, they were all in line of his duty, no more important than treating his patients. Until he went to the hospital for the last time, he treated his patients. Though he was unable to go to his office, it was kept open with his office nurse in charge. He treated those patients who came to the office by telephonic instructions to the nurse. Others were asked to come to the house where, sitting in his chair, he treated them.

In spite of his modesty about himself and his work, his reputation spread across the oceans and continents. I could visualize how thrilled the Koreans at home and the world over were to hear of a man like him. An example of that was the reaction of two thousand elderly Korean emigrants in Siberia. Their communication to him, with their signatures affixed thereto, was as follows:

> December 10, 1919, His Excellency, Dr. Philip Jaisohn:
>
> We are informed that Your Excellency has been making every effort to devoting your time and energy for the cause of the independence of our Fatherland, that you have helped to establish various organizations in America for furtherance of our cause, that you have brought to the attention of the world the true conditions in Korea, whereby our nation, with the history of over forty centuries, may not be forever buried in oblivion, and that our race, numbering 20 million, may be delivered from bondage by arousing the moral consciousness of the civilized nations.
>
> We have the utmost confidence in your ability and zeal to lead our struggle to a successful conclusion, and we hereby entrust this noble task in your hands.

This organization is composed of elderly people of the Korean race now residing in Siberia. It was organized eight months ago and has a membership of over two thousands whose signatures are appended hereto. Our aim is to encourage Korean youth everywhere to devote their lives to our great national cause.

In a recent meeting, our members agreed that you are the only one qualified to lead us along the path of wisdom and justice and unanimously elect you as Honorary President of this association. We hereby request your acceptance of this office. By so doing, you will gladden our hearts and inspire us to go on with our work with greater determination.

May God's rich blessings be on you.

The (Korean) Old People's Association of Siberia.

Photo: The Philip Jaisohn Memorial House in Media, PA, just south of Philadelphia (2023 photo). He lived here from 1926 to 1951.

(**Editor's Note:** After Philip Jaisohn 's death, his daughter, Muriel, continued to live in the house until her passing in 1984. It is now preserved as the Philip Jaisohn Memorial House by the Philip Jaisohn Memorial Foundation and is open to the public. Address: 100 E Lincoln St, Media, PA 19063)

On January 5, 1951, one week after my visit with 'the warrior of peace and democracy', I received a telegram from his daughters informing me that Dr. Jaisohn had passed away that morning. After a hurried call to extend my family's condolences to Stephanie and Muriel and to consult on whom to notify of his passing, I took the train to Media. Though the message had been long expected, its actual arrival stunned me.

As I sat on the train, chugging along over the Allegheny Mountains, feelings of sorrow and anger welled in me alternately. Sorrow because so great a benefactor to so many people - Korean and American - should have suffered so much and died an unsung hero; anger because his fidelity to noble principles was consistently distorted and those who could have helped lessen his financial worries toward the end so casually ignored him.

General John R. Hodge was among the many friends who mourned Philip Jaisohn. His letter of condolence, the first message to arrive, shows the depth of his admiration, it was addressed to Muriel:

I received your message late this afternoon. I have no word that will or can ease your sense of loss of your father. I know how close you two were and how much you meant to each other. Also, I know something of how you feel. My mother, widowed

445

since I was six years old, passed away late May at the age of 88 after a full life of service to her family and neighbors.

Your father was a great man, broad and full in his perceptions and loyalties to his people, his friends and his family. He loved Korea and he loved his adopted country. One point in the whole Korean picture has been my wish that he could see the problem settled. I have loved him and admired him since I first saw him in Washington D.C. in 1947 and while he was in Korea. I wished a thousand times he had been 30 years younger. He lived a full life, and I wish I could when my time for release from this troubled world arrives, that I have done as much as he has to make it better.

Of all the Christmas cards I received, I prized most the one signed by him and shall always keep it. God bless you and comfort you and the rest of the Jaisohns.

Sincerely, John R. Hodge

In addition, there were numerous messages of condolence, including a cablegram from President Rhee and General Helmick, Deputy Military Governor in Korea. It was also learned later that at the time of his death all flags throughout South Korea were flown at half-mast.

On January 8, 1951, his funeral - a simple, private and dignified ceremony - was held in a funeral home, where a decade earlier his wife's funeral had been held, with a small group of his relatives and friends in attendance. There was no reading of messages of condolence. There were no eulogies either. While the eyes of some were red and moist, there was no other display of grief in the gathering. In heavy silence, the mourners sat listening to an Episcopalian clergyman as he read some

Biblical passages and prayers. It was an Episcopal burial service. In half hour the ceremony was over.

Thus did the small group of men and women who had loved and admired Philip Jaisohn bid him their last farewell. They were speechless, for their sense of loss was too numbing. Nor do they need to hear of his achievements. They were all too familiar with them. The editorial of The Media News that morning was the only exception to the dignified silence. It was as follows:

Dr. Philip Jaisohn of Media, one of the most active advocates of Korean independence in the world, is being buried today.

From the time of his youth in his native Korea, Dr. Jaisohn was imbued with the fierce desire for liberty and independence for himself and his people. And he translated his desire into action. Unfortunately, his little homeland was in a spot on the globe that made his fight against his aggressors an almost endless and even insurmountable battle. But he never gave up the work for Korean independence, even after becoming a naturalized citizen of the United States.

Dr. Jaisohn's life was marked by a zeal for freedom and justice in his native land and for his adopted land. In this he differed from many stormy figures in the histories of nations, whose actions are motivated by desire for personal power and are against systems of government that vest control in the people.

Dr. Jaisohn, like most truly great men of history, was appreciated more at his adopted home community with the coming of death than he was while living.

Photo: Obituary article announcing Philip Jaisohn 's death, published in the Media News (January 1951).

Photo: Personal belongings of Philip Jaisohn .

Photo: Memorial monument to Soh Jai-pil located in Rose Tree Park, Media, Pennsylvania, USA.

Photo: Statue of Philip Jaisohn in front of the Embassy of the Republic of Korea in Washington, D.C.

Photo: His remains were transferred to Korea in 1994 and are now interred at the National Cemetery in *Dongjak-dong*, Seoul

Inscription on the Monument at the Independence Hall of Korea
(*Cheon-an,* South Korea):

To the People of Korea:

If we unite, Korea will live. But if we divide, Korea will perish.
Without Korea, there will be no people of the South,
and no people of the North.
Is there any wisdom in doing things that lead to death?
Choose the path that leads to life.

On the occasion of the March 1st Independence Day, 1949

Photo: The Independence Hall of Korea (*Cheon-an,* South Korea):

450

CHAPTER SIXTEEN:
CONCLUSION

An old adage has it, 'a leopard dies, leaving behind his skin; a man dies, but his name lives on.' Exactly. The 'Assumer of Service,' which Dr. Jaisohn's Korean name (Jai-pil) denotes, lives on. He was born a high aristocrat and was entitled to command the services of not only his own servants, but also the common people of his native country. Instead of reveling in such privileges, however, he led a revolution aiming at a fundamental change of Korea that was to sweep away her ancient social evils such as hereditary aristocracy of which he was a beneficiary, and an absolute monarchy.

But the Jaisohn revolution was unlike any other in history. In the first place, the changes he sought were not for his own benefit. Though he had initiated and directed it, he kept himself scrupulously in the background. He wanted it strictly for the benefit of and by the masses. Secondly, it was not to reduce his people to the level of commoners, but to pull them all up to the high end of equality and liberty under Jaisohn's clarion call: 'All of you are *yangbans*!' Pointing out man's creative and ennobling qualities, he asserted that 'all who apply these qualities to the creation of wealth and happiness for themselves and of justice and might for their country were *yangbans*.' These words made the people wide awake to see what they truly were as human beings.

In that sense, Jaisohn was the torch-bearer of his people, yes, the light. As light cannot be hidden under a bushel, the life of so unique a man as Philip Jaisohn cannot remain buried for long. It shines through the fog of time, exposing the truth from a sham and challenging all who are conscientious to emulate him. His championship of the cause of the deprived masses cost him dearly, but in the end he emerged victorious. It cannot be said that he won the fight to make Korea reunified and truly democratic country. But his unshakable faith that it will be realized, and that the way lies in peaceful and mutually cooperative endeavor by all concerned - the people of the North and South and of the United States - stands as a challenge to us all.

There were ups and downs in his fortune during his life, spanning over four-score years. In good times as well as bad, his bearing was the same - dignified, serene and simple - except for a brief period in the 1920s when his disappointment and failure to help Korea achieve her liberation was aggravated by his business failure. Even then, only those closest to him sensed the depth of his suffering. However, he quickly pulled himself together and, braving staggering odds, took the offensive for the recovery of his financial solvency as well as health. By the end of World War II, he was free of all debts. His medical practice was thriving, and, given more time, he might well have saved up enough money to enable him to retire comfortably.

But he was not left alone. General John R. Hodge, Commander of the U.S. Army of Occupation in Korea, sent him an urgent invitation.

Hard pressed for a well-qualified adviser, the General turned to Jaisohn. Never a man to decline a call for public service, Jaisohn accepted the invitation although he was well aware of how onerous his undertaking would be - a month long transcontinental and transoceanic journey and a highly sensitive and burdensome role awaiting in Korea. His position in Korea was much more difficult than he had anticipated, and he was unable to please everyone, but he discharged his duty with truthfulness, selflessness and fidelity to principle, which guided him throughout his life.

He could not be bought. He was not interested in high office, be it political or civic. He despised opportunists. But he was a man of love. He loved Korea and the Korean people. He loved America and its people. Because he loved them, he wanted them to be free, prosperous and respected.

When Jaisohn walked on the streets of Media, people could not help noticing him twice. He was a man of charismatic bearing, but it was more than his physical appearance that made him a man of charisma. They saw something radiating from inside of him. So did the Koreans who saw him a living wisdom. Hence his advice: '*Saltori hasio* (Earn your livelihood), then you will become not only your own master, but also the builders of a new and better Korea.'

He practiced it himself. Before his medical practice became prosperous in the 1930s, he raised potatoes and green vegetables in his garden for recreation, but also for food. In his office he washed test tubes and sterilized needles himself. Even when he had an army of clerks and assistants at his disposal while he served as the Chief Adviser on Korean affairs to the U.S. Military Command in Korea, he was a do-it-yourself man, as much as his time and energy allowed. He usually wrote out his speeches with his own hand before sending them to the typist. He treated his office staff as colleagues, not orderlies. The assessment of South Korean leaders by American reporters in Seoul during the Military Government revealed what manner of a man Jaisohn was in their view. According to one of them of the big four, Syngman Rhee, Kim Koo, Kim Kiu-sik and Philip Jaisohn,

- Rhee was a Tammany politician,
- Kim Koo a warlord,
- Kim Kiu-sik a political scientist and
- Jaisohn a saint.

To the end of his life, Jaisohn loved his fellow men without expecting anything in return for himself. However, he demanded that they practice what they knew to be just and good. To a visitor near the end of his life, who had asked whether he had a message for the people of Korea and of America, he answered: "I hope they love and respect the rights of one another and remain friends."

Jaisohn not only lives on but is admired more widely with each passing year. This makes him a temptation as well as an inspiration. Self-seekers are tempted to take advantage of his name. It is hoped that there will be no such persons as they will be dishonoring him by so doing. Those who are inspired by him and accept his challenge to follow his example will become the Philip Jaisohn in spirit.

APPENDIX

Appendix 1:

Philip Jaisohn Memorial Foundation

The Philip Jaisohn Memorial Foundation is a nonprofit organization established in 1975 in Philadelphia, with authorization from the U.S. federal government and the state of Pennsylvania. Its mission is to carry on the noble spirit of Dr. Soh Jai-pil (Philip Jaisohn), the first Korean to become a Western-trained physician and a lifelong patriot who dedicated himself to both his homeland, Korea, and his adopted country, the United States.

The Foundation began with the opening of the Philip Jaisohn Medical Center, founded through the collaborative efforts of eight Korean American doctors residing in the Philadelphia area—Yoon Doo-hwan, Oh Dong-yeol, Yum Geuk-yong, Park Kyung-ji, Oh Sung-gyu, Hong Geum-soon, Kim Jung-sun, and Lee Kwan-woo. Dr. Yoon Doo-hwan served as the Foundation's first president, and Dr. Hyun Bong-hak as its first board chair.

In addition to cultivating the next generation of leaders, the Foundation provides a wide range of services to Korean-Americans and other local ethnic communities. These services include medical care, social welfare, home health care, senior employment assistance, health insurance support, legal and mental health counseling, and more. It also offers educational scholarships and sponsors the Philip Jaisohn Award, among other active programs.

The Philip Jaisohn Memorial House, located in the wooded hills of Media, 24 kilometers southwest of Philadelphia, is a wooden residence where Dr. Soh lived from 1925 until his death in 1951. After the passing of his daughter, Miss Muriel, the home was transferred to the Foundation in 1987 and opened to the public in 1990.

Philip Jaisohn Memorial Foundation

Philadelphia Office
Address: 6705 Old York Rd, Philadelphia, PA 19126
Phone: (215) 224-2000

Lansdale Office
Address: 51 Medical Campus Drive, Lansdale, PA 19446
Phone: (215) 997-2101

Jaisohn Wellness Center:
Address: 1290 Allentown Rd, Lansdale, PA 19446
Phone: (267) 638-9500

Media Memorial House Address
Address: 100E Lincoln Street, Media, PA 19063
Phone: (610) 627-9768
Phone for Reservation: (610) 241-6582

Website: www.jaisohn.org

Appendix 2:

Acknowledgments

I extend my heartfelt thanks to the board members of the Philip Jaisohn Memorial Foundation for their valuable input during the editing process of this book.

I also express my deep gratitude to Joseph Cho for transcribing the now out-of-print English original by Professor Channing Liem (임창영) into a Microsoft Word file.

Editor
Young-il Cho, Professor
Drexel University, Philadelphia, PA

www.ingramcontent.com/pod-product-compliance
Lightning Source LLC
Chambersburg PA
CBHW020914140626
46545CB00015B/37